THE COMPLETE BOOK OF
AQUARIUM PLANTS

Robert Allgayer and Jacques Teton

WARD LOCK LIMITED · LONDON

CONTENTS

First published in France in 1986
under the title *Plantes et Décors d'Aquarium*
© A.T.P. – Chamalières – France – 1986

English Text © Ward Lock Limited 1987

Text filmset in Optima
by
M & R Computerised Typesetting Ltd., Grimsby, England

Printed and bound in Spain

British Library Cataloguing in Publication Data
Allgayer, Robert
The complete book of aquarium plants.
1. Aquarium plants
I. Title   II. Teton, Jacques
III. Plantes et decors d'aquarium.
English
635.9'674   SF457.7

ISBN 0–7063–6614–X

INTRODUCTION

At one time or another, we have all found ourselves mesmerized by the lush plant life of an aquarium, oblivious to even the most colourful of the fish weaving in and out among the aquatic plants.

After the initial surprise reaction, we may think about creating something similar and this is when a number of questions arise: what quality and amount of light do the plants need? what kind of water and sub-stratum is best?; which plants to choose?; which fish to select?; and what is the most effective decoration for the aquarium? An elementary knowledge of the natural sciences and physics will not provide the answers, in fact the rather obscure terminology will probably just seem daunting: photosynthesis, mercury vapour, pH, carbon dioxide.

The jargon may create the impression that the task is impossible, achievable only by a doctor of botany or a specialist in plant biology. But in practical terms, the most successful aquariums are the handi-work of aquarium enthusiasts fond of aquatic flora. By respecting and applying some simple rules reflecting the laws of nature, anyone can acquire enough expertise to produce successful results.

We hope that this book will help you to discover the natural living conditions of plants and to analyse the reasons for their require-ments. We hope it will enable you to give them the care they need. Finally, we hope to guide you towards a choice of plants which can live alongside fish to create an effect which is in keeping with the natural harmony of the environment.

Nonetheless, the advice, ideas and tricks of the trade collected in these pages will need to be backed up by your diligence and your love of plants for your venture to be successful.

FROM NATURAL HABITAT TO AQUARIUM

The majority of plants gracing aquariums originate from the tropical or sub-tropical regions of the world. The surviving specimens of the long, and sometimes fatal, journey from natural habitat to aquarium should be both selected and planted with the utmost care.

The natural environment of plants

The scarcity of aquatic plants in the natural environment may come as a surprise to aquariophiles. Many rivers and streams contain none at all for one reason or another. The rivers' seasonal floods and the scarcity of materials vital for the plants' growth or dispersal means that their spread is effectively hampered. Very specialized species are local and have only a very limited distribution, while other plants are confined only by continent. Some are cosmopolitan, or have become so as a result of man's intervention, in some instances to such a degree that they obstruct navigation or local flora. The temperature is the main reason why these plants have not shifted northwards. Tropical and subtropical flora remain between the thirty-fifth parallels, while the more hardy of them reach as far as the temperate zones. On the other hand, species from temperate zones adapt very well to warm-water aquaria.

■ Specific conditions for life

Distribution

Many aquarium plants come from South America, South East Asia and, to a lesser extent, Africa. It is worth knowing even a little plant ecology as this can improve aquarium management. The larger groups of plants currently available in the specialized market number: some floating species, strictly aquatic plants, and amphibians (or paludals). The first group is represented primarily by *Eichhornia crassipes*, *Pistia*, *Salvinia* and some species of duckweed. In most cases the plants are cosmopolitan, as a result of their dispersal by means of aquatic currents.

The second group comprises the numerous, strictly aquatic species valued by aquariophiles, and their spread is very limited. Some genera are found only on one continent (for example, the genera *Cabomba* and *Henianthus* are found on the North-American continent [Nearctic plants]) but the majority are spread across inter-tropical zones. Finally, the third group, amphibious or paludal plants, tolerate alternating floods and dry seasons. The better known belong to the genera *Echinodorus* from America, *Anubias* from Africa and *Cryptocoryne* from Asia.

Special adaptations

Each type of plant is suited to a particular environment because of its individual characteristics. Thus, the aquatic fern *Bolbitis heudelotii* is perfectly suited to torrents and spring tides because its scalloped leaves offer minimum resistance to the pressure of the current. Its rhizome root system means that it holds perfectly to the substratum when the plant is constantly sprinkled by whirls of water. Nevertheless, there are some species whose morphology is not in keeping with their environment. Thus, Aponogeton from Madagascar has scalloped leaves but is happier in stagnant or calm water in a shady spot. Everything would have us believe, however, that it would adapt easily to running water and intense light. In fact, the spaces between the veins offer very little resistance to water and many plants exposed to the sun tend to develop leaves with a smaller surface area. These are extreme cases; the majority of the plants prefer calm, stagnant or very slow moving water. Some even prefer a regular eddy. Stagnant waters basically harbour the genera *Cabomba, Myriophyllum* or *Aponogeton*.

Few species are truly suited to the brutal conditions of the Amazonian, Central American or African rivers. The speed of the current, heavy floods or muddy waters limit their growth. So it is more rewarding, when looking for plants in their natural environment, to try on flooded ground, along the lateral arms of a river or in small streams. *Eichhornia crassipes* shows many of the characteristics typical of surface plants. Its shell-like leaf can pick up the slightest breeze and the whole foliage acts like a ship's sail. The spongy petioles have loose fibres which retain air and so prevent the plant from being submerged. According to the dominant wind, the plants will travel from one bank of a pond to the other. They can cross the most turbulent of rapids, like those in the lower Congo without danger; in fact, brackish water and defoliants are the only natural enemies of this plant. Other species can be developed by aquatic cultivation as in the Mexican paddy-fields and 'chinampas', where marshland cultivation is practised.

Growth according to rain cycle

In the tropical forest the seasonal rains (or the monsoon in Asia) are responsible for the cyclic variations in the water levels. Plants suddenly become submerged under muddy water highly charged with particles, and the large size of their leaves means that they attract more sun and obtain more energy. During the dry season, they are often a long way from river beds; those few who manage to survive these conditions are then torn up by the violence of the currents. At the start of the dry season, the water level drops. This is the time when the amphibious species emerge, their tender leaves disappearing rapidly as they are replaced by rigid laminae.

■ Plants across the planet

Africa

Most African species known to the aquariophile are from West Africa, located in the areas where fish for aquariums can be found. Flora varies widely according to local ecology. As in South America, the tropical region is covered with humid forests, but there is also bush and savanna. Some streams cut through shady forest glades, while others are exposed to the blistering sun. A typical plant genus found in these glades is *Anubias*. The species flourishes along shaded banks and grows only in the rainy season when it is under water. The galleries are also the home of *Crinum natans*, which can be recognized from its lovely white flower which is so reminiscent of the lily. Many species need a great deal of sunlight and grow profusely in exposed areas, like the bush country or savanna. Here you will find the cosmopolitan genera: *Ammania, Brasenia, Cyperus, Myriophyllum, Nymphaea. Aponogeton* is a genus more representative of Madagascar, where its various species are found in places with varying degrees of shades. Only two or three of these species are found in Africa. The most Southern of them, *A. distachus*, can also be found in the South of France and in Spain. Along the West African coast from Senegal to Angola, wide breaches appear in the forest, which unfortunately means there is very little in the way of endemic aquatic flora and fauna.

Central America

This section also includes the southern part of the United States. From the Tehuntepec isthmus to the

The natural environment of plants

Mexican river bordered by lush plant-life

south, the strip of land which joins North and South America is very narrow. Streams run fast and short and there is very little plant life in these. However, plants abound, both in mass as well as species number, in wide stretches of stagnant water and lagoons. In northern Mexico and to the south of the United States, aquatic plants are more plentiful in the temperate zones. Large groupings of *Cabomba caroliniana, Certophyllum demersum, Myriophyllum alterniflorum, M. hippuroides, Lobelia splendens,* or *Marsilea quadrifolia* can be sighted in stretches of stagnant water. There are no heavy floods in this region but the land is rich in minerals (although it gets poorer towards the south of Central America).

South America

The gigantic Amazonian basin forms a huge plain on the Eastern side of South America, but it is not an area of marshland. In the rainy season, vast stretches of land are under water; but in the dry season, although the soil is damp and muddy, it does not become waterlogged since it drains very quickly into the major rivers and streams. Some 20 m (22 yd) of rain falls annually in daily showers, mostly on the slopes of the Andes; the stagnant pools and ponds contain some interesting flora for aquariophiles. The genera *Cabomba, Myriophyllum* and some rare species of the genus *Echinodorus* can be found here. Broadly speaking, the genus *Echinodorus* does not comprise many aquatic species, as the majority tend to grow away from water in the dry season. This means that they are ideally suited to the aquaterrarium, where their foliage will adapt and they are able to flower.

Variations in temperature are also extremely important. They reach

15°C (59°F) in undulating areas and 35–38°C (95–100°F) in stagnant pools where ectreme temperatures are normal. On the other hand, the fact that they adapt to transitory minimum temperatures of 15–18°C (59–64°F) means that they can very easily be maintained in an aquarium kept at a temperature of 22°C (71°F). Many South American species that attract the aquariophile—like, for example, *Echinodorus horemannii, E. Longiscarpus, E. osiris, Cabomba australis, Heteranthera zosterifolia.* —originate in more southerly regions, such as south Brazil, Paraguay, Uruguay or Argentina. As these plants are accustomed to cool temperatures, they do very well in tanks with a maximum temperature of 25°C (77°F).

Asia

Asia contains the largest number of aquatic plants, both in terms of species and quantity. Most of them come from aquatic horticultural farms in Sri Lanka, Singapore and Malaysia but the natural environment itself is also a rich source of plants for the aquariophile. The Celebes Islands, off Borneo, and New Guinea are both rich sources.

These regions are characterized by the fact that they contain no major rivers and changes in temperature are only very slight because of the effect of the sea and absence of seasons. The paddy-fields have not yet encroached on the tropical forest and thousands of watercourses, streams, lakes and marshes drain away the water. Rainfall is greater in Asia than in South America with 20–35 m (22–38 yd) annually; but the rainfall is spread evenly throughout the year and the day, and the water later drains towards the sea. Changes in level are not very noticeable—a matter of two or three metres. Both air and water temperatures are constant at 26–28°C (79–82°F), and the same goes for insolation which is around twelve hours a day. On the whole, the flora react quickly and often unfavourably to any slight change,

one way or the other.

Once in the aquarium, these Asian species are even more sensitive to changes in light, heat, physio-chemical qualities in the water, as well as to other factors which are not present in the natural environment. Species of the genus *Cryptocoryne* are the best known from these countries. They grow in all kinds of natural environment there and include species which are strictly aquatic, as well as paludal and

Typical Sri Lankan vegetation

amphibian. *C. ciliata* can be found alongside rivers where there is plenty of sunshine and they react quite well to the sea's influence. In tropical forests, small watercourses can become heavily flooded and the resultant change in water-level (from 1–2 m [1–2 yd]) has a direct influence on the growth and appearance of some species. The water level can, however, also fall very rapidly. Amphibious species like the *C. wendtii* from Sri Lanka, are polymorphous. The best known, strictly aquatic Asian plants are the hygrophiles, myriophylles, blyxas and potamogetons. Some plants come from large islands, such as the giant Vallisnerie from New Guinea, ot? ies from the Celebes islands and false tenellus from New Zealand and Australia.

■ Characteristics of the Environment

Varieties of Water

In the aquarium, plants can benefit significantly from modern maintenance techniques, in the same way that fish do. In its natural environment, climatic, physical and chemical conditions affect a plant's location. Heavy floods carry down suspended muddy particles which settle on the plants, covering their laminae with an opaque and muddy film. Fast-moving currents pull up river-beds, exposing rocks and pebbles. These factors ensure that few plants are happy on ground disturbed by spring-tides.

Of equal importance to plant growth in the natural environment is the chemical composition of the water. For example, the murky waterways in South America which have a low pH level, lack minerals and are heavy with humic acid, contain very little plant life. At the same time, clear fast-running waters which have no mineral salts, are also devoid of plant species. It is the lightly mineralized, clear waters of South America with their almost neutral pH content which provide the most propitious home ground for plants. Plants are not happy in the rivers of Mexico, where the water has a high basic pH content and is heavily mineralized. Plants found in lagoons where the water has a mineral content are subject to precipitation containing calcium and magnesium. This is particularly the case for *Ceratophyllum demersum*, whose leaves feel like sandpaper brushing against the legs of an unsuspecting walker.

The main role of carbon dioxide gas

Non-sulphurous underground water-beds encourage plant development, and the carbon dioxide gas which accumulates there is important to their growth. Where this occurs in rivers, plants grow downstream—thanks to the presence of carbon dioxide; however, when the gas disperses they wilt very quickly, as it is essential to their photosynthesis. The large East African lakes are devoid of plant life that may be of interest to aquariophiles. The main reason for this is the particular composition of the water, which is basically lacking in minerals. Another possible reason is that coastal winds disperse the carbon

Station in Cabomba, Mexico

dioxide gas and thus set up intense oxygenation. Lakes Tanganyika, Malawi and, to a lesser extent, Lake Victoria, have no plant life at all. On the other hand, Lake Victoria is covered in *Papyrus, Typha* and *Nymphaea* in its marshy regions. The rocky coast is covered by greenish-yellow algae called Aufwuchs, the staple diet of thousands of Cyclides (exotic perch). The sandy coast will occasionally see crops of stunted *Vallisneria*. Obviously, when maintaining plants artificially, the environment differs greatly from that provided by nature.

	SOUTH AMERICA		CENTRAL AMERICA		AFRICA		ASIA
	Black water – Peru	Clear water – Guyana	Lagoon Ignacio Allendé	River Rio Candela ria Mexico	River Mungo Cameroon	Lake Tanganyika	Small Malayan river
pH	5,80	7,2	7,2	7,3	7,5	7,8 à 8,2	6,3
Total hardness THf°	0,20	7	17,5	63	6	20	3,5
Carbonate hardness THf° .	0,12	4,5	12,5	40	4,5	5	2,5
Nitrites mg/l	0	0	0	0	0,5	0	0
Nitrates mg/l	1,50	1	25	0	3	4	0
Temperature °C	24	23	28	25	27	27	26
Transparency m	2-3	3-4	1,0	10	1,0	20	1,0
Colour.	Tea	Blue	Brown	Green	Brown	Blue	Tea
CO_2 mg/l	1	12	18	0	8	0	2
Conduct. uS/cm² at 20°C.	17	150	620	2 300	75	600	140

Physico-chemical characteristics of some water types found in the natural environment.

■ Acclimatization of the plants

Certain precautions must be taken when 'wild' specimens are introduced into the aquarium. In fact, the conditions in which plants were picked, transported or sold, may give cause for some disappointment once they are in the aquarium. Rare species, brought home by aquariophiles or botanists who have exercised the utmost care when picking and transporting them, are rarely a problem. However, those which are available on the market —Myriophylles, *Bacopa, Vallisneries* and *Echinodorus*—often are. These plants come to us from distant farms where optimum conditions of cultivation and profitability are sought. Transportation costs represent a major expense and economies are often made with this to the detriment of the plants.

Selecting and packaging

When they have been collected, plants are selected and bunched tightly in quantities of 250 or 500. These are then packaged in polystyrene boxes and kept moist with wet newspaper. In the best conditions, the plants will be refrigerated at a temperature of 18°C (64°F) and transported quickly to avoid a journey longer than thirty-six hours. The most fragile specimens are put into lightly inflated nylon bags, to prevent them being crushed.

The overcrowding of plants, packaging them at an atmospheric temperature around 28°–30°C (82–86°F) in tropical countries, and journeys longer than forty-eight hours are all detrimental to healthy acclimatization. This kind of treatment causes plants to ferment. Crates containing the bunches often reveal scorched plants, generally with about a hundred undamaged ones on the outside which have been saved by their proximity to the air circulation. Importers should choose their suppliers according to the quality and care practised in their packaging techniques. Then, there follows the equally difficult task of successfully acclimatizing plants under glass. Ideally, the plants should be put under water, in units of sale, in the best conditions of light and heat, so they reassume their 'natural' appearance.

Good health and selection

Some of the rarer plants, such as the *Echinodorus*, are cultivated in Europe underwater and, in principle, should be acclimatized in this immersed state before being sold. But, in most cases these species are found on the market with their spike still intact. They usually receive a supply of weakly-diffused carbon dioxide gas at this point, because the water often has an acid content which contains very few minerals. This artifical stimulus quickly restores the health of the plant so that it looks good enough for the retail market. It will depend on the retailer's ability and sense of responsibility as to whether the plants will be allowed to continue their convalescence under good conditions, or whether they will have to suffer a second trauma in quick succession. The aquariophile or aqua-cultivator will have to be able to assess the condition of plants and to pick those which have suffered least down the commercial line.

When making a choice, the expert will check that:
- the specimens do not have spikes;
- the plant tissues are a light green colour, unless yellow or red is the natural colour of the plant in question;
- the foliage of *Cabomba* and the Myriophylles species are erect;
- the foliage of *Cryptocoryne* plants have no brown markings;
- the edges of the thin leaves of *Vallisneria* are not torn;
- the *Aponogeton* has no leaves (the absence of foliage points to plant having recently gone through a resting phase, which indicates a good recovery is under way);
- bulbs are firm and do not emit gaseous bubbles when squeezed.

Opposite: Black water in French Guiana

An importer's glass-house showing above-water cultivation

Plants in the aquarium

There is no compulsion to keep plants and fish together in an aquarium. Only a few piscicultural species need plants on which to lay their eggs. Often, the aquariophile chooses plants for an aquarium simply because he or she prefers aquatic plant-life to fish-life, in which case, a Dutch tank will be the choice. Often, for purely aesthetic reasons, the choice will be to combine fish and plants.

■ Some technical grounds and aesthetic points

It used to be the case that plants were important in an aquarium for the health of fish, but this is no longer true, thanks to sophisticated technology and reliable aquarium equipment. Our predecessors did not have the use of functioning filters or air pumps. It was the plants who used to do the work of this equipment, by supplying oxygen and filtering the water.

Modern techniques, in particular the drip system, restrict toxic matter found in a tank. Until now, many people wrongly thought that this role could be filled by plants, thus justifying their presence in the aquarium. To avoid any real disaster to fish, it is best not to count on plants as filtering agents. Over the last ten years the opinion of aquariophiles has changed a great deal on this subject. Tanks with too many fish are less common today. Aquariophiles leave no stone un-turned where the well-being of their fish is concerned, and often they will respond to the specialized market by acting against the interests of the plant.

However, it is difficult to picture a freshwater, or even seawater tank devoid of plant-life. Without plants any tank would look singularly unattractive. Moreover, plants give fish somewhere to hide and define their boundaries. They bring life and movement, particularly to the top of the tank, which is never an easy area to fill.

Some tanks, which have no plant-life are maintained by cichlidophiles (Cichlid enthusiasts), in which case the effectiveness of the physio-chemical conditions has to take precedence for the well-being of the fish. The same kind of plant 'desert' will be seen where aquariophiles keep plant-eating fish or natives of brackish water.

■ Organizing the aquarium: a question of taste, trial and error

The variety of colours and shades to be found among aquatic plants makes it possible to create a real masterpiece. Different shades of green, yellow and red, when combined with various natural or artificial materials, can produce some quite striking contrasts. It is very difficult to give advice in this field but vital plant requirements must be taken into account. Suggestions for their position in the tank should be looked on as a guide only; putting a tall plant in the foreground of the tank will ruin the aesthetics but will certainly not stop the plant growing and reproducing. The arrangement of plants is a question of good sense, personal taste, and knowing the needs of plants and fish, in order to maintain the balance of the miniature world of the aquarium.

A sense of the aesthetic will probably banish the use of divers in rocking chambers, plunging sub-

Piranha tank

marines and other such water-garden ornaments. Artificial plants are sometimes a good copy and could be used to decorate a tank containing occupants which are destructive plant-eaters. On the whole, the use of a plant in the aquarium is less important than its aesthetics. The ability of plants to detoxify or to oxygenate is often quite limited compared to currently available aquarium technology. No plant will obviate the necessity of changing the water or of using air-diffusers. Without the contribution of technology, a tank, no matter how well planted out or populated, will in the long-term prove unrewarding. An exception to this is the water hyacinth which makes a highly efficient pump but is extremely difficult to keep in an aquarium...or Elodes, which are genuine oxygen diffusers but wilt in the heat of the tank.

Shelter and defining territories

Aquarium plants contribute more than just aesthetics. For example, small, surface or floating plants offer a partial covering, so that an Amazonian tank can be created. *Cryptocoryne*, which are small with wide leaves can shelter small fish near the substratum of the tank. Curtains of plants can be used to define boundaries, so that several species of fish can live together. The question of chemical changes and a final analysis on the profitability of keeping plants in the aquarium, will be discussed in the next chapter.

■ Plants and fishes

Co-existence

Aquatic plants present no danger to fish; in fact, the converse is true. Certain species of fish feed on plants, while others even attack them. However, by their very presence, fish supply plants with the carbon dioxide required for growth, and some species clean off the parasitic algae which grow on their leaves.

Although they are herbivores, some fish steer away from plants which are too leathery or taste 'bad'. This tends to be the case for the Java fern, *Microsorium pteropus*, as well as various species of the genus *Crinum*. The African fern, *Bolbitis heudelotii*, is usually left alone too. In short, plants and fish can live together within a well-planned framework.

Food sources

The most fragile of the aquatic plants which fish find appetizing, are those which have foliage which

Plants in the aquarium

Families of fish (H=Herbivores)	MAJOR PLANT TYPES hardy ———————————————————— frail						
	Crinum Bolbitis Microsorium	Spathi-phyllum Vallisneria	Cryptocoryne Echinodorus Anubias	Pl. flottantes Fougères flottantes	Apono-geton Ludwigia	Rotola Hygro-phila	Cabomba Myriophyllum Limnophila
POLYPTERIDAE	+	+	+	+	+	O	O
ALESTIDAE	+	+	+	+	+	+	+
CITHARINIDAE (H)	O	O	–	–	–	–	–
ANOSTOMIDAE (H)	O	O	–	–	–	–	–
CHARACIDAE	+	+	+	+	+	+	+
CHARACIDIIDAE	+	+	+	+	+	+	+
CURIMATIDAE (H)	O	O	–	–	–	–	–
ERYTHRINIDAE	+	+	+	+	+	+	+
GASTEROPELECIDAE	+	+	+	+	+	+	+
HEMIODIDAE	+	+	+	+	+	O	–
LEBIASINIDAE	+	+	+	+	+	+	O
SERRASALMIDAE (H)	O	O	–	O	–	–	–
COBITIDAE	+	+	+	+	+	+	+
CYPRINIDAE	+	+	+	+	+	+	O
BAGRIDAE	+	+	+	+	+	+	+
CALLICHTHYIDAE	+	+	+	+	+	+	+
CLARIIDAE	+	+	+	+	+	+	+
DORADIDAE	+	+	+	+	+	+	+
LORICARIIDAE	+	+	+	+	+	+	+
MOCHOCIDAE	+	+	+	+	+	+	+
PIMELODIDAE	+	+	+	+	+	+	+
CYPRINODONTIDAE	+	+	+	+	+	+	+
POECILIIDAE (Poecilia)	+	+	+	+	+	O	–
POECILIIDAE (others)	+	+	+	+	+	+	+
ANABANTIDAE	+	+	+	+	+	+	+
BELONTIIDAE	+	+	+	+	+	+	+
CICHLIDAE ≅ (H)	+	+	O	+	O	–	–
CENTRACHIDAE	+	+	+	+	+	+	+
CENTROPOMIDAE	+	+	+	+	+	+	+
LOBOTIDAE	+	+	+	+	+	+	+
MONODACTYLIDAE (H)	+	O	O	+	O	–	–
NANDIDAE	+	+	+	+	+	+	+
SCATOPHAGIDAE (H)	+	+	O	+	–	–	–
TOXOTIDAE	+	+	+	+	+	+	O
ATHERINIDAE	+	+	+	+	+	+	+
CHANNIDAE	+	+	+	+	+	+	O
GOBIIDAE	+	+	+	+	+	+	+
HEMIRHAMPHIDAE	+	+	+	+	+	+	+
MASTACEMBELIDAE	+	+	+	+	+	O	O
MELANOTAENIIDAE	+	+	+	+	+	+	O
MORMYRIDAE	+	+	+	+	+	+	+

Co-existence plants – fish (+ good; O possible; – poor).

is finely separated or thread-like, such as the *Cabomba*, *Myriophyllum* and *Limnophila*. Even *Poeciliids* such as guppies, which are supposed to be non-aggressive towards plants, attack these. The non-herbivorous members of your tank may also find it difficult to resist the temptation offered by the young shoots of these genera. Some species of herbivorous fish — in particular Anostomids, some algae-eating Cichlids, or Curimatids — are very fond of them, just sprinkle a handful of the foliage onto the surface of the water, to see how they hurl themselves at it. Spinach or lettuce are suitable alternative foodstuffs for the fish but many aquariophiles cultivate the plants in order to meet various dietary requirements, as the other greenery is often refused.

The best way to keep these 'feather-duster plants' is to place them in a Dutch tank, as their position in the communal tank is not viable in the long term.

Props for egg-laying

Many breeders make use of plants for a particular purpose. Belontiids enthusiasts (Belontiids belong to the family of fighting and Paradise fish) use floating fern, which offers many advantages. One of these is its capacity for cutting down water-surface movements, so that nests can be made out of bubbles. It is very common for the male of this particular species to build the nest with his own 'saliva'. The bubble sticks to the plant and uses it as an anchor. Later, when the fry swim around freely, plants offer shelter to them among their own radicles, which lie near the surface. The micro-organisms which develop in their midst provide the first food for the young fish.

Plants make useful breeding grounds for species with reproductive difficulties, and also for those who reproduce quite spontaneously. Species from various families like the small Charicids, Cyprinids,

some Cyprinodontids and the Melanotaeniids, lay their eggs on or between the slender leaves of the plants. Moss like the Bogor (*Glossadelphus zollingeri*), the Fontinalis (*Fontinalis antipyretica*) or even the Java (*Vesicularia dubyana*) prove very suitable for this purpose.

On the other hand, tall plants with slender foliage are preferred by fish which lay their eggs in open water. The plants should be carefully cleaned, so as not to contaminate future fish spawn with the bacteria and fungi that they harbour. This should be done by bathing them in a solution of potassium alum, (6 g to 1 l) for one hour at 35°C (95°F). This treatment is also recommended for plants housed in communal or ornamental tanks so as to free them of undesirable molluscs or the colourless, gelatinous eggs that are laid. The eggs of some species of fish are particularly fragile. The breeding places would then need to be sterilized, either thermally or chemically (using a 10% solution of hydrochloric acid) which the plants could not tolerate. In this case, substitute with materials which can withstand such an operation. An example is the 'mop', a floating island of cork, on which threads of green synthetic wool have been secured by means of a rubber band. A filtering moss of green nylon can also act as a good substitute. These materials stand up very well to successive sterilizations. Many fish will lay their eggs on them: the *Phenacogrammus interruptus*, the *Aphyosemion*, or Characids, and the *Hyphessobrycon erythrostigma*.

Plants of the genera *Anubias*, *Echinodorus* and *Cryptocoryne*, have wide leaves which remain rigid against the pressure of the fish's abdomen, when it is laying its eggs. The leaves are oval, spear-shaped and spatula-like on a stalk which is fairly stiff, so they are able to stand up to a firm pressure when the eggs are being laid. The female can therefore attach her oviduct and perfect the way the egg sticks to

Leaf-fish: Monocirrhus poly-acanthus

example is the egg-laying habit of the 'leaf-fish' (*Monocirrhus poly-acanthus*) which strangely resembles a leaf in shape and colour. It attaches its eggs to the foliage by means of a filament and then watches over their hatching without being observed by other occupants.

Fossil plants: peat

A group of fish belonging to the Cyprinodontids family, lays its eggs in peat. This is true of some types of *Aphyosemion*, the African *Nothobranchius* and the neo-tropical *Cynolebias*, which in captivity will bury itself in a layer of peat-moss (*Sphagnum*) to lay its eggs. Peat-moss grows in successive layers in acidic marshland and it is the accumulated layers which create the peat. The matter which contains the eggs is dried but left slightly moist and then stored in nylon sachets and date-stamped. After a resting period, which is determined according to the fish in hand, the peat and eggs are replaced in the water where the fry quickly hatch. Aquariophiles find many applications for peat, and it is perfectly suited to horticultural uses, provided that no preservatives or nitrogen products are added to it.

plant tissue. Subsequently, the larvae attach themselves to the underside by means of a filament or their cephalic glands. These plants make the best breeding ground for certain species of the Cichlid family, which sometimes use the plants simply as a base to which the larvae can attach themselves. Callichthyids (*Corydoras*), some of the Locariids and Cyprinids (*Barbus* some and *Rasbora*) are unique in that they lay their eggs on the underside of the plants' leaves. The most stunning

■ General advice

It is sensible for the aquariophile to find out about the habits of a fish before each purchase. Consult an authoritative text for this information to avoid some nasty surprises. When magnificent fish like the *Leporinus*, *Anostomus* and *Abramites* clean out a well-planted tank within the space of one day, it is enough to reduce even the most sanguine person to tears for being unfamiliar with the habits of the latest addition to the tank.

Some species are particularly recommended as cleaner-fish or 'window washers'. The best known of these, the *Gyrinocheilus aymonieri*, along with the small *Ancistrus*,

Otocinclus or *Garra* carry out numerous tasks for the aquariophile and for the plants. These fish move quickly between the stems, shaking off particles which have settled on the leaves. The particles are then suspended in water and drawn towards the filter. These fish tend to be plant-eaters with a quite specific diet; they are particularly fond of the algae layer (periphyton) which grows on the leaves of higher plants. It would be a mistake to regard these fish simply as effective cleaners; their prime function is to feed! They are no substitute for proper water changes and glass scraping.

Planting

Successful planting is not as easy as it seems at first; even under the best conditions there is no guarantee that plants will survive. Some substrata are better suited than others for securing plants. Should plant species with strong roots be used? If so, should these be pruned or left whole? Should the foliage be left complete or should it be trimmed? Should plants be indiscriminately placed in the tank or should their size when fully grown be taken into account? The list of questions is endless and each can only be answered in relation to the individual plant.

■ Substratum problems

Planting is a relatively easy matter, if make-up and structure of the substratum are considered. Plants which have roots or suckers survive well in sand, thanks to its inherent properties. In a more granular substratum, planting is a bit more difficult, depending on the size of the grains and how densely packed they are.

Plants fare much better in gravel, for example, than they do in Natalit, where there is always the risk that they will rise to the surface shortly after being planted. If this is the case, protective moss or various lead ballasts (such as bands or grips) should not be used in the aquarium, particularly when an acid environment is planned. It is always possible to ballast plants, particularly if they are tall. Do this by placing a small pebble on one of their leaves.

■ Should roots be cut?

Special attention should be paid to roots, as there are many aquarium enthusiasts who have the wrong ideas about them. Many believe that strong roots will guarantee a thriving plant and so they ask suppliers for plants with long roots. But this is not necessarily the case. Strong roots do not always point to a healthy plant; what good are they if the heart of the plant is itself weak?

If a plant does have strong roots, should these be cut before placing it in the aquarium? The answer here will depend on whether the plant was cultivated in or out of water. Plants grown out of water should have their roots well trimmed before being put into the aquarium, but this is not necessary for those grown under water.

Some timely answers

Plants which have rhizomes, such as *Echinodorus*, *Aponogeton* or *Cryptocoryne*, may be trimmed as long as there is enough left for them to be held in the substratum; their roots will then develop on the new section of the rhizome. Plants with stalks, like *Cabomba*, *Myriophyllum* (and generally all those which are sold in sprigs of four or five), are sought with their roots by aquarium enthusiasts, but this is a grave mistake. The roots are not only superfluous, but can also give rise to a number of problems. Simple stem suckers form quickly under the joints of the roots all along the stalk and this growth is inhibited when the stalk is planted in the substratum. So the plant uses its

Planting

Opposite: Marshland in Cayenne Island (Guiana)

reserves to create strong roots and to anchor itself, thus creating a solid basis for future growth. If this stem sucker is pulled out of the of the substratum and later replanted, its roots will go rotten. Plants with stalks should not, therefore, be replanted with their roots and this is why, when overhauling the aquarium, it is a good idea to shorten the stalks of these plants by a few centimetres.

■ Successive transplants

The information above is a help in understanding the problems encountered when trying to revive plants which have been bought from the shop. Multiple transplants during each stage of their journey to the market often exhaust the plant's ability to form new roots. So how can these plants remain healthy? The aquarium lover can solve this problem to some extent by gauging the arrival of the plants. Aim to purchase them as soon as they arrive at the shop and certainly before they are planted out and have time to develop new roots.

■ Should leaves be retained?

A decision should be made quickly as to whether to retain or remove the leaves from the plants before planting them.

For the large *Echinodorus*, eight to nine central leaves will suffice. If there are more leaves than this, it will be enough to remove some of the external ones, as the plant will then have more energy with which to manufacture roots.

Dwarf plants and *Cryptocoryne* should have five to six healthy leaves.

On the other hand, *Aponogeton* should be chosen with a leafless bulb, or one where the leaves are only just beginning to grow.

Dutch tank

■ Choosing species and organizing the tank

When establishing a new tank or overhauling an aquarium, it is always best to buy all the plants in one go. This is not always possible, either for financial reasons or because it may be difficult finding exactly what is required in the shops. Not all aquatic species can be bought: some one hundred and sixty species are listed by specialist wholesalers.

Plants are selected according to requirement and taste, but also for biological reasons.

Plants which grow very quickly, like the *Vallisneria*, can harm neighbouring species if they are put in the background near the aquarium's filter. Their ribbon-like leaves, buoyed up by the water current which is emitted by the pump, monopolize much of the light. On the other hand, species of the genus *Cryptocoryne* are very much at home around the base of these same *Vallisneria*, where the light is quite sufficient for their growth. Natural decorative elements, such as a coconut shell, make good breeding grounds par-

ticularly for the small Cichlids. There is no point placing plants too near the opening of the coconut, as they are likely to be unearthed by fish in an attempt to establish a clear field of vision over the territory. All these possibilities should be borne in mind before any actual planting. Before establishing the tank, it is best to start by making a small sketch marking in the position of the various plants; also mark in other factors, such as spray from the filter or static items of decoration (roots, rocks) etc. Plants should be arranged in an irregular fashion so that they do not end up looking like rows of soldiers on parade.

Fast-growing plants are better placed in the background or at the sides. Bear in mind the natural colour of each species, so that the overall effect is harmonious.

Finally, avoid overcrowding the plants when planting. As long as growing conditions are good, the spaces left empty during planting, will quickly be filled with healthy foliage.

■ Planting techniques

When you have decided which species to buy and how to arrange the decoration, pay a visit to your retailer, preferably carrying a polystyrene box!

Plants with stalks should be selected in quantities above ten, while any exotic-looking types should be picked singly. Select five to seven of the Amazonian plants, *Cryptocoryne* and *Aponogeton*, according to how much space there is in the tank. Once the plants have been purchased, do not accept them wrapped in damp newspaper, instead ask to have them placed in a slightly inflated plastic bag containing a little water: this prevents them from becoming crushed and chilled. At this point, the polystyrene box comes in useful as a means of carrying the plants home.

Before putting them in the aquarium, plants should be bathed in a solution of potassium alum for one hour at a temperature of 35°C (95°F), for the sake of plant hygiene. They should then be rinsed in clear water at a slightly lower temperature. Plants with stalks should be grouped into bunches of two or three and their stems shortened by two or three centimetres.

Hold them between your thumb and second finger and plant them by pushing with the index and ring fingers. They should be laid out in clumps of the same species, rather than scattered around in the tank.

Establishing species with roots requires a little more attention. The heart or neck of the plant should, under no circumstances, be covered by gravel or any other kind of

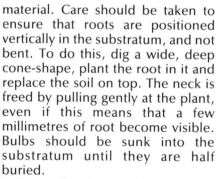

Species with roots, like Vallisneria asiatica, *should be planted with necks above the substratum*

Rhizome of Microsorium pteropus *should not be buried*

material. Care should be taken to ensure that roots are positioned vertically in the substratum, and not bent. To do this, dig a wide, deep cone-shape, plant the root in it and replace the soil on top. The neck is freed by pulling gently at the plant, even if this means that a few millimetres of root become visible. Bulbs should be sunk into the substratum until they are half buried.

Generally plants with rhizomes are anchored solely by their roots. But some plants of the genera *Bolbitis* and *Microsorium* should not be buried in the substratum. Their particular kind of root will not tolerate this sort of treatment and they should be attached to a prop of some kind in the open water. For example, the rhizome could be attached with a paper-clip which could be stuck into the polystyrene decor, thus holding the plant in position. Three to four weeks later,

the paper-clip can be removed; by this time the plant will have taken hold naturally (the paper-clip won't leave any trace). Alternatively, use a rubber band to hold the rhizome up against a peat-bog root or a rock. Once the plant has anchored itself to the substratum with its roots, the rubber band can be broken and removed.

Planting aquatic species which have a bulb, like those of the genus *Crinum*, is much more difficult. When purchased, their roots are often short, and as their density is lower than that of water, they are often drawn towards the surface. The only way round this is to bury the roots in the best way possible and to wedge the bulb to the substratum with a small flat stone, which should remain in place until the roots develop.

Possible layouts for planting are discussed in the individual sections on each species.

THE REQUIRE-MENTS AND MAINTEN-ANCE OF PLANTS

The aquarium enthusiast is devoted to creating living conditions which approximate those of the natural environment of the plant. But, it is also important to pay attention to the special requirements for maintenance and growth essential to plant-life which needs chlorophyll to survive.

Light

In the natural environment, the sun provides all the light energy necessary for plants which use chlorophyll for the process of photosynthesis. In the aquarium this source of light is too irregular and difficult to control, so artificial light has to be installed. To meet the requirements of the plants, the amateur should ensure that the light source is adequate in terms of quantity, quality and duration.

■ Quantity of light or illumination

Most imported aquatic plants originate from tropical or inter-tropical zones. In fact, many of them inhabit shady environments in forest glades, or damp tropical forests, so they actually need very little light.

The inevitable question comes to mind: how much light should be supplied to aquatic plants?

Illuminating plants

Under natural conditions, illumination on the water surface and under a slightly overcast sky is between 15,000 and 20,000 lux at midday. Under 30–40 cm (12–15 in) of water this falls to around 700 to 3,000 lux. But in shady areas, at the same depth, lighting is restricted to around 150 to 500 lux.

The table below sets out the quantity of light requirements for the major plant groups housed in a tank. The values are applicable to isolated subjects. They would be slightly higher for a tank comprising mixed plants or for a Dutch tank. Also, surface plants and tall plants cast a significant shadow over those immediately below them.

Loss of light

Even pure water acts as an obstacle to the penetration of light. The amount of light which reaches the centre of a liquid will be weaker, the higher the water column to be crossed. Any particles suspended in the water of the aquarium act as an additional barrier to light penetra-

Plants (genera)	Amount of lighting in lumen/m^2
	0 500 800 2 000 4 000 8 000
Surface plants	
Myriophyllum	
Bacopa	
Hottonia	
Ludwigia	
Aponogeton	
Ceratopteris	
Nomaphila	
Rotala	
Vallisneria	
Echinodorus	
Sagittaria	
Cryptocoryne	
Marsilea	
Microsorium	

Lighting requirements of some genera.
● *optimum per group*

28

tion. For this reason, an effective filter should be installed and the water changed regularly. Moreover, the various wave-lengths which constitute white light, are absorbed selectively in terms of depth. Thus, the red is absorbed by the level just under the water surface, the green a little lower down, and finally the blue. This means that a change has been made to the original light quality, from the surface downwards. Wherever possible, avoid using glass or plexiglass lids on top of the aquarium, as much of the light is reflected from the surface. Also, the lid could eventually become covered in algae or scale which would act as a barrier to the light source. The loss of light through a glass lid could be estimated at around 7–9%, according to the quality and thickness of the glass in question.

The idea of using an illuminating cover over the aquarium is becoming more popular. In order to limit the loss of light, the angle formed by the edges of the aquarium and the centre of the light source should be at 120°. This can be achieved by dividing the width of the tank into four so as to position the height of the light source in relation to the water surface. The inside of the cover should be lined with a perfectly smooth layer of aluminium foil or a layer of chromium paint (obtainable in spray cans for use on hub caps). Both precautions reduce light loss.

Calculating the light flow to be installed

The level of power for illumination, or light flow, has to be calculated in terms of data available on aquatic plants and disturbances to the light from its source down to the bottom of the tank. An easy formula would be to install one power of 1 W per 2 l (3½ pt) of water. But for a large volume of water and for a water level higher than 50 cm (20 in), this formula would use up a vast amount of energy, especially if fluorescent tubes are utilized. For water levels

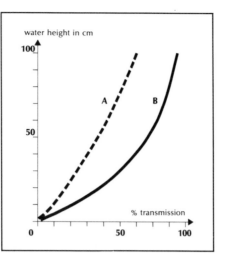

Light loss in relation to depth.
A – in pure water
B – in the aquarium

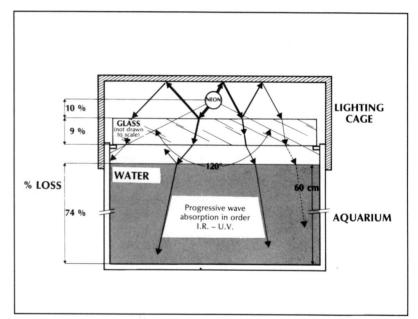

Conception of lighting cage and various light losses in %.

higher than 60 cm (24 in), use high-pressure fluorescent bulbs (1 to 10 bars) whose light density is as much as 5 candelas as against 0.8 for the classical fluorescent tube.

A simple formula for calculating the light flow to be installed, taking into account the various losses, follows:

Light flow = 20.S.H.P. where:

S = surface

H = height

P = losses (via water level, cover, lid)

20 = constant expressed in lumen

Aquarium in cm surface × height	Lighting 20 lm/dm²	Coefficient of water height loss in cm	9% cover loss	10% lid loss	Lighting flow to be installed	lm/l lm/dm²
100 x 40 x 40 160 litres	40 dm2 800 lm	x 2,5 2 000 lm	180 lm	218 lm	2 398 lm	14,98 0,37
140 x 60 x 60 504 litres	84 dm2 1 680 lm	x 3,8 6 384 lm	574 lm	695 lm	7 654 lm	15,18 0,23
240 x 80 x 80 1 536 litres	192 dm2 3 840 lm	x 5,0 19 200 lm	1 728 lm	2 092 lm	23 020 lm	14,98 0,24
350 x 150 x 100 5 250 litres	525 dm2 10 500 lm	x 6,25 65 625 lm	5 906 lm	7 153 lm	78 684 lm	14,98 0,28

160 litre tank	2 tubes of 90 cm/60 W theoretical, 66 W actual (power absorbed on installation)
504 litre tank	3 tubes of 120 cm/120 W theoretical, 144 W actual or two 80 Watt bulbs
1536 litre tank	5 tubes of 150 cm/325 W theoretical, 390 W actual or 3 × 125 watt bulbs
5250 litre tank	6 bulbs of 250 W/1,500 W theoretical, 1,800 W actual

Light power required according to tank volume.

■ Quality of light

Plants not only need a certain amount of light, but also a certain quality of light. Their green pigment, chlorophyll, picks out very definite wave-lengths from the sun's light. By giving the plants access to wave-lengths which are found in the blue and red spectrums, they will be better able to accomplish the process of photosynthesis.

White light spectrum

The white light spectrum can be visualized by splitting it by means of a prism. From 3,800 Å to 7,500 Å visible waves appear corresponding to colours which follow this order: violet, indigo, blue, green, yellow, orange and red. At the two extremities, 3,800 Å, the ultra-violet (U.V.) rays and 7,500 Å, the infra-red (I.R.) are invisible. The largest amount of energy absorbed by the chorophyll process is found in the blue and red rays. So, it is important to select light sources which predominantly emit these two wave-lengths, that is 4,200–4,500 Å and 6,300–6,800 Å. However, many aquarium lovers have noticed that plants will adapt quite well to a non-specific emission spectrum. There are many tanks around which are illuminated by a collection of tubes which comprise only the industrial white kind, and these tanks contain a very prosperous plant-life, provided of course the other factors required for plant growth are respected. This extreme solution is not to be recommended; it is always better to select a tube which resembles solar emission by referring to the colour rendering index (CRI) or to the chromatic index, for which 100 represents the total solar spectrum at the zenith. The global spectrum of light sources is then compared to solar light, by conferring on them a value related to the standard of 100. A note relating to this should be supplied in the documents which come with the tubes, so that the user when making his purchase can see immediately

Photosynthesis effectiveness curve.

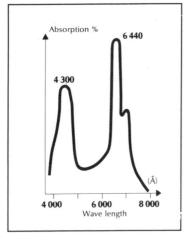

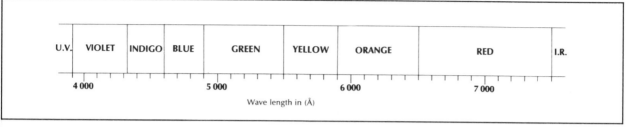

| U.V. | VIOLET | INDIGO | BLUE | GREEN | YELLOW | ORANGE | RED | I.R. |

Wave length in (Å)

4 000   5 000   6 000   7 000

White light spectrum.

the spectrum value of the lamp by referring to the 100 index. After all, the purchaser is not necessarily a specialist in interpreting the spectrum curve!

Specialized (often described as horticultural) fluorescent tubes contain a majority of blue and red waves in their emission spectrum, and are therefore closer to the spectrum for assimilating chlorophyll. But the tubes emit a very faint light, which is not generally satisfactory for the aquarium enthusiast. Also, they rarely show off the decoration in the tank to its best advantage and their emission spectrum is deficient in yellow waves, which form a major part of visual sensitivity. Because of the two dominant colours, this kind of fluorescent tube highlights the red and blue colouring of fish, plants and decoration, producing a garish effect.

Try for a compromise on all sides, while keeping sight of the requirements in hand: assimilation of chlorophyll, colour of the fish, personal taste, and the quest to reproduce a natural world in the aquarium. The fluorescent tubes with a CRI index to 100 will produce the most natural looking aquarium. Curiously enough, but perhaps for good reason, most Dutch tank specialists make little use of these tubes.

Also, take into account the aesthetics of the fish themselves. Under the yellowish light which you get from Wotan Colour 30 or Daylight tubes, the blue hues of the African Cichlides or marine fish, look very pale. Here again, the visible spectrum can be corrected by adding a dominant-blue tube in the foreground of the aquarium.

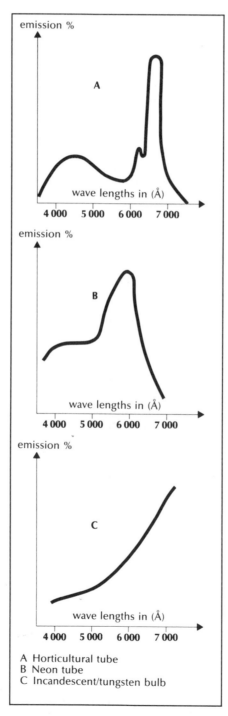

A Horticultural tube
B Neon tube
C Incandescent/tungsten bulb

Emission spectrum of some light sources.

Choosing the light source

It is extremely difficult to recommend any of the various types and brands of lighting sources, especially given the fast-moving technology in this field. Moreover, there are very few scientific works available on light sources and their influence on aquatic plants. With this subject, we must rely on results, the experience of the aquarium enthusiast, and the information supplied by the manufacturers.

Recent progress in the industry which covers lighting for aquariums concerns the increase in light output (1m/W) of fluorescent tubes in relation to the decrease of energy consumed.

Low-power discharge lamps with an acceptable CRI, some of them higher than the 90 index, are coming onto the market. Given a similar light output for both sorts of lighting, the light density is higher in the discharge lamps. This will mean better lighting in deep water. Unfortunately, discharge lamps are mainly designed for use in industry and public lighting. The few models taken for use in the aquarium are fairly mediocre. The lamps are in fact based only on the chlorophyll-absorption spectrum. The same can apply to horticultural tubes, where the visual spectrum curve of the aquarium enthusiast seems to have been ignored. Designed for germinators and horticultural conservatories, they have not been given much aesthetic consideration.

Wherever possible, it is best to select a standard-length tube with a wide scale. For example, tubes of 0.60 m (2 ft) (590) for an 80 cm (2 ft 6 in) tank, or 1.2 m (4 ft) for a 1.6 m (5 ft 2 in) tank, even if they end up being used in an orthodox manner in the lighting cover.

Tube length in mm	Nominal power in W	Tube diameter in mm	Length of aquarium in cm
136	4	16	20
212 (1)	6	16	27
288 (1)	8	16	35
360	14	26/38	46
437	15	26/38	54
517 (1)	13	16	60
590 (1)	18/20	26/38	70
641	18	26	75
691	18/25	26/38	80
742	18/25	26	80
818	25	38	90
895	30	26	100
1 047	38	26	110
1 200 (1)	36/38/40/115(2)	26/38	130
1 500 (1)	58/65	26/38	160
1 760	55/85/110(2)	38	190
2 370	75	38	2 500
2 385	110/215 (2)	38	2 500

(1) European standard length tubes
(2) Super-power tubes

Choice of tube length according to aquarium length.

■ Various types of tube

Fluorescent tubes

The length of fluorescent tubes available on the market will determine the chosen length of the aquarium frontage. The latter should be slightly longer, so as to allow for the thickness of the connecting bases. The standard 1.2 m (4 ft) and 0.60 m (2 ft) tubes offer the widest choice in quality of light.

Budget tubes can be easily spotted from their 26 mm (1 in) diameter as compared to the usual 38 mm (1¾ in), particularly for the standard 1.2 m (4 ft) tube. Their power is weaker than the nominal 40 W. As for the majority of fluorescent tubes, they last approximately 6,000 hours. This corresponds to a daily use of fourteen hours for a period of one year.

Some tubes have a life which is sometimes four times as long (over 24,000 hours). These long-life tubes have the advantage of a high colour-rendering index (IRC or CRI). They may seem expensive, but the investment is perfect justifiable. These tubes are also known as full-spectrum tubes, because their temperature is close or identical to that of natural light. The latter has a CRI of 100 for a temperature of 5,500 K. By comparison, an incandescent lamp has a temperature of 2,200–3,000 K.

According to brand, the colour rendering is given in detail (e.g. CRI 91) or marked from 1 to 4. These numbers indicate levels corresponding to the following CRI values:

- Level 1 = 85 to 100 (Exceptional CRI)
- Level 2 = 70 to 84 (Good CRI)
- Level 3 = 40 to 69 (Fair CRI)
- Level 4 = 2 to 40 (Poor CRI)

This numbering system is only meaningful to the aquarium-owner. Bear in mind that the choice of tubes for major illumination should be made from full-spectrum light sources.

TYPES AND BRANDS	CRI or Ni.	Temperature (K)	Lighting in lumens	Life expectancy in hours
Trucolor 30 PHILIPS . . .	98	5 000	2 350	6 000
Maxilux 22 WOTAN . . .	96	3 800	3 750	7 500
Maxilux 21 WOTAN . . .	85	4 000	5 400	7 500
Northlight Colour Matching THORNE . .	94	5 800	1 700-2 700	—
Maxilux de-lux Daylight Color 12 WOTAN . . .	98	5 000	3 750	—
True Lite DUROTEST. . .	91	5 500	2 180	24 000
True Lite POWER TUIST .	91	5 500	2 400	24 000
Optima 50 DUROTEST . .	91	5 000	2 200	24 000
Colorite THORNE	90	4 000	1 800-3 000	—
Dayleight 5 000 DE LUXE .	85(1)	5 000	2 000	6 000
Lumière du jour OSRAM .	85(1)	5 000	3 250	6 000

Characteristics of some full spectrum fluorescent tubes
Tube (1): 2 m, 36 or 40 W.

Horticultural fluorescent tubes

When used on their own in the aquarium, these tubes emit an artificial light which exaggerates blue and red tones. Their light rendering is not very good, because green and yellow wave-lengths tend to slide towards the blues and the reds. If the power (W) is effectively increased, this is done to the detriment of the visual perception curve (see table). As the aquarium owner is not trying to obtain a productive rendering, but simply a natural rendering of colours and optimum growth for the plants, these tubes cannot be used as the principal means of lighting the tank. They are, however, recommended for the aquarium foreground, but always in conjunction with one, or several, full-spectrum tubes. This is known as a multiple-tube lighting system.

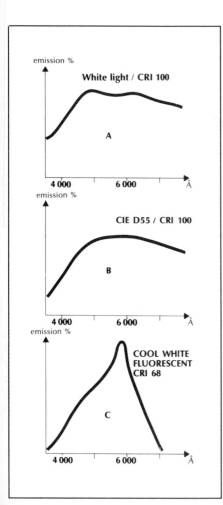

Comparison between two emission spectra of tubes available on the market and a white light spectrum.

Hot and Wotan Colour 30 tubes

These tubes emit wave-lengths corresponding to prevailing yellow or orange colours. When placed in the foreground of the aquarium, they enhance decorative plant arrangement. A large selection is available on the market; high-scale tubes have a high CRI, and also the best light rendering.

TYPES AND BRANDS	CRI	Tempera-ture	Lumens	Life expect-ancy in hours
Sylvania Homelight de lux F36W/HLX	85	2 700	3 150	6 000
Sylvania Warm-White de lux F36W/WWX	85	3 000	3 200	6 000
WOTAN Maxilux 31	85	3 300	3 450	6 000
WOTAN Maxilux 32	90	3 300	2 350	6 000
WOTAN Interna 41	85	3 300	3 250	6 000
THORNE Polylux 3500	85	3 500	3 450	6 000
THORNE Polylux 2700	82	2 700	3 450	3 200
Natural de-lux	92	3 500	1 750	1 500
PHILIPS Color 83	85	3 000	?	6 000

Characteristics of some hot or Wotan Colour 30 (tubes of 1.20 m).

Replacing fluorescent tubes

Whatever the life of a tube (6,000 to 24,000 hours), replacements should be on hand. When doing this, whether it is because they are used up or in order to change the emission spectrum, try to change one tube at a time. When three or four tubes are replaced simultaneously, the abrupt alteration to the light intensity and the restored total-lighting-spectrum can prove fatal to aquatic plants. It is better to replace two, three, or four tubes over the period of one month, say one tube a week.

Discharge Lamps

Unlike fluorescent tubes, which have an internal pressure lower than 0.1 bar, discharge bulbs and lamps have a high pressure. They cannot be directly connected to the mains supply; it is necessary to connect the two through a self-induction coil.

The lamps often have a week CRI. Depending on the gases, metals or minerals used in their make-up, the emission spectrum can often be improved, but this may have an adverse effect on the light rendering. So-called de-luxe lamps are corrected by an internal filter of fluorescent material which transfers some of the violet rays to the visible, yellow and red wave-

TYPES AND BRANDS	CRI/Ni	Temperature K	Power W	Lumens
SYLVANIA HSI/T.70 .	75	3 000	70	20 000
SYLVANIA HSI/T.150	75	4 300	70	28 000
WOTAN HQI-TS/NDL . . .	1	3 300/5 000	70	5 000
WOTAN HQI/D . . .	1	5 000	250	17 000
WOTAN HQL de lux	2	3 000	80/125	3 000/5 000
THORNE Arc-Stream 3000	80	3 000	150	19 000

Characteristics of some discharge lamps.

lengths. Discharge lamps have a life-span of 6,000 to 10,000 hours according to type. They lose about 20% of their light intensity over this period of time.

The lamps and bulbs discussed above are well suited to the aquarium because of their excellent colour reproduction and because

their colour temperature is closest to that of natural light. Discharge lamps are available with a power range from 50 to 3,000 W, but most are entirely unsuitable for the aquarium or the terrarium; their CRI is very low because of the dominant yellow of their emission spectrum.

■ Lighting time

Day-night rhythm

The most important influence on plant life is lighting time. Any artificial change in light rhythm or regularity is harmful to plants and the aquarium enthusiast should never under-estimate the importance of this aspect of plant biology and physiology. Lighting time must be adapted to the original latitude of the plants and to its regular rhythm. The light rhythm for tropical and sub-tropical plants is between eleven and thirteen hours, depending on the season. Tropical species are accustomed to short days and temperate zone species to long days. The latter will flourish in summer, with fifteen to sixteen hours daylight, but tropical plants can suffer from too much light. The natural environment of the majority of plants in the tank will dictate the lighting time. In the cases quoted, the minority population will be able to adapt to a surplus or deficit of one or two hours.

Time clocks and 24-hour cycle

It is equally important for the 24-hour, day/night cycle to be a regular one. Plants are used to fixed hours for light and darkness, and their vital functions (photosynthesis, respiration, opening and closing leaves and corollae) operate in a regular fashion like clockwork. We have all seen the corollae of the water lily and red poppy close before sunset. It is in the plant's vital interest to receive as much

energy as possible at the right time. The aquarium owner can solve the complex problem posed by the day/night cycle by integrating a time-switch into the electrical circuit, programmed to start at a pre-set time for a lighting time of twelve to fourteen hours. A multiple switch would serve to control several light sources.

A more sophisticated device imitates sun-rise and sun-set. Connected by the timer, this is an electronically controlled rheostat, which will progressively increase the light intensity from a lamp or the whole lighting system. The device should not be used when connected to fluorescent bulbs, which require full electrical power.

Just how useful progressive lighting is for aquarium plant biology has not been proven, but it does at least mean the owner is less of a slave to the aquarium.

A word of advice before purchasing any of this equipment. The time-switch should be a reliable one with a power rating compatible with the electricity supply. The most common units run on 15 amps.

For a circuit comprising three or four different light sources, it might be worthwhile investing in a multiple-function time-switch, which could control four light sources. Some time-switches are available with digital programmers or mechanical contact studs on a revolving dial. Simple time-switches generally come with plastic studs or one revolving dial.

Programming example

In a tank which has many tubes, the lighting can be arranged so that it reproduces the sun's intensity and spectrum. A Wotan Colour 30 tube in the background will emit a warm light with contrasting hues, while a Gro-Lux in the foreground will add blue and red tones. At midday, two major tubes, similar to Tru Lite, would provide full lighting-power for about eight hours. As the lights are switched off in reverse order, a sun-set, albeit somewhat jerky, is simulated and this does at least produce a gentler effect than if all the lights suddenly turn off.

There is nothing to stop you from altering the clock altogether and lighting the tank by night, when electricity rates are usually half-price, just as long as strict attention is paid to the rhythm and regularity of the light/dark cycle.

Number of tubes per tank	Switched-on	Switched-off
Simple time-clock on tank with 1 – 2 tubes	10 h	23 h
Programmable time-clock multiple tubes	9 h 30 Wotan Colour 30 or Aquaglow 10 h 30 Gro Lux 12 h 00 Chosen tubes	20 h Chosen tubes 22 h Gro Lux 23 H No lighting

Example of 13-hour programming.

Lux	Aperture	Exposure (sec.)	Compatibility of amount of light for aquatic plants
75	2,8	1/2	Insufficient light
150	2,8	1/4	*Cryptocoryne* and others
300	2,8	1/8	Species adapted to weak light
600	2,8	1/15	Other plants in tank centre
1 200	2,8	1/30	Good lighting
2 400	2,8	1/60	Surface plants
4 800	2,8	1/125	Surface plants
9 800	2,8	1/250	Plants in their natural environment
38 000	5,6	1/250	Plants in their natural environment
75 000	8,0	1/250	Plants in full sunlight in aerial environment

Controlling lighting

It is unlikely that the aquarium owner will overdo the lighting for his plants. On the contrary, he may not provide them with enough light. To measure light quantities (in units of lux) reaching plants, various methods may be used, particularly a camera. From outside the tank, position the camera at the height of the substratum with the lens directed towards the light source. Under these conditions the camera cell, adjusted to 50 ASA, will allow you to monitor the amount of light present in the tank, with a relatively precise global value.

Water quality and dissolved elements

Water is vital to both aquatic and terrestrial plant-life, but especially to aquatic plants as it carries the carbon dioxide gas (CO_2) essential for photosynthesis. Water contains elements which nourish a plant's growth: nitrates, phosphates and trace elements.

The aquarium is a confined environment, in which the physico-chemical qualities of water (pH, hardness: d.GH, carbonated hardness: d.KH) are subject to important changes brought about by plants, fish or external agents. Its various parameters should, therefore, be monitored regularly if ideal conditions are to prevail for plant-life and animals in the tank.

■ The pH content of water

The pH content has a strong influence on plant behaviour. It corresponds to the amount of hydrogen ions (H^+) present in 1 l (1.76 pt) of water and its values (without units) range from 1 to 14. With a value of 7 it is neutral, which means that basic acid Hydrogen ions (H^+) are present in equal number to basic Hydroxide ions (OH^-). Where the pH value is lower than 7, the water solution will be acidic; for values greater than 7, it will be basic. Any basic or acidic change to the water modifies its pH content.

Carbon dioxide has the greatest influence on pH content. It is highly soluble in water and will combine with it to form carbonic acid (H_2CO_3). This acidic factor will diminish the pH value and render the water acidic. This is not the end of the story, though, as calcium salts in the form of carbonate ($CaCO_3$) will react with carbonic acid to make calcium bicarbonate ($Ca(HCO_3)_2$) which neutralizes the excess acid. This resistance to any change in the pH is known as buffer capacity. Highly mineralized water, which is rich in calcium carbonate and magnesium, has a high buffer capacity.

pH modification in relation to CO_2 in two water types.

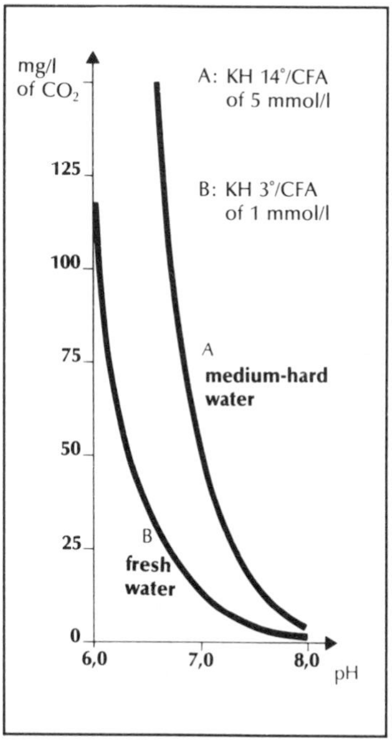

mg/l of CO_2

A: KH 14°/CFA of 5 mmol/l

B: KH 3°/CFA of 1 mmol/l

125

100

75

A
medium-hard water

50

25

B
fresh water

0

6,0   7,0   8,0

pH

■ Water hardness

The calcium and magnesium salt content of water is expressed in mg/l. This measure is known as the total hardness or hydrotimetric strength. It represents total temporary hardness (KH) and permanent hardness. Temporary hardness corresponds to the measurement in mg/l of calcium and magnesium carbonate salts; permanent hardness corresponds to the measure, expressed in the same units, of calcium and magnesium sulphate salts. Hard water represses any sudden change in pH and will prevent plants and fish from being poisoned.

37

	alkaline earth ions mmol/l	alkaline earth ions mEq/l	German degree °d	ppm of CaCO₃	English degree °a	French degree °f
1 mmol/l alkaline earth ions	1,00	2,00	5,50	100,00	7,02	10,00
1 mEq/l alkaline earth ions	0,50	1,00	2,80	50,00	3,51	5,00
1 German degree	0,18	0,357	1,00	17,80	1,25	1,78
1 ppm of CaCO₃	0,01	0,020	0,056	1,00	0,0702	0,10
1 English degree	0,14	0,285	0,798	14,30	1,00	1,43
1 French degree	0,10	0,200	0,560	10,00	0,702	1,00

Conversion table for units of water hardness.

■ Carbon dioxide

We are aware of the important role played by carbon dioxide in the complex phenomenon known as photosynthesis or assimilation of chlorophyll. We can represent its function for chlorophyll plant-life as an equation:

$$6 CO_2 + 6 H_2O + E \rightarrow C_6H_{12}O_6 + 6O_2$$

where:
CO_2 is carbon dioxide
H_2O is water
$C_6H_{12}O_6$ is a sugar
O_2 is oxygen
E is energy from the sun in the form of photons.

Evidently, a deficiency in carbon dioxide will impede the synthesis of sugar, which is the plant's source of energy, and will consequently restrict its growth.

Signs of carbon dioxide deficiency

Traces of calcium carbonate on the aquarium walls and decoration indicate a shortage of carbon dioxide in the tank. To understand where these traces come from we have to revert to the following equation:

$$CaCO_3 + H_2CO_3 \rightarrow Ca (HCO_3)_2$$

This reaction will only take place where carbon dioxide is present. In its absence, it works the other way round. The soluble bicarbonate yields carbon dioxide to the water and the insoluble calcium carbonate forms a precipitate in the tank.

Under balanced conditions, where there is neither a deficit nor an excess, there is a permanent exchange between carbon dioxide and bicarbonate. But if there is a shortage of carbon dioxide, the bicarbonate has to yield a lot of this gas so that a large amount of insoluble carbonate will be formed — and as a result calcium deposits will appear.

Causes of deficiency

There are several reasons why carbon dioxide can be lacking. The most serious cause is the use of diffusers, whereby the water column produced in the aquarium stirs up the water. The effect of this is that the lower levels of water are brought into contact with the surface where any free carbon dioxide escapes. Filter or turbine jets positioned just beneath the water surface can produce the same effect. Water injection introduces a lot of air and releases a certain amount of oxygen which drives out carbon dioxide. The apparatus may be extremely good for fish and will maintain a high pH content, but it is not very good for plant growth. Where carbonate hardness is between 6 and 8° KH, carbon dioxide must be diffused artificially. Increasing the fish population, which produce carbon dioxide naturally, is really not the answer. The extra carbon dioxide produced by fish is in fact disproportionate to actual requirements. On the other hand,

Acid fixation capacity (AFC) in two water types.

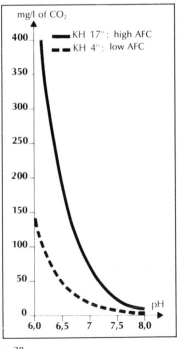

mg/l of CO₂

—— KH 17": high AFC
- - - KH 4": low AFC

slightly mineralized water with a sparse fish population often produces enough carbon dioxide to maintain an equilibrium with bicarbonates.

Rapid plant growth in the tank can also give rise to a deficiency, and here the carbon dioxide shortage is indicated by a slowing down in the growing pattern and the appearance of carbonates on the aquarium walls. If other elements for plant growth are also lacking, the deficiency will be all the more apparent.

It can also be the result of the variation between day and night photosynthesis activity. During daylight hours plants will absorb carbon dioxide so as to assimilate chlorophyll, and at night their respiration, like that of fish, releases carbon dioxide. It is quite easy to check this variation by taking day- and night-time pH readings. The pH factor will be higher in the morning than in the evening, so in a densely planted tank, with a large fish population, a measurement of pH 6 in the morning will compare with pH 8 in the evening.

If a tank is continually aerated, for the good of the fish, such a discrepancy in the pH will not occur, but plants are often found in such tanks. This is particularly true of aquariums which house fish from Lake Malawi and Lake Tanganyika, where a pH level above 7.5 must be maintained. Plants have little chance of a long life in this kind of evironment, because there is a shortage of free carbon dioxide and

the physico-chemical constants of the water are as follows: (15KH, pH: 7.5 = 19 mg/l of H_2CO_3).

Measuring the deficiency

Before artificial carbon dioxide is diffused, the aquarium's biological equilibrium should be properly evaluated. In order to pinpoint any possible carbon dioxide shortage, the pH should be measured first, preferably by means of an electric pH-meter or a good chromometer; then the carbonate hardness should be measured with the use of reagents and the solution should be made up with a standardization pipette. The results can be interpreted by using a chart showing the amount of carbon dioxide present in water. If the level shown is lower than 8 mg/l, then the aquarium owner should artificially introduce carbon dioxide. But then, as no two aquariums are alike, it is quite possible for plants to grow well, despite a free carbon dioxide rate below the norm.

The analysis should be carried out as soon as signs of a carbon dioxide deficiency manifest themselves, either by carbon deposits, a slowing down of growth or a change in plant appearance, such as a yellowish colour. If the measurements obtained are lower than 8 mg/l and there are one or more of the above deficiency signs, then carbon dioxide should be introduced artificially.

Carbon dioxide production

There are several ways of obtaining carbon dioxide. It is very difficult to

d°KH	C.F.A. mmol/l
1	0,4
2	0,7
3	1,0
4	1,4
5	1,8
6	2,1
7	2,5
8	2,9
9	3,2
10	3,6
11	3,9
12	4,3
13	4,6
14	5,0
15	5,4
16	5,6
17	6,1
18	6,4
19	6,7
20	7,2

Carbonate hardness conversion table/acid fixation capacity.

pH	factor	pH	factor	pH	factor
6,0	118	6,7	24,0	7,4	4,7
6,1	94	6,8	19,0	7,5	3,7
6,2	75	6,9	15,0	7,6	3,0
6,3	59	7,0	12,0	7,7	2,4
6,4	47	7,1	9,4	7,8	1,9
6,5	37	7,2	7,5	7,9	1,5
6,6	30	7,3	5,9	8,0	1,2

Calculation of dissolved CO_2 in relation to pH (to each pH value there is a corresponding factor which will give the carbonic acid content expressed in mg/l, by multiplying this factor by the AFC).

Water quality and dissolved elements

Equipment for producing CO₂ by chemical reaction method

CO₂ diffusion system with simple pressure-reducer and canister

produce and the end result is often an output of gas which is quite low and of doubtful purity.

It can be bought in specialist shops in gas form or as a liquid, bottled or in canisters. To produce carbon dioxide by anaerobic fermentation, water, sugar and baker's yeast are used. In a 1 to 10 l gas bottle, the three components are added in the following proportions: 1 l of water to 100 g of crystallized sugar and 20 g of yeast. Fermentation produces a small amount of gas which is only enough for a small tank. The process is somewhat lengthy, taking eight days to a month according to the quantity of the mixture, and the resultant carbon dioxide is not pure. When it is diffused in the tank, it leaves a greasy film on the surface, even if mixed properly with water in the aquarium.

Carbon dioxide can also be produced chemically under similar conditions. In this case, chalk and hydrochloric acid are used in a thermal glass bottle, but here again the purity of the gas leaves much to be desired.

Bottled carbon dioxide comes in liquid form weighing between 8 g and 75 g. The gas is maintained at a pressure of 60 bars. In containers, carbon dioxide comes in gas form under low pressure. Both types of carbon dioxide are of feed-pump quality. Unfortunately, the small amount of gas contained means that

a supply lasting eight days to one month only is possible for a tank of 80–100 l, depending on the plant's requirements. The bottles should only be used as a top-up supply, when the main supply is turned off, or for refilling bottles of industrial gas.

Carbon dioxide is also available in industrial bottles. Depending on the bottle size, the weight of the liquid gas will vary from 1.5 kg to 10 kg. Bottles should be fitted with an escape valve so that the gas, which is under high pressure, can be used regularly and in complete safety. A 1.5 kg gas bottle could supply a 100 l tank for one year, depending on water hardness and density of plant-life. The industrial size bottle of liquid gas, weighing 10 kg, will provide an almost endless supply to an aquarium operating under normal conditions.

When using carbon dioxide from a high pressure container, the following guidelines should be followed:

- when installing the container, check the water-tightness of the escape-valve and connections by using soapy water;
- do the candle test, if you suspect a leak;
- keep the container away from sunlight and any heat source;
- adhere to any annual safety tests recommended (the container should not be filled after the date stamped on it);
- never transfer gas from one container to another;
- always keep the container in an upright position when in use.

Connecting the carbon dioxide supply

A section of plain nylon, flexible piping, much in use among aquarium owners, carries the carbon dioxide (produced either by fermentation or another chemical reaction). The very low pressure of the gas means that it can be directly linked with the diffuser device, and the required pressure reduction to

Industrial CO₂ bottle

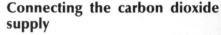

KH Hardness	1	2	3	4	5	6	7	8	9	10	11	12	13	14	15	16	17	18
1 000	100	120	140	160	180	200	220	240	270	300	320	340	360	380	400	420	440	460
900	100	100	120	140	160	180	200	220	240	270	290	310	330	350	370	390	410	430
800	50	70	90	110	140	160	180	200	220	240	270	290	310	330	350	370	390	410
700	30	40	60	80	110	130	150	170	190	210	230	250	270	290	310	330	350	370
600	30	40	40	60	80	100	120	140	160	180	190	210	230	250	270	290	310	330
500	30	30	40	40	50	70	90	110	130	150	170	190	210	230	250	270	290	310
400	30	30	40	40	50	50	70	90	90	120	140	160	180	200	220	240	260	280
300	*	30	30	40	40	50	60	70	90	100	120	140	160	180	200	220	240	260
200	*	*	*	30	30	30	40	50	50	60	80	100	120	140	160	180	200	220
100	*	*	*	*	*	30	30	30	40	40	50	70	90	110	130	150	170	190

(row header: volume in litres)

Diffusion surface in cm^2 of CO_2 in relation to aquarium volume and water hardness.
* Amount of CO_2 produced by fish population is sufficient under normal conditions.
30: standard apparatus available in the shops is suitable for this surface.

0.02 to 0.2 bar will be achieved by a simple two-stage escape valve for gas in canisters or bottles. The two-stage escape valve with pressure gauges ensures complete control over the gas, but this instrument is very expensive and is a bit of a luxury. Specialist shops will be able to advise on this equipment.

The valve can be adapted to the cannisters or bottles by means of screw connectors. Pressure can be lowered by 60 bars to 0-0.7, using the control tap. Gas required is carried from the escape valve through nylon piping, which is controlled by a simple tap. This valve is particularly recommended as its price is very reasonable considering its function and how easy it is to use.

Diffusion devices and methods

Carbon dioxide diffusers available in the shops are often badly fitted and unattractive. Most of them have an upright perspex or plexiglas tube, with a very small opening to separate carbon dioxide from water. They fit to the side wall by means of suction cups and look unattractive. The device could be used in a compartment of the decanting tank, where used water is sifted off.

Tanks which use decanting filters do tend to be extremely large and dozens of diffusers would be needed to properly spread the carbon dioxide. The type of diffuser mentioned above is best suited to a small tank of less than 100 l, but where there is less chance to hide it. The contact surface of these tubes is no more than 30 cm^2 (12 in^2), which will probably do for larger tanks, but here the carbonate hardness must also be lower (see chart showing diffusion surfaces).

Continuous carbon dioxide diffusion with a wooden or pottery diffuser is to be avoided at all costs. The dispersal of carbon dioxide cannot be controlled and the amount of gas consumed is prohibitive, with more than 99% of it rising to the surface and escaping into the air.

Diffusion by bubbles from a separate tank connected in series to the outlet of a centrifugal pump, is equally difficult to regulate. By this method, in contrast to continuous

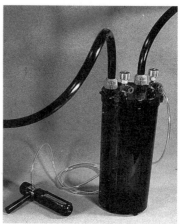

Vat for forced CO_2 diffusion through washer (on right).

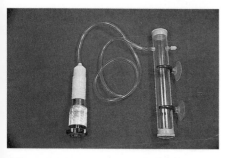

CO_2 canister, pressure-reducer and diffuser.

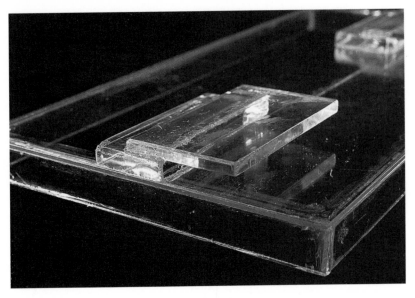

CO₂ bell jar

a carbon dioxide chamber can be made out of existing backing in the aquarium. For the latter method, if the surface area meets current needs, a glass rod can be stuck vertically on the supporting area. This should be 2–3 cm (¾–1 in) high and it will lie under the water, hidden by the lighting cover. It must also be fixed into this position on the front and back walls, so as to retain carbon dioxide. A reduced opening should be made for the flexible connection piping which brings gas to the upper surface. A piece of 4 mm (³⁄₁₆ in) rigid tubing is slipped into the opening and this is made water-tight with silicon glue. Flexible connection piping is fixed on to the coupling which feeds the chamber with carbon dioxide.

Using diffusion

A detachable bell-jar should be filled with water and returned to the tank; when in position, its water-tightness should be checked. It is working perfectly when the water remains inside it even though it is at a different level from the tank's surface. If it is not detachable, a flexible hose should be slipped into the air pocket and the air sucked out. The water will then rise in the chamber. Both methods save on carbon dioxide. The aquarium owner who has an ample supply of gas can use it to expel excess water or air.

gas diffusion, carbon dioxide is forced through the water. Both methods can be poisonous to aquatic life, because saturation point is reached very quickly.

The perfect method of diffusion was invented by Mr P. Isseman, an aquatic-plant lover. His method is to bring carbon dioxide freely into contact with water over a fixed surface in a bell-jar. The gas spread over the surface meets the exact biological needs of the plants, no more and no less, according to the water carbonate hardness. Despite its size, the bell-jar is practically invisible, as it blends in with the mirror formed by the water's reflective surface. It is made out of glass, 4 mm (³⁄₁₆ in) thick and stuck together with silicon; it must be absolutely water-tight. It is made-to-measure for each aquarium and can be square or rectangular in shape, and of any suitable height. It can be mounted with backing against the side of the aquarium, or permanently stuck to one of the side or back walls. Its height will be decided by the average water-level in the tank and the lower edge of the lighting cover.

If properly positioned in the aquarium, this simple, cheap, easily operated device is very discreet. It can be placed in the background underneath fast-growing plants, or

Diffusion control is carried out in two stages. When installed, the carbon dioxide chamber is completely filled with gas by opening the escape-valve tap a little way and the tap to its fullest extent. When the gas starts to overflow and rise to the surface, its output is reduced so that surplus bubbles rise to the surface at a rate of ten an hour. As plant growth increases and the carbonate–carbon dioxide–bicarbonate exchange becomes stable, the bubbles diminish. Often when a lot of carbon dioxide is needed, the bubbles stop and the water-level in the bell-jar rises. The carbon dioxide output can then be adjusted using the control tap. In time, when plant requirements are stable, the aquarium-owner can easily assess the optimum output for carbon dioxide needs. This particular implementation is not possible for carbon dioxide in canisters, as diffusion time is limited by the small amount of gas available.

The bell-jar should then be refilled with carbon dioxide, as required, when the water level reaches its maximum height after the gas has run out. So as to diffuse the carbon dioxide in the best way possible throughout the aquarium, a water current should circulate beneath the layer of the gas.

When diffusing carbon dioxide, the water's physico-chemical parameters must be followed. For a week following its installation, a pH reading must be taken night and morning. After a week's diffusion, the carbonates–carbon dioxide balance will stabilize with only plants and outside leakages using up the gas. A weekly reading of the pH and carbonate hardness will be sufficient to monitor the water.

It is sensible to use carbon dioxide gas thoughtfully, after carefully assessing the real needs and deficiencies of the aquarium water.

■ Trace elements

The term 'trace elements' is applied to all substances in low concentration needed for life and plant growth. In essence, they consist of metals, and to a lesser extent, nitrates and large molecules which are found in the soil's argillo-humic compounds. Their presence is vital, even though they play a small part in plant metabolism. If one trace element is missing, even if all the others are there in sufficient numbers, plants will perish. This basic concept is known as the law of the minimum. This also applies to those elements equally important and vital to plants, such as carbon dioxide, light, pH, and carbonates.

Assimilation

In the earth, plants draw trace elements through their roots; while in water, special organs (hydropods) situated on leaves are used by plants for assimilation. Before they can be assimilated in water, trace elements will need to be there in an ionized and soluble form, and the ionized form will have to be right for the plants.

Let us take the case of iron (Fe), a metal element vital for chlorophyll assimilation. It is found in two ionized forms:

- Fe^{++} : ferrous iron;
- Fe^{+++} : ferric iron.

Only the first form can be assimilated by plants, and only if it is linked to an organic compound which can maintain it in soluble form. Organic molecules, which in this state release iron and other metals such as magnesium or manganese, are known as chelators.

Chelators

These are complex organic molecules, capable of binding with metal ions or certain proteins, to render them soluble and acceptable to plants. The compounds are found naturally in the aquarium, especially in the substratum. Often they are humic acids which result from argillo-humic compounds. Some experts recommend that filtering be carried out with material rich in humic acid, such as turf, so as to incorporate the clay or argillo-humic compound in the tank. Unfortunately, these substances deteriorate quickly.

The best solution is to artificially chelate trace elements, with a chelator synthesis. E.D.T.A. is the most popular with aquarium owners and hydroculturists. It is marketed in different countries by several manufacturers, Merck, BASF and Dow Chemicals are some of these. A specialist dealer will be able to advise on the types available, but only the disodium type should be used.

Iron deficiency

Regular water changes ensure a sufficient supply of most trace elements, but cannot meet the plant's need for iron (Fe). Yellowing leaves are a sure sign of iron deficiency, which can also arise when iron chelation is ineffective. In very hard water calcium and magnesium are chelated first, and the iron is ignored. First, extra iron should be added, and second, chelators. There is absolutely no point in introducing iron in solid form, as nails or granules.

Iron additives/chelators

Hard water generally has an average concentration of 2 mg/l. The element can be checked by using a test (Merck: Aquamerck no. 14 404) which determines the deficiency and controls the introduction of additional chelates. Where iron is naturally present in a concentration higher than 1.5 mg, there will be no need to supplement it. But this concentration could be raised to 2.5–3.0 mg/l, accompanied by the chelator (E.D.T.A.). Iron present in mains water (from the tap) will be chelated alone, because of its concentration.

Bivalent iron can be added to the aquarium in various forms: as tetrahydrous chloride Fe $C_{12}4H_2O$; as dihydrous gluconate $C_{12}H_{22}FeO_{14}2H_2O$; or as hydrous sulphate $FeSO_4H_2O$ accompanied by a chelator. The amount of E.D.T.A. required as chelator on the iron and other metal ions will be slightly optimized, in keeping with the amount needed for iron alone. Chelates for professional hydroculturists can be obtained in a product called Everplant D obtainable from Everglades Aquatic Nursery, Cirencester.

Excess chelators

If the trace elements/E.D.T.A. proportions are not right, the plants will suffer physiological disturbances. An overdose of E.D.T.A. implies that a certain amount of chelator in the aquarium has not been combined. It will do so in a preferred order: calcium, magnesium and manganese, and finally bivalent iron. With an overdose of E.D.T.A., chelation continues and it can happen that large amounts of trace elements, in the form of various metallic ions, will be caught up, and this applies not only to metallic ions in the water and substratum, but also to those stored in plant tissue. It is possible, therefore, for iron oxide which is stored in the aquarium to be suddenly mobilized by excess E.D.T.A. Bivalent iron, in excess can supersede other trace elements important to vital plant processes, such as phosphate or manganese. The result will be a deficiency caused by an imbalance between the various trace elements. These problems will not arise if the chelates–chelators proportion is strictly observed, and a close check kept on iron content.

Commercial products have certain drawbacks: the first is the price; the second is their presentation in dilute form; and third is the absence of indication as to quality and quantity. This makes it virtually impossible to measure the correct amount of trace elements for healthy plant growth, as so many factors have to be taken into account.

You should also guard against adding chelates very suddenly to an area which has been chronically deficient. Overdosing will not revive stunted plants, for which the proper dose has already been suplied. As we have seen, it will merely produce a negative effect, and sudden chelate treatment can cause under-nourished plants to suffer a kind of alimentary collapse, particularly those of the genus *Cryptocoryne*. This is probably a contributory cause of the mysterious illness from which they suffer. In fact, this practice is tantamount to forcing a banquet on someone who has endured a long hunger-strike.

Aquarium chelation should be carried out cautiously after due consideration of the energy balance. In a newly-installed tank, the dose is calculated on total contents, and thereafter it should be measured with weekly or monthly water changes. Plants which show signs of a long-term shortage should be introduced to them gradually, when the water is changed.

In the same way as for carbon dioxide, light or any other element, a sudden and excessive change in the environment is just as harmful as a prolonged shortage.

Fertilizers and chelates which are suitable for garden and indoor plants will not be appropriate for aquatic plants. Apart from iron, these chemical additives contain large amounts of nitrates, phosphoric anhydride or potassium oxide. These substances are too rich for an aquatic environment in which they are already well represented.

Measuring iron

The chelation ratio of E.D.T.A. to trace elements is molecule to molecule. The molecular mass of products used should be known, and some used by aquarium owners are listed below. Remember that the molecular mass corresponds to the mass of N molecules of any one product. N is the number of Avagadro-amperes and is equal to $6,023 \times 10^{23}$. Molecular masses of the following products are:
E.D.T.A. (Titriplex III®) M = 372.24 g (00002)
Iron sulphate ($Fe SO_4$) M = 151.91 g (00002)

Iron chloride ($Fe Cl_4, 2H_2O$) M = 198.81 g (00002)
Iron gluconate ($C_{12}H_{22}FeO_{14}, 2H_2O$) M = 482.18 g (00002)

This amount would be sufficient for an aquarium of 1,000 l (220 gallons) with a proportional amount of E.D.T.A. Unfortunately, some unstable factors, like the pH or a preferential fixation order conditional on E.D.T.A., can disturb iron chelation. Preferential constants mean that first the chelator combines with magnesium, then calcium. In principle, chelation in hard water will mostly affect carbonate hardness elements, such as calcium and magnesium.

Fixation order	0 Kmz	5	10	15	20	25	30
9	≥≥≥≥Fe⁺⁺⁺≥≥≥≥≥≥≥≥≥≥≥≥≥≥≥≥≥≥≥≥≥≥≥≥≥≥ 25,1						
8	≥≥≥≥Cu⁺⁺≥≥≥≥≥≥≥≥≥≥≥≥≥≥≥≥≥ 18,8						
7	≥≥≥≥Zn⁺⁺≥≥≥≥≥≥≥≥≥≥≥≥≥≥ 16,5						
6	≥≥≥≥Cd⁺⁺≥≥≥≥≥≥≥≥≥≥≥≥ 16,5						
5	≥≥≥≥Al⁺⁺≥≥≥≥≥≥≥≥≥≥≥≥ 16,1						
4	≥≥≥≥Fe⁺⁺≥≥≥≥≥≥≥≥≥≥ 14,3						
3	≥≥≥≥Mn⁺⁺≥≥≥≥≥≥≥≥≥ 13,8						
2	≥≥≥≥Ca⁺⁺≥≥≥≥≥ 10,7						
1	≥≥≥≥Mg⁺⁺≥≥≥ 8,7						

Table of EDTA constants conditional on trace elements shows that some trace elements will be chelated before trivalent iron, and in strict rotation. Excessive doses of EDTA mean that trace elements stored in plant tissue will be transformed, and this sudden change will be fatal to the plant.

The substratum

It is not absolutely necessary to have a substratum in an aquarium devoted to fish, and many owners of the more delicate species prefer to do without, for hygienic reasons. The substratum is made up of aggregates which make a home for host-seeking pathogenic agents, like *Ichthyosporidium* cysts. But one of the reasons it is a vital ingredient in the planted aquarium is because it gives a natural appearance.

The substratum is supposed to represent a river-bed or the bottom of a tropical lagoon. The following two criteria should be borne in mind when making your choice:
- it should be chemically neutral and this applies to limestone and to its toxicity;
- it should look as natural as possible. Any artificial appearance should be avoided which means excluding quartzite tinted red, black or any other colour.

■ Natural quartz or quartzite

This is the most popular material used for substrata by aquarium owners, but unfortunately it has no real advantage to offer the fish, or the plants, or even the owner. Its bright white colour makes the surroundings look pale in the light and as its brightness does not light up other parts of the tank, the fish feel disorientated as the bottom of the tank is lighter than elsewhere.

Quartz grains have flat sides and cutting edges and tend to overlap so that they form hard, compact blocks, making it hard for water to circulate between them. When restoring the tank, the owner will note that quartz tends to subside and thicken after a period of time, and waste products will form binding material to which roots will attach themselves. Unfortunately, as the water circulation is hampered by lack of space, the environment will suffer from a shortage of oxygen.

■ Sand

Sand always has the same properties, whether it comes from the Loire or the Rhine, and its creamy yellow colour is beautifully effective. But, like quartz, its top layer will clog with time and prevent the passage of water. Roots take very well in it and it is particularly recommended for tanks designed for earth-eating Cichlids of the genera *Geophagus*, *Acarichthys* because, when looking for food, these species filter the substratum through their gill rakers. The same can be seen in species of the genus *Corydoras*, who search the ground with their barbs. A coarse substratum would be a handicap to feeding.

Sand does not provide a sound foundation for constructing any relief in the aquarium. The nature of the substance ensures that movements of fish and water currents constantly smooth it down to an even, surface.

■ Gravel

Round gravel with 2–4 mm diameter grains is the most suitable material for an aquarium substratum. It has no sharp edges and its rounded structure allows plenty of space for water to circulate freely. Roots can easily take a hold in it and benefit from the nitrate-charged water.

The addition of a heating cable will render the substratum an oxidizing environment. Gravel can be laid quite thickly (more than 10 cm) in the background of most tanks. Its colour makes it suitable for all kinds of decoration, and time will see it hidden with single-cell algae or diatoms. The large Cichlids prefer a larger-grained gravel (10–12 cm diameter) which will prevent them from instinctively digging it up. Another important advantage of gravel is its very modest price.

■ Pozzolana

This is a dark-brown, volcanic, siliceous rock which makes the best substratum of all for aquariums and filters. The alveolar structure and rounded shape of the ground pozzolana along with its colour make it the perfect choice. It has all the advantages of gravel, but on top of that its reddish colour helps recreate the lighting found naturally in tropical rivers and lagoons. Fish feel more secure without the bright- ness found with a sandy substratum and pozzolana's porous construction makes an excellent terrain for plant roots. Uneven grains allow water to circulate freely and the substratum is an oxidizing environment where colonies of de-nitrifying bacteria flourish. Because it is so porous, it is usually less dense than other materials. Aqualite, while similar and offering the same advantages, is more expensive.

Mining pozzolana

Pozzolana goes very well with polystyrene resin decoration, although it may look rather too regular on its own. The dark background throws plants into relief and the resulting effect is realistic and does credit to the talents of the aquarium-owner.

The substratum may be particularly thick, especially if water is drained by simple convection or slow filtering.

Pozzolana used as decoration

■ Composite substratum

There are publications aimed at the aquarium specialist or owner, which describe compounds which can be utilized for the substratum. Turf, humus, clay pellets, organic—even faecal matter—are suggestions, with no distinction made between aquarium and garden, terrestrial or aquatic plants! Aquatic plants are not familiar with these substances and will not use them as a food source. Their nutrition, for the most part, is derived from water soluble elements and is assimilated by their leaves. The sole function of their roots is to attach plants to the substratum.

Some people recommend an argillo-humic complex, which is not considered a fertilizer, but rather a chelator which binds with bivalent iron. Unfortunately, clay is compacted in the substratum and cannot inter-change with the water in the aquarium. The same is true of any turf buried in the substratum; it ferments and creates a range of problems for the aquarium-owner.

It is better to put turf in the filter, where humic acid in an oxidizing environment is of greater benefit to the aquarium as a whole.

Clay pellets are beneficial to plant-life but should not be treated as fertilizers. They have been heated almost to boiling point, and any active ingredients are destroyed in the process. But in this perfectly neutral new form, clay reacts like zeolites storing excess substances and supplying plants according to their needs. Some plants sold in containers or with their nutritional bed intact, still have zeolites between their roots. For them, compacted clay pellets may be placed over a heating cable and covered with a layer of gravel or pozzolana. By this means they are turned into a real storehouse of trace elements. The heat promotes a thermal exchange between the substratum and the water which supplies plants with necessary trace elements.

■ How to make a choice

As a general rule, the simplest substratum is the best and it is important to opt for one with large granules. Substrata with wide interstices will guarantee clear water, for however good the filters are, they do not remove all the particles. Wide gaps also serve to hide particles before they are broken down. Aquariums which have a constant display of suspended particles are generally those with a fine sandy bottom, where fish and water movement ensure that waste constantly rises to the surface. They are not recommended.

■ Snails for substratum maintenance

A colony of molluscs can be very valuable in maintaining the substratum. *Melanoides tubercularia* with its conical and helical shape is a good choice. It only moves around at night in visible sections of the aquarium and as the species is ovoviviparous, it will not lay eggs on plants and decorations. It does not eat plants or roots and by day it buries itself in the substratum, where it moves around looking for edible particles. As its habits are clean, the interstices remain open and allow water free passage, so the substratum retains its oxidizing properties and related advantages. Gastropods indicate the substratum is biogenically sound, but if they abandon the area, it generally means there is some imbalance or pollution present. Either the soil is acting as a reducing agent or, more seriously, hydrogen sulphide is being produced.

Unfortunately, snails have two particular disadvantages:

- they flatten out the relief in the decoration;
- they multiply at a phenomenal rate.

The first disadvantage you will have to accept, unless you want to live without them. But you can deal with the second and limit the population by trapping them at regular intervals. Small pieces of meat should be placed on the substratum before the lights are extinguished and one or two hours later you will find a mass of snails stuck to the pieces. Do not use chemical products to dispose of them, as their destruction in any large number could easily pollute the aquarium.

Molluscs like lymnaea can do valuable work in the aquarium

DECORATION

Once the aquarium enthusiast has designed the decoration for the aquarium, it is time to select plants for it, and by doing so to create a Dutch tank. Another option is to aim for a good balance of both plants and fish.

Artificial decoration

Enthusiasts whose aquariums have a capacity of 200 l or more (whether fresh- or sea-water) tend to make use of artificial décor). The first designs used in the early 1970s were made of expanded polystyrene and were designed by the sea-water section of France's oldest aquarium club, Friends of the Aquarium of Strasbourg 1932. These early styles were not for the tank's interior, but were designed to fit behind the rear glass, which was kept scrupulously clean, and the decoration was touched up with ordinary, toxic paint. When non-toxic paints were invented, the décor could be moved to the tank's interior, but the paint was not highly water-resistant and in some cases, was found to be harmful to fish. The discovery of epoxy resin solved these problems and meant that colours would stay fixed and the surface would be protected.

At about the same time, the Aquarium at Nancy devised a similar decoration using a matt gel-coat, made of glass and resin on polystyrene, but this was soon abandoned because it was too difficult to implement. Research in energy-saving then led to the use of insulating materials which proved to be excellent raw material for aquarium decoration. Polyurethane foam, added to certain types of polystyrene, formed the basis of artificial decoration. In all these cases, the raw material was coated with epoxy resin (a method used in viticulture to insulate the inside of concrete wine vats). The technique, which began in Alsace, is now in use world-wide.

■ Making polystyrene decoration

Choice of thickness

The largest manageable blocks of polystyrene are available in a standard size 2.50 x 1.50 x 0.50 m (8 x 5 x 1½ ft), and in slabs 10 to 150 mm (½–6 in) thick. Because of its granular composition, polystyrene has a density of between 20 and 35 kg/m^3. The heaviest type consists of very small granules and this is the one to choose for the aquarium, as it will contract very slowly and is extremely rigid.

The volume of polystyrene needed depends on the type of aquarium. A Dutch tank will take a slab with dimensions similar to the rear glass and about 10 cm (4 in) thick. It should not be so thick that it will encroach on the planting area, although there are some exceptions. For example, where the effect of an uneven bank of a South American river is required, the polystyrene should be at least 30 cm (12 in) thick.

Working polystyrene

Before working polystyrene, make sure you have the necessary equipment: handsaw, kitchen knife, fel pen, Stanley knife or large screw-driver, portable blow-lamp or hot-air stripper and sheathed, electric wire.

The first job is to cut the block to the internal dimensions of the aquarium. The original, chiselled surface will be the side which goes against the rear glass. Large blocks which are more than 1 m (1 yd) cannot be cut with a handsaw; an electric wire with joint at every 8 to 10 cm (3 to 4 in) will produce a far superior job. The block should be cut slightly longer than the aquarium, to compensate for any shrinkage as a result of heat. A flame should be run smoothly over the side which is to be in contact with the glass, to ensure a good surface. The same should be done for the sides which, when shrunk, will reduce the block to the width of the aquarium. When this has been done, the block can be put inside the aquarium.

When all contact surfaces have been singed, the real sculpture can start. Before starting, you must know what kind of decoration you want, and decide on the effect you want to create. It would be unrealistic to carve great masses and then put layers of schistous rocks in the foreground. But the same forms would combine with volcanic cinders to convey a lovely reddish-brown geological tone, which would look very life-like. Obviously, the way the visible side of the block is carved will provide the tank's character. The beginner should first make a rough outline with a pen. Try out the drawing in the tank as you go along to see how the work is progressing. Make rough-hewn decoration with a saw, and create details like caves, relief and indents with a screw-driver. But the best tool of all for detail work is your hand or finger. If you rub hard with the palm of your hand, layers of granules can be removed bit by bit and by inserting a screw-driver into the polystyrene block and prising it up, you can dig out a small

A

B

C

D

Working with polystyrene:
A – Singeing the back fascia
B – Sculpting the block
C – Singeing large areas
D – Satisfaction with the finished article

conical section.

The art is to create maximum relief using the minimum volume of material, but there is no point in carving work which will not be visible through the front glass of the tank; leave out what cannot be seen. The minimum thickness to use is about 1 cm (½ in) and any hollows should be accessible by using a resin-coated paintbrush. When the decoration is sculpted, it should be singed and a hot-air stripper which operates at 100°C (212°F) will be ideal for the larger surfaces. It will not be suitable for the smallest corners though; you will need an adjustable blow-lamp for these jobs. But do take care, because polystyrene is inflammable and gives off toxic fumes!

There is another variety of polystyrene decoration, known as sandwich-décor, where a layer of natural rock alternates with polystyrene slabs. This kind of design must be put together in layers but, fortunately, it is all detachable. Natural stones steady the whole structure and the decoration works well in tanks where accessibility to fish and their fry is important.

Polystyrene back-drop

■ Polyurethane decoration

Double-component polyurethane

Using double-component polyurethane means that the decoration can be coloured using a universal dye in one of the two components. Polymerization does, however, cause smooth mounds on the surface, so your material will have to be re-roughened after this stage.

The two components should be mixed by weight in equal parts. It is rather difficult to pour on the vertical back glass of a very large tank and is better suited to an aquarium with detachable glass sides, where the surfaces to be coated can be placed flat. However, it can be done in a large tank, by starting at the bottom of the pane of glass and by building fixed means of support, such as hollow bricks, into the décor. Layers of polyurethane can be applied in successive horizontal colours, right up to the top. The operation is much easier for a small tank, as the back wall is coated with polyurethane after being laid flat. The covered surfaces are cleaned with a diluting agent like acetone or trichlorethylene and covered with a silane base primer.

Polyurethane foam has distinct advantages. When it expands to twenty-five times its original volume, it spreads everywhere, filling up all the holes, thus preventing water from getting into any corners where it can stagnate, once the tank has been filled.

A decantation tank can be included in the decoration, and for this you will need a glass container, which has not been covered with primer but instead with a thin layer of vegetable fat, or margarine. When the polyurethane is polymerized, the container can be removed with a suction cup and the impression it leaves in the decoration will act as a decantation tank. Water inlets and outlets can be pierced directly into the polymerized foam. Glass joints can be laid in channels which have been dug in the mass, and these are made water-tight with silicone glue.

Single-component polyurethane

Single-component polyurethane is marketed in one container, unlike the double-component variety which comes in two. It is much simpler to use and you just have to shake the container for a few minutes and then press the attached spray-gun. It will expand to its fullest extent within ten minutes at a minimal temperature of 18°C (64°F). Detailed work is much easier with this product, because the foam can be piped through tubes; caves can be modelled by coating flower-pot holders or the bottoms of plastic bottles. It also serves to insulate the aquarium, limiting heat loss; this is even more effective when three sides of the tank are coated.

Polyurethane decoration showing decantation tank

■ The finishing touches: resin

Both polystyrene and polyurethane will, in time, emit styrolene. This is why it is imperative to coat them with one or two layers of epoxy resin and to ensure the long-term chemical neutrality of the decoration. Resin provides the best finishing touch for surfaces which will be in contact with water and for all polystyrene surfaces. Resin makes the surface hard and can be inlaid with mineral micro-elements (sand, quartz dust, shells or coral for seawater tanks).

Implementation

Two basic rules must be followed when using resin:

- follow the manufacturer's instructions for use;
- work at a mimimum temperature of 20°C (68°F).

When they are separate, the two constituents of epoxy-resin are toxic, and it is only polymerization which neutralizes their toxicity. For this to be successful, the following guidelines should be noted:

- weigh measures of resin and its catalyst, as proportions need to be strictly observed;
- work only at a minimum environmental temperature of 20°C (68°F).

Aquarium owners only have problems using the product when they do not follow the correct procedure.

The good polymerization of the resin means that a universal dye can be combined with it and will be neutralized in the coating.

The tools you will need to apply the resin are: a hard-bristle paintbrush, a glass jar, a wooden stick, dyes, and something with which to sprinkle the resin.

As polymerization will start shortly after the mixture is prepared, make a quantity suitable to the surface you are covering and the time you need to do so. It is a good idea to slightly alter the dyes for each preparation, so that colours are not too regular. The colour of

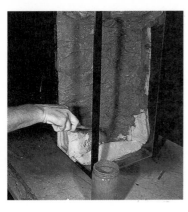

Applying resin to a poly-urethane decoration

the resin should be as close to that of natural elements as possible. Lava should be coloured red and black, millstone is best reproduced using yellow and red, for bauxite use sienna and a little black, and for sandstone, use yellow, red and black. A little sand sprinkled on the top, helps to lighten the shades.

Application on polystyrene

Start the application on the back of the polystyrene decoration, which will not be sprinkled with sand. The resin layer fixes the granules in the polystyrene, particularly in the places where the silicone glue is applied to stick the decoration to the rear window of the tank. When rear and side walls have been polymerized, the visible side can be coated with resin. Work on surfaces 40 x 40 cm at a time, using 35 to 45 cl of prepared resin. When the surface has been treated, it should immediately be sprinkled with sand, which will stick to it. Then turn the whole thing over to remove any excess. It can be coated in successive stages, but do check that all crannies and waterways have been done properly.

Application on polyurethane

Unlike polystyrene, polyurethane does not require singeing when being worked, and its internal structure is very different. It has very small pores which protect it from being torn. Resin is applied as above, but it is more difficult to do, as you are working on decoration already in the aquarium. The front glass has to be protected, because resin will stick to it and once something is coated and polymerized, it is very difficult to remove. One careful application of tinted resin should be enough for a fresh-water tank, but two are better for sea-water tanks and only the last layer should be sprinkled with minerals. The second layer will afford better protection against marine species like the parrot fish and balistidae who tend to nibble at the decoration.

■ Installation of the polystyrene decoration

After three days in a well-ventilated room, the resin will be completely polymerized, and the finer details can be adjusted; channels for heating cables (front or rear) or for glass supports on the bottom can be cut with a handsaw and then coated with resin. A few hours later, the decoration can finally be installed in the tank.

Remember to fix the decoration tightly to the base and rear of the tank, so that it won't bob about as its density is different to that of water. The best way to do this is to first clean the surfaces thoroughly with a diluting agent and then glue the base and rear of the decoration. (It is not advisable to attempt to do this job on your own.) Squeeze the decoration tightly against the back wall and bottom of the tank and forty-eight hours later it can be filled with water.

Natural decoration

When the background has been completed and the floor of the aquarium installed, it is time to think about arranging the rest of the decoration; we recommend natural materials, like rocks and wood, which can be found in our environment. Natural materials could also be used to decorate the backdrop, if they are preferred to artificial materials. Naturally we are not going to discuss colours and taste, but we expect you will want to avoid gadgets like divers and water-mills, there being little connection between these synthetic models and the real world!

■ The role of natural elements

Apart from the floor of the aquarium which comprises minerals in a different form see (chapter on substratum), rocks and wood make up the solid components of the tank's internal decoration. Rocks provide the skeleton for the substratum, stabilizing it and protecting it to some extent from some fish species, while also giving them somewhere to take refuge and lay their eggs. It acts as a territorial marker and enables mountain-stream plants, such as the *Microsorium* and *Bolbitis* to take root in open water. It also benefits other plants by tempering the effect of the waste current, filter or jet.

■ Choosing materials

Some materials available will not be quite right for your display. Certain minerals will be too calcareous for the aquarium you have in mind, others release toxins. The tank's general appearance really depends on the structure, size and colour of rocks in use. Although some are suitable from the chemical point of view, they may not be right visually; white, green, red or blue will be too bright for example. (Although they are all very well for a minerals exhibition or a jeweller's shop window.) Nonetheless it is possible to achieve the right kind of geological mix in an aquarium, but it is better to aim for this in a large tank, where various small sections can be combined to form an overall picture.

■ Different rock types

Rocks are distinguished according to their origins and can be divided into three major categories: sedimentary, metamorphic and magmatic (igneous). Sedimentary includes limestone, marl, sandstone and sand; metamorphic comprises slate and gneiss; and magmatic includes granite and lava basalt).

A metamorphic rock: gneiss

Sedimentary rocks

Some types of sedimentary rocks used in environments where water hardness is either irrelevant or preferred. For example, in brackish water aquariums, in those designed for species from salt lakes in the Rift Valley or North Mexico, and in marine aquariums. These types should not be used with river species from South America, Africa or Asia. Remember that they produce a chemical reaction when in contact with certain cleaning agents such as disinfectant.

The best known and most popular types are travertine and Karstic limestone. The first looks like round chalk stone and the second is pitted with irregular cavities and sharp edges. They are often very heavy, but this varies according to their place of origin. Another variety suitable for decoration is hollow tufa, which is not very dense and can be found tinted with iron oxide. Sometimes it contains crystallized calcium carbonate in prism form, which is known as aragonite, and is quite safe for aquarium use. The variety is indigenous to Eastern France, Spain, and the Caroline Islands.

Other suitable rocks for decorating are fluorite or fluorspar which is made up of large, green or blue crystals sometimes showing white veins; and calcium carbonate calcite, which is usually colourless, but often white or pinkish from iron oxide deposits. Marble and dolomite are suitable too and have the

Decoration achieved with metamorphic rocks

added advantage of serving as filters and stabilizing an alkaline pH.

Sandstone is made up of compacted sand which can look very attractive in the aquarium. Quartzose sandstone in hard water will absorb a great deal of the water's calcareous content. On the other hand, calcareous cement sandstone does tend to harden fresh water, so it is better to choose the neutral quartzose or silicious variety. It is usually laid in horizontal layers or obliquely in the tank and, like red slate, it can be crumbled by tapping the surface with a wooden mallet. A large, thick plate can be cleft in two to form two surfaces, but this should be done with considerable care, and only when it can be split evenly.

Metamorphic rocks

Slate, which is a form of shale, adds interest to the aquarium. Thin slabs of black and green slate can be arranged in horizontal layers on the bottom of the tank or against the back wall. It is particularly suitable for small Cichlids from African lakes, that cannot survive without contact with stone, and its structure means that a large surface area can be obtained with very few stones. On the substratum it can be used as a foundation for sand or gravel terraces, but with its black, flat surface it does not always look very appealing. Watch out for slate slabs which are shot with gold, because this is pyrites or fools' gold, which dissolves in water and is poisonous to living organisms.

The most popular shales among aquarium enthusiasts are the red and green varieties from Thailand. They can be arranged in slabs and used in the same way as slate. They are quite neutral and harmonize well with South American, African and Asian aquariums. Their red or green colour contrasts strongly with aquatic flora, creating a varied atmosphere in the tank. Slabs should be positioned carefully so that they look natural.

Gneiss is made up of thin leaves of black mica and quartz. The larger blocks are excellent for big aquariums and provide caves and hideaways for large, territorial fish.

Magmatic (igneous) rocks

Granite is marketed under various names, such as granilite, syenite, deiorite, which correspond to proportions of its constituent elements: feldspar, quartz, mica. It is very dense with bright lines and usually light in colour.

Basalt is a volcanic, compact, black rock which makes a splendid back-drop for plants, but it is very sharp and should be rubbed down before being positioned in the tank. As it is very dense, it is best not to use too much of it in the aquarium.

Various materials are grouped under the heading of lava, such as obsidian, rhyolyte, clinkstone, andesite, porphyry, pumice and lava itself, in the form of volcanic bombs, slag or pozzolana. The term lava, which is used frequently by aquarium owners in fact only applies to granular volcanic ashes. Lava is the best material of all for decorating the aquarium. Large slag blocks with vacuoles can be used to build high structures, as they are very light-weight. Their natural dark colour, characteristic of the tropical aquatic environment, blends perfectly with plants, but their round shape makes them difficult to arrange and it is a good idea to create a graduated land-slide towards the front of the tank. They can also be partially buried in the substratum, to form terraces at different levels. In its powdered form, it is the best kind of material for a substratum and filtering base. Its dark colour tones down bright lights. As a filtering medium, its rugged surface with vacuole will harbour rich bacterial flora, vital to an efficient nitrogen cycle.

Quartz, flint and pebbles can also be used. Although quartz is relatively rare, flint and pebbles can be used to re-create a model river-bed. This sort of decoration is recommended for fresh water, European tanks and Central American river tanks. It also looks good in aquariums designed for rheophile species from the Congo region, where heaps of large, round or oval pebbles offer shelter to smaller fish and their fry.

Other rocks

We come finally to industrially processed, natural materials such as coke, which is produced by distilling bituminous coal and can be very decorative. It should be soaked for a long time before use, as it tends to float and its porous channels need to be completely water-logged before being placed in the aquarium. Its matt, black, colour contrasts effectively with plants and it is inexpensive, light and harmless in an aquatic environment.

Blast-furnace slag makes a good decorative tool in a flat, pebble-like form and looks good when it is swollen and hollow. Heavier than coke, but lighter than rock, this is another processed, natural material which is harmless but should be rinsed before use to eliminate impurities. It can contain iron deposits which oxidize quickly in water, forming rust, but this is quite harmless.

Terracotta can add volume to the decoration of a large tank and is neutral in water. Hollow bricks provide a foundation for natural rocks in the substratum and a skeleton for very big decorations. A pile of bricks can support a façade of natural stones and provide hiding places for fish.

It is also possible to construct artificial hiding places, for example, in expanded polystyrene. A large, round block is partially coated with a centimetre thick layer of concrete. The polystyrene that is left uncovered is removed with acetone when the concrete is hard. Hollow shells, in which the fish can hide, are left in the concrete. However, this surface will need to be coated with epoxy-resin.

Decoration using volcanic rocks

■ Wood

Choosing wood

Tropical-river and European aquariums generally include a piece of root, a stump, or a branch of dead wood, but as with rocks, not every sort is suitable. The best type for aquarium decoration is fossilized or petrified wood; some tree bark is also suitable, and so are bamboo shoots.

Usable	Toxic
Oak	Resinous (all species)
Willow	Elm
Beech Poplar	Wood thrown up by the sea*
Birch	Bark except from cork-oak

Usable or toxic materials for aquarium use.
* Wood thrown up by the sea may be used in brackish or even sea-water tanks.

Where to find wood

As forest wood is often decayed by natural biological processes, wood found submerged in an aquatic environment is more suitable and ready for use. A small cord with a hook on the end will guarantee a good catch for you. You will need to brush the wood thoroughly to free it of algae and then soak it in a sterilizing solution of unconcentrated disinfectant (20 cl for 20 litres) or copper sulphate (1 g per litre) for one or two hours. It should then be rinsed thoroughly using a nylon brush; do not use metal as this will damage the wood.

The best preserved pieces of wood are found in sphagnum acid peat-bogs, often from the peat birch *(Betula pubescens)*. The wood is protected from decay by its acidic environment but try looking in a bog, which is unlikely to be legally protected. The small amount of acidity the pieces of wood contain can be harmful to plants and fish in

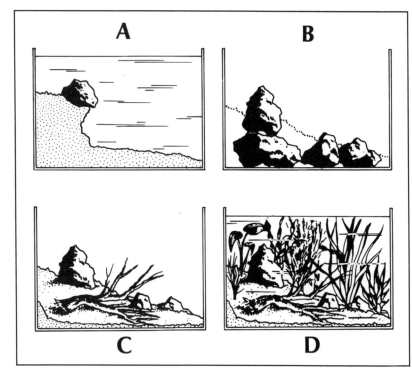

a small tank, so it is advisable to soak them for a few days in fresh water, changed daily, before placing them in your tank. You can also obtain wood in specialized commercial outlets. They are classified according to their origin, regardless of whether they are pieces of branch or trunk, or roots; they are referred to as Scotch Wood, Moorkienholtz or Bogwood.

Peat wood looks good in all different kinds of tank, but especially those with a South American or African river theme.

Installation

A little ingenuity is required to install and maintain the wood in its desired position. Ballast it with a rock or pebble, wedging the ballast into a cavity in the wood, or use thread to hold it down. If you use thread, it must be made of pure nylon.

A long branch can be wedged up against a rock with its upper side against the aquarium itself. It looks perfectly natural to have a branch lying diagonally in the aquarium like

Installing decoration
A Never put a rock directly on to the sand as it will fall.
B Put rocks on the bottom.
C Enhance mineral decoration with roots or branches.
D Install plants when natural decoration is complete.

this, as many live or dead ones fall in such a position in the natural environment.

Using bark

Many aquarium owners use cork-oak bark as decoration, as it makes an excellent trimming for the back window of the tank. Using the rounded edges, supporting terraces can be made for the substratum. Before use, it must be boiled and dried thoroughly, then insulated with a layer of epoxy-resin to protect the surface from water. It can be stuck to the back of the tank as background decoration or fixed onto the bottom, as a foundation, with silicone glue.

Fossilized wood

Some types of fossilized wood will not be suitable, such as lignite, a wood undergoing carbonization, or fossil wood from calcic peat-bogs, which is decaying.

You should concentrate on fossil wood from sedimentary layers; some lovely examples are often unearthed from deep layers in sediment by ballasting dredgers; these can go directly into position in the aquarium after simply a brief rinse.

The wood should not be allowed to dry and will not affect the water in the aquarium, as it has lain for millions of years in underground water.

Decoration using dead-tree branches and roots

Silicified or petrified wood

Petrified wood has a hard, ligneous surface, as its plant cells have been replaced by silica. It originates in hot, desert regions and like many rocks, it is quite neutral. Brush it lightly under tap water before using it for decoration.

Using bamboo

Bamboo shoots are resistant to decay in water and recreate zones of reed-beds. They can be coloured any shade from black to light-yellow, as well as any shade of brown, and are the perfect choice for a typical Asian setting. But don't overdo it: a small background corner for about ten shoots coupled with helical or striped *Vallisneria* should be sufficient.

Before use, bamboo should be disinfected in a potassium alum solution, which will eliminate germs and fungi which grow in a gelatinous, white mass particularly around the joints.

Combining wood and plants

Tropical waterways are often littered with dead wood

The Dutch tank

Unlike the standard aquarium, the Dutch tank is designed almost exclusively for plants and is planted in one go with careful selection. The living room makes an ideal spot to display the beautiful, finished glass-house.

It will come as no surprise to discover that this kind of aquarium was an invention of the Dutch, whose natural fondness for indoor plants influences their national love of aquariums. However, even beginners can create perfect examples—provided they follow advice and instructions carefully.

■ Positioning the Dutch tank

Before you rush into anything, work out a place for the tank, bearing in mind its size and particularly its weight. You have to take the same precautions and make the same checks before installation, as for any other tank. But a Dutch tank can be heavier than others of similar dimensions because of the volume of its substratum. If a tank holds more than 500 litres, check the floor where it is to be positioned. A wooden parquet floor on joists is always a problem. If the tank is to go perpendicularly to the joists, it is a good idea to reinforce the base of the aquarium with IPN-type welded iron bars. Underneath this you can place a compressed Novopan slab and a sheet of polystyrene, in the same way as you would for a standard aquarium.

■ Tank dimensions

The aquarium's dimensions have an important aesthetic effect. The width is particularly significant as it must allow for a field of vision deep enough to show off the decoration to its best effect. A Dutch tank should be at least 130 x 60 x 60 cm (51 x 24 x 24 in). Length and width can be greater, but it is best to keep the height to 60 cm (24 in) which, bearing in mind the depth of the substratum, will make it easier to tend the plants frequently. The height is also important for proper lighting in the tank.

A length of 130 cm (51 in) is important because it allows much greater flexibility in terms of the types of standard 40 W fluorescent tubes that can be used.

■ Dressing the rear pane

There are many ways of dressing the rear pane of an aquarium. One idea is to stick a photographic cardboard cut-out with pictures of common aquatic plants on the outside, but don't use one which includes fish as they don't move around! It is unfortunately difficult to get hold of a photograph taller than 50 cm (20 in) but allowing for the depth of the substratum at the back, and 'by' sticking the photo to the top edge of the tank, you should not be able to see the missing section in a 60 cm– (24 in–) high tank.

Another way of decorating the

rear glass is to cover it with a coat of black or dark-blue paint. Use a paint spray for this job, because it is very fiddly to do with a paint-brush.

Both types of decoration will leave the internal face of the back pane visible, and this can mean reflected light will distort or disturb the general effect, especially if plants at the back are not planted out very densely, or if they are still quite small.

The best solution is to use polystyrene or polyurethane, which is installed inside the tank against the back pane. Its implementation is very like that outlined in the chapter on artificial decoration and it should take up the minimum of room, so as

not to encroach on the plants' growing space. Avoid projecting ledges. The material you use should be 3 to 4 cm (1 to 1½ in) thick and worked in discreet, horizontal strata, then coated with dark, almost black, resin and sprinkled with quartz dust or fine sand. The whole artificial decoration should be coated with tinted resin.

Leave it to polymerize for four or five days, and before it is properly installed, give it a thorough rinse. This decoration can incorporate an internal decantation tank, although sometimes these take up too much room; other filtering methods are possible and we shall be looking at these later.

■ Equipment for the tank

Heating through the substratum

This method of heating is carried out by installing a heating cable on the aquarium floor, with a power of 15 to 180 W, according to the volume of the tank. Cable lengths can vary from 3 to 10 m (3 to 11 yd) and double cables can be used for similar heating power, for example 50 W for 3 m (3 yd) or 60 W for 10 m (11 yd). In a Dutch tank it is best to install two 60 W cables of 10 m (11 yd) each, rather than a single 120 W of 9 m (10 yd) length. Heat diffusion will be better and there will be no plant-damaging hot spots. Most plant species with strong roots like to feel the warmth beneath them. The major advantages of cables is the heat exchange that is set up between the hot water of the substratum and colder water above it. By conduction, the resulting heat exchange spreads well-oxygenated water and maintains the substratum in aerobiosis. This exchange is of prime importance when a thicker substratum is utilized, as in a Dutch tank. Also, the slow-rising current of warm water prevents any superficial clogging, which can arise when

a crust forms on the substratum surface. In aerobiosis, all matter filtering through the cracks in the substratum is broken down by colonies of *Nitrosomonas*, and then by *Nitrobacteria*. These bacteria are involved in the nitrogen mineralization cycle, which in turn promotes the production of the nitrates that are absorbed by plants.

A thick substratum maintained in an aerobiosis through the absence of oxygen, often quickly produces pockets of hydrogen sulphide (H_2S). At the same time, the substratum will turn blackish at the bottom. Heating cables improve the general atmosphere of a Dutch tank and mean that they require much less overhauling.

A heating cable maintains the substratum in an oxidizing environment, so there is no need for a clay or peat foundation. Trace elements, in particular iron, will no longer be present in their trivalent state, but will be oxidized throughout the aquarium. Treatment with chelates (chelates + Fe^{++}) is recommended for an oxidizing substratum.

Dutch tank

Filtering

Filtration of the aquarium can be carried out in a variety of ways. Chamber and turbine filters are located outside the aquarium, preferably underneath in the supporting structure. If the suction and output pipes are fitted with taps, their maintenance is greatly simplified; those which run between the tank and the wall look unattractive and mean that tank support structure needs to be unwedged at the front. The aquarium owner can overcome this problem by concealing the equipment. Turbine filters operate very smoothly in a tank and a Dutch tank should be provided with one with a low turbine output, for example 350/l hour for a volume of 500 l. Plants do not like fast waste currents, and where there are fish around there is no need for any strong suction. Filtering chambers should always be as large as possible and you should replace the one which comes with the standard turbine, with a larger one, unless you can purchase them separately in the first place. Turbine outflow should be below water level, where

the suction is, as it will diffuse water through the tank this way. If it is positioned opposite the suction, a direct water current will be set up between them.

Another method is to use a decanting filter. This will take up a certain amount of space in the aquarium, so you should allow for at least 10 cm (4 in) width, unless there is already sufficient room for it. Water should pass slowly through the filter, which should be 50 to 60 cm (20 to 24 in) long, according to the length of the tank. It can be employed for specific jobs, such as light filtering beneath the substratum. Water is collected in PVC tubes, designed to protect the heating cables, and punctured with 3 to 4 mm ($^3/_{16}$ to $^1/_4$ in) holes, so that the substratum is not sucked in. The tube used will be led into the first filtering chamber through a hole in the filter partition, or through several openings, depending on the size of the installation. Water releases larger particles in the first compartment, then crosses into a second compartment containing filter wool.

The wool serves as a mechanical pre-filter, which can be removed for a weekly rinse. The third compartment is filled with crushed pozzolana and acts as a biological filter. The fourth contains accessories, like immersible pump(s), main or secondary heating, and possibly also a back-up diffuser for the summer. Over a 60 cm (24 in) length the four compartments take up an area of 15 x 10 cm (6 x 4 in) of the overall aquarium depth. This makes it easy for you to reach in to carry out any adjustments. The biological substratum will be colonized by denitrifying bacteria and the area should be constantly protected from macro-particles with filter wool.

There is no need to clean the pozzolana in the third compartment, unless the water flow is checked for any length of time.

Passageways between the compartments should allow water to circulate freely.

Pump outlets should also be below water level, preferably via the separation partition of the decanting filter. Thus, the water outlet will lie in the upper corner in front of the filter, and the suction in the lower back corner. This is an excellent arrangement for water circulation in the aquarium. The suction opening can be hidden by polystyrene decoration, through which a small tube is bored. A PVC grill protects the water entry when it is not connected to a substratum filter. The decanting filter is operated with one or several immersible pumps, but take care as filtering in a Dutch tank should not be too forceful.

Even the smallest external turbines produce too forceful a current and small immersible pumps from 200 to 300 litres per hour do the job very well, aside from which they are quiet and easy to maintain. However, water resistance means that water cannot be filtered into a very long pipe, so it is better to lead it out into the aquarium when it emerges from the decanting tank. Under these conditions, outlet power is the best for a Dutch tank. Commonly-used filter-gutters are unsuitable for Dutch tanks, as constant falls in water level create distorted lighting effects and have the added disadvantage of depriving plants of their vital carbon dioxide quota.

When the filtering system has been installed, the aquarium decoration, if it is a polystyrene one, can be glued into place in the tank.

Dutch tank

The Dutch tank

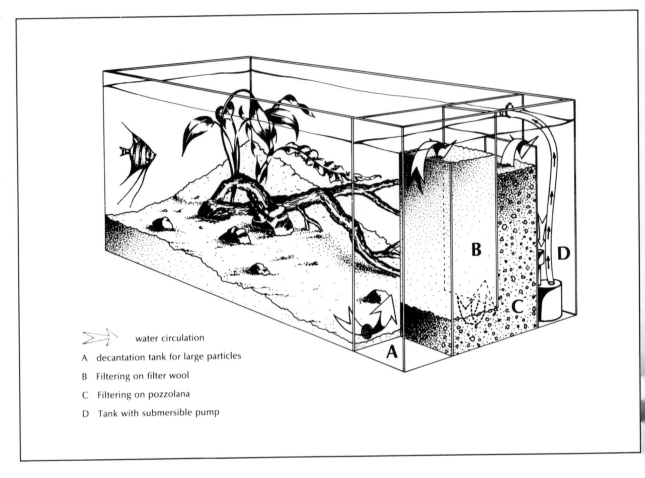

water circulation

A   decantation tank for large particles

B   Filtering on filter wool

C   Filtering on pozzolana

D   Tank with submersible pump

Components of a decantation filter.

Lighting

For tanks up to a height of 60 cm (24 in), it is best to choose fluorescent tubes; beyond that, discharge lamps are the best choice.

In a 60 cm (24 in) wide aquarium, six or seven tubes can be installed and although this may seem too powerful, a Dutch tank does actually need more lighting power than a traditional tank. Bear in mind that this kind of tank is mainly designed for cultivating plants, which come in large numbers, sometimes concentrated into small areas. It is important to ensure that the aquarium as a whole gets enough light and that shady spots are eliminated wherever possible. A Dutch tank with dimensions 140 x 60 x 60 cm (55 x 24 x 24 in) will need four tubes distributed as follows:

- 1 Gro-Lux tube in the foreground;
- 2 Full spectrum tubes in the middle;
- 1 Wotan Colour 30 tube in the background.

Lighting is adjusted according to the decanting filter, but placed centrally where there is an external filter.

For an aquarium where the water level is higher than 60 cm (24 in), discharge lamps are positioned over the tank, either suspended from the ceiling, or fixed to the wall. A lighting cage is not recommended in this case, as the heat given off by the lights would be harmful to the aquarium, and the emission cone means that they must be positioned some way from the water surface. You can leave this aquarium uncovered, as it is usually very large with a drip system and overflow and there is no need to worry about evaporation. Nor is a cover needed to stop fish jumping out, if you keep them. It is a well known fact that in larger aquariums, fish do not jump out. If the aquarium is established, plants will eventually spread over the whole surface.

To obtain the best diffusion results, look at the technical characteristics of each kind of discharge lamp. The lamp should be positioned according to the angle of emission cone and aquarium width, somewhere in the region of an emission angle of 90° to 120°. A low emission cone angle means that the lamp should be moved away; if it is higher, it should be moved closer to the tank. But a lamp with an angle of 120° which is too far from the aquarium surface will have a light-flux which shoots across the area to be lit up. It should be integrated into a diffusion cover with an identical angle of opening.

Water qualities

If the Dutch tank has a drip system, there will be no option; water will preferably be semi-hard between 5 and 13° dGH, that is from 9 to 24° fTH. In all cases, total water hardness should be between 3 and 18° dGH. Conductivity up to 600 uS/cm^2 is quite acceptable. Harder water can be softened by using lightly mineralized water at source, or demineralized water. Never use permuted or bi-permuted water, because this has undergone mineral transfers, rather than demineralization.

In most European towns, ordinary drinking water will be suitable, but mountain regions could have water which is too soft, for example in the Lake District and Snowdonia.

■ Arranging the Dutch tank

Before laying the substratum, choose the permanent features of the arrangement, bearing in mind that a Dutch tank is designed principally for plants. Avoid any exaggerated use of size or colour, such as brilliant white quartz, tuff which has been tinted by iron oxide, travertine with unusual contours, syenite, brilliant black obsidian or red and green porphyry. We would recommend neutral-coloured lava or matt-black coke; see that peat-bog roots are played down in much the same way as rocks. A slim, branch shape is preferable to large, compact masses. In principle, rocks and roots rest on the bottom of the tank, but as the few fish chosen for this kind of tank do not dig into the substratum, this arrangement is not compulsory.

Installing the substratum

In a Dutch tank, the substratum should be arranged in a particular way and not slightly raised towards the back, as for other tanks. The substratum itself must be deep, about 7 cm (3 in) at the front, and about 10 to 12 cm (4 to 5 in) at the back, but a relief back-drop is superfluous, as plants will serve for this purpose. As far as possible, decorate the visible section of the substratum in front of the aquarium, so that it is in keeping with the rest of the tank. A good choice would be round gravel with 3 or 4 mm (³⁄₁₆ or ¼ in) grains, or crushed pozzolana over a layer of clay pellets, which can be purchased from a horticulturist shop or florist.

For boundaries between different sorts of plants use rocks which are fairly thin but have large surfaces: for example, fast-growing, medium-sized or dwarf foreground plants. Rock height should not be more than 10 cm (4 in) higher than the highest part of the substratum. In a word, don't make it look like an Alpine garden. Make sure when you put the rocks in that they do not interfere with the heating cable in any way. Then, once all the permanent fixtures are in place, you can fill the tank with water.

■ Filling the tank

The tank should be filled with running water and if the tap is fitted with a modifier, regulate the temperature to approximately 25°C (77°F). If the tank is fitted with a decanting filter, fill the first compartment. It will run from there into the cross tank via a suction opening or via pipes which run beneath the substratum. In this way, the decoration itself is not moved. If you are going to pour water directly into the tank, put a shallow bowl on the substratum and pour it into that. When full, the water will overflow very gently.

As it is being filled, you will see the decoration appears to sag because of the water and air exchange in the substratum, but this will be corrected automatically when you put the plants in.

■ Operation

When it is full, tank accessories are put under tension. This is the time to check that the whole tank is water-tight and to adjust heating and pumps. Let the aquarium operate on a test-run for a week. This will give you time to check heating regularity, filter efficiency and, very importantly, decanting filter baffles. Empty the tank after a week and fill it with fresh water. Now you can concentrate on the plants. As we have already mentioned, it is a good idea to plant the tank as soon as you receive the plants, so order them in advance when you have prepared a layout sketch. Almost all the species that you could want can be obtained from plant wholesalers, who supply over 250 aquatic species and their varieties.

A Dutch tank can be designed for plants and fish from the same continent, or to show a diversity of fish and plant life from all over the world.

Dutch tank

■ Some plants for the Dutch tank

Species quoted are merely examples chosen for their position in the tank. Numbers of plants indicated are to be treated as a minimum per species for a tank size of 500 litres (110 gal) (140 x 6 x 60 cm) (55 x 2 x 23 in). Aquarium enthusiasts should give full rein to their creative abilities with this kind of tank, bearing in mind the fact that plants are living things which often have very strict maintenance needs.

Foreground plants

Number	Species
20	Echinodorus bolivianus
20	Echinodorus paniculatus
20	Echinodorus tenellus
15	Acorus gramineus var. pusillus
20	Anubias nana
15	Aponogeton natans
20	Cryptocoryne costata
20	Cryptocoryne gracilis
20	Cryptocoryne parva
20	Cryptocoryne petchii
50	Lilaeopsis novae-zelandiae
20	Marsilea crenata
15	Saururus cernuus

Plants for the centre of the tank (medium height)

Number	Species
20	Alternanthera sessilis
10	Anubias afzelii
7	Aponogeton crispus
7	Aponogeton undulatus
7	Barclaya longifolia
20	Bacopa monnieri
15	Cryptocoryne affinis
15	Cryptocoryne becketii
15	Cryptocoryne korthausae
15	Cryptocoryne willisii
10	Echinodorus major
20	Ludwigia alternifolia

Certain species suitable for the centre of the tank can also be planted diagonally, with the first few near the front window.

Background plants

Number	Species
20	Bacopa caroliniana
20	Cabomba caroliniana
3	Crinum sp.
10	Hygrophila stricta
20	Limnophila aquatica
15	Ludwigia palustris
20	Myriophyllum sp.
20	Vallisneria sp.

Main plants for the tank centre

Number	Species
1	Aponogeton bolivinianus
1	Aponogeton madagascariensis
2-3	Aponogeton ulvaceus
2-3	Cryptocoryne balansae
2-3	Cryptocoryne retrospiralis
2-3	Echinodorus cordifolius
2-3	Echinodorus osiris
1	Eichhornia azurea
1	Nymphaea lotus

The monographs at the end of the book will give readers further information on each species.

■ Planting

It is best to do this all in one go, but if you don't have all the plants to start with, keep those you have in warm water (30 to 32°C [86 to 90°F]), grouped in species on the surface. They will keep like this for a few days until you get the second delivery.

Before you start planting, let out about a quarter of the water in the aquarium and turn off all the electrical accessories. This will enable you to work in the water up to your armpits without getting electrocuted!

The actual planting is crucial, so get some help if you can. First plant the background or alternatively the main plants for the centre of the tank. If they are planted parallel to the back panel, keep background plants an identical height (unless they have stalks, in which case grade the rows slightly).

Most background plants have stalks and before planting you should remove any band or grip tying them together. Plant them in the substratum in twos and threes with spaces of 3 to 4 cm (1 to 1½ in). The same method can be used for planting species with stalks in the centre of the tank. A red tinted species could be alternated with a green one.

Before going on with the planting, adjust background decoration; a badly placed rock or root should be moved to its proper place before you start on the middle section. Medium-height species with roots usually come in containers on a base of growing medium. The container should be removed before planting, leaving the actual bed intact. Cut about 1 cm (½ in) of this away, so as to expose the centre of the plant and cover it with a small layer of substratum, without covering its stem or rhizome.

Foreground plants are extremely tricky to handle. The smallest species, like *Echinodorus tenellus* or *Lilaeopsis novae-zelandie* are generally supplied on a base of growing medium tied with nylon string. Planting is easier when this has been removed, but if they are delivered singly, planting is laborious to say the least. Often, when you've got three in place, you will find ten others floating to the surface. You will need all your dexterity to bring them into line.

Arrangement for Dutch tank with clumps of plants.

1 Limnophila aquatica
2 Ammania senegalensis
3 Cryptocoryne petchii
4 Bacopa caroliniana
.5 Barclaya longifolia
6 Lilaeopsis novae-zelandiae
7 Echinodorus major
8 Nymphaea lotus
9 Myriophyllum spicatum
10 Marsilea crenata
11 Vallisneria spiralis
12 Rotala rotundifolia
13 Anubias nana
14 Cryptocoryne korthausae
15 Alternanthera lilacina

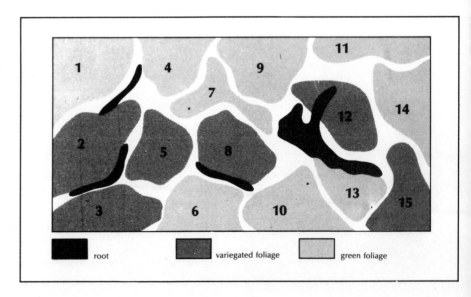

root   variegated foliage   green foliage

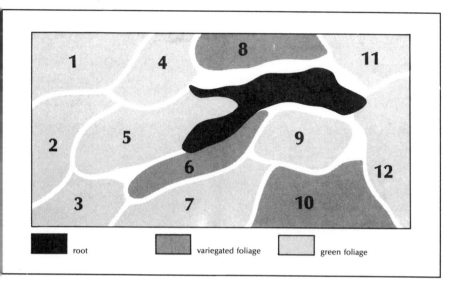

Arrangement for regional Dutch tank.
1. Aponogeton crispus
2. Limnophila indica
3. Cryptocoryne undulata
4. Ceratopteris thalictroïdes
5. Hygrophila corymbosa
6. Barclaya longifolia
7. Marsilea crenata
8. Rotala rotundifolia
9. Nymphaea lotus
10. Cryptocoryne petchii
11. Vallisneria asiatica

■ Initial care and maintenance

Once the plants are in place, fill the tank up again with water and start up the maintenance equipment, so that you can control water currents from the turbine. The current should not be so strong as to make plants bend or wave about. At this point the tank will not yet look like a Dutch tank and the most important job is still to be done. Plants may still have crushed leaves and twisted stems; there could be some debris floating on the surface which needs fishing out.

You should now add a dose of chelates appropriate to the tank's volume, check various accessories (especially the carbon dioxide diffuser), and adjust the time-switch for the lighting to last 14 hours. Plants should now be left alone for a month, unless you have to re-plant the odd escapee.

After a month plants will have taken root and spread out their leaves; fast-growing species will have reached the top of the tank. Plants with stalks should be shor-

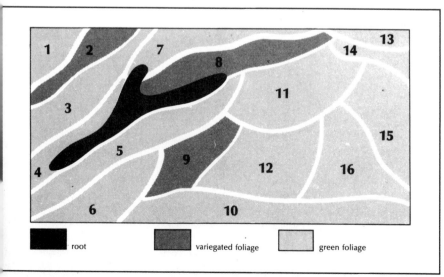

Arrangement for Dutch tank with plants in oblique strips.
1. Vallisneria sp.
2. Alternanthera lilacina
3. Cabomba aquatica
4. Alternanthera reineckii
5. Samolus floribundus
6. Cryptocoryne wendtii
7. Limnophila aquatica
8. Ammania senegalensis
9. Barclaya longifolia
10. Echinodorus tenellus
11. Aponogeton madagascariensis
12. Cryptocoryne beckettii
13. Ludwigia palustris
14. Rotala rotundifolia
15. Hygrophila stricta
16. Ludwigia alternifolia

tened by several centimetres and overhanging lateral cuttings can be replanted in free space reserved for the same species. Take off the old, yellowed leaves, particularly those rising to the surface (*Nymphaea* *lotus*). At this point, you could take the opportunity to change the water and rinse out the filter wool. The substratum should be siphoned, although there won't be many particles for about four to six months.

Dutch tank.

Fish for the Dutch Tank

To bring some life into this Garden of Eden, choose lively, but innocuous fish, preferably gregarious, small and coloured; they can occupy the bottom, top or open water in the tank. If the whole tank is filled, there shouldn't be any competition among various species and hopefully no debris left on the tank's bottom.

Surface-swimming species	Bottom-living species	Open-water species	Fish useful for plants
Carnegiella sp.	Corydoras sp.	Lepidarchus adonis	Gyrinocheilus aymonieri
Gasteropelecus sp.	Botia sp.	Boehlkea fredcochui	Ansistrus leucostictus (8 cm)
Dermogenys pusillus	Apistrogramma sp.	Hyphessorbrycon sp.	Farlowella sp.
Epiplatys sp.	Rineloricaria parva	Rasbora sp.	Hypoptopoma thoracatum
Colisa chuna	Stigmatogobius sp.	Moenkhausia sp.	Otocinclus affinis
Trichogaster leeri	Pelvicachromis sp.	Phenacogrammus sp.	Homaloptera zollingeri

Some species for the Dutch tank.

Maintaining the tank

Look after the plants carefully and attend to them regularly. A total overhaul of the aquarium is only neccessary after three or four years. Summer is a critical time, as an increase in water temperature could harm plants. So, if you are away for long periods, slow down their metabolism by slightly lowering the temperature to 22°C (72°F).

Tanks for plants and fish

The aquarium owner may well choose to keep an aquarium with plants and fish together; this is a common preference.

There are a number ways of organizing this sort of aquarium:

- the collector will opt for a communal tank which groups a variety of fish and plants from diverse bio-geographical regions;
- the purist will create a geographic tank, where fish and plant species from the same bio-geographical area can be brought together.

Whatever the choice, the aquarium owner must be sure to look after the interests of the fish as well as providing for the requirements of the plants.

Communal tank

A communal tank is often a 'collective' tank where you will find all varieties of fish and plants, irrespective of their country of origin.

The aquarium is often arranged in terraces with rocks to hold the substratum in place.

Sometimes, the geological composition is an unusual one, combining a mixture of plants, a peat-bog root and multicoloured fish. Even in a communal tank it is important to make a careful selection of your fish population. Whereas mixing plants together is relatively unimportant, if you do this with the wrong kind of fish, the consequences can be disastrous.

As a general rule, try to combine species which do not compete over territory or food. Whenever possible, follow the advice of aquarium clubs, associations and specialist magazines if you want to achieve the best results. Studious research will be well-rewarded.

Community tank comprising for the most part Cryptocoryne *and* Trichogaster

Position	Species or genera	Number of individuals
Plants		
background	Vallisneria spiralis	10
	Limnophila aquatica	5
	Rotala rotundifolia	10
centre	Nymphaea lotus	1
	Ludwigia brevipes	10 (at side)
	Lobelia cardinalis	10 (at side)
foreground	Cryptocoryne wendtii	10
	Lilaeopsis novae-zelandiae	15
surface	Ceratopteris cornuta	2
Fish		
surface	Trichogaster (toutes espèces)	4 à 5
	Xiphophorus (toutes espèces)	10 (including two males)
open water	Hyphessobrycon flammeus	20
	Brachydanio rerio	20
tank bottom	Coydoras (toutes espèces)	5 à 6
	Botia (toutes espèces)	4 à 5
	Gyrinocheilus aymonieri	1 à 2

Example of flora and fauna composition for a community tank (suitable for a tank of approx. 300 litres).

■ Geographic tanks

A geographic tank is one which aims to combine plants and fish coming from the same continent or geographic region (for example, a Guianese tank). Thus plant and fish species are defined by hydrographic boundaries and the tank may contain species from a particular lake, river or its tributaries. Remember that you will not only have to check origins of plant and fish species selected, but also recreate their environment to a certain extent. For example, an Amazonian aquarium requires dim lighting, while a Tanzanian aquarium needs to be lit quite brightly. All these points depend on observations of the natural environment, so the beginner would be well advised to do some research on specific fauna and flora characteristics.

The regional tank offers optimum conditions for maintaining plants and fish. When you come to stocking it, avoid artificial plant and fish varieties, like fish with sail-shaped fins, albinos or xanthoics.

Specialized clubs and associations (with particular interest in killies, cichlids, labyrinthi fish and ovoviviparous species) will enabl the aquarium owner to obtain rar species and local varieties, as we as common species which hav been bred from wild specimen similar to the natural ecotype.

Central America

In Central America, waterways ten to be short with fast-running cu rents. From northern Mexico dow to Panama, water becomes steadi

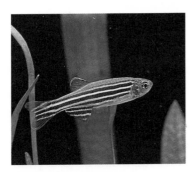

Brachydanio rerio

Corydoras julii

Botia macracantha

softer. For example, Rio Panuco in Mexico has a conductivity of 2,000 uS/cm² while in Costa Rica water is softer at 150 uS/cm². Fast streams and large rivers have practically no aquatic plants at all, as they only thrive in stagnant water. Water is always highly oxygenated (80 to 95% oxygen saturation), alkaline pH varies from 7.0 to 8.0. Waterway beds are often littered with wood and covered in gravel with large pebbles. Fish in this region are most fond of fast currents, although some

Water: pH	7,0-7,5
dGH	5-15°
uS/cm²	150-1 000
Temp	23-26 °C
Filtering	intense
Light climate	intense
Substratum	gravel – pebbles
Decoration	rocks – wood
Plants	none
Fish	Xiphophorus Priapella Rheophilus Astyanax fasciatus Rhamdia guatemalensis

Arrangement for river type aquarium

species are happy in calmer sections of water.

Central America has a second biotype made up of stagnant water lagoons. The aquatic environment is totally different, with a rich variety of plant life. Surface plants of the genera *Eichhornia, Pistia, Salvinia* etc. and foliage of *Nymphaea* spread across wide areas. Fish are often broader as there is no current, and their colouring is brighter as the environment is a duller one; this is particularly the case for Cichlids. Water temperature ranges from 25 to 30°C (77 to 86°F) and is less oxygenated (60 to 80% saturation) but still alkaline. Substratum is mostly mud, but sometimes sandy near the banks. The design of a lagoon-type aquarium whether with

Water: pH	7,0-7,8
dGH	5-15°
uS/cm²	150-1 000
Temp	23-30 °C
Filtering	medium
Light climate	diffused
Substratum	coarse sand
Decoration	wood
Plants	Salvinia Myriophyllum Ceratophyllum Cabomba Marsilea
Fish	Xiphophorus Poecilia Thorichthys meeki Dorosoma petenensis

Arrangement for lagoon type aquarium

fish or plants can of course be adapted and the owner may choose other species from the same region.

South America

Waterways in South America are known among aquarium enthusiasts for their high level of acidity and soft water; but this is only partly true. In some regions, near Pucallpa in Peru, for example, water can in fact be alkaline and of average hardness; the same is true of llanos in Colombia. But, in the wide expanse of the Amazon, water is acidic and extremely soft: pH is

Water: pH	5,5-6,8
dGH	1-5°
uS/cm²	30-100
Temp	23-26 °C
Filtering	medium on turf
Light climate	diffused
Substratum	powdered lava, pozzolana
Decoration	roots, dark rocks
Plants	preferably none
Fish	Gastéropélécidés Tétragonoptérinés Ptetrophyllum altum Apistogramma sp. Corydoras sp. Otocinclus sp.

5.5–7.0, dGH: 0 to 2. It may be dark brown and transparent (known as black water), milky brown (brown water) or transparent and colourless (clear water). The colouring and physio-chemical condition of rivers depends in part on the geological make-up of basin slopes. Rivers and streams in forest glades have no submerged aquatic flora but river beds are covered with leaves and dead wood. Along the river route, water may be stagnant or rough. Shallow-water regions of the latter will often reveal small characids, cichlids and *Corydoras*.

Arranging a South American tank

As a general rule, the tank should not contain submerged aquatic plants, but for purely aesthetic reasons, some plant species of the genera *Echinodorus, Cabomba, Myriophyllum* can be used to embellish the tank. Make the decoration out of polystyrene to represent a dark-brown hollowed bank, with peat-bog roots and rocks, like shale and lava.

Certain species are best kept in special tanks, in particular, genera *Serrasalmus* (piranha), *Colossoma, Mylossoma, Myleus, Metynnis* (false piranha), and all larger species of the families Cichlidal and Loricariidal. But the physio-chemical conditions of the aquarium are the same.

Africa

The African continent can be divided into several regions of fish life, corresponding to various hydrographic basins. Unlike the neotropical continent of Central and South America, several ecosystem types can be distinguished. Rivers and streams in the savanna are exposed to the sun, while those in forest glades are well protected. Areas like this are common along the Atlantic coast. East Africa holds a certain fascination for aquarium owners, because of the rich fauna contained in its large lakes. Inland seas like these contain fauna but virtually no aquatic plants.

The inherent physio-chemical water qualities make it difficult to look after these aquatic plants. Small lakes which occur in active volcanic land present exceptional physiochemical conditions, which are difficult to reproduce in the aquarium. This applies, for example, to Lake Natron in Kenya which has a pH of 10.5, density of 1,020 and temperature of 40°C (104°F). Fauna coming from small lakes are less well-known among aquarium enthusiasts. The region is famous for Lake Malawi, Lake Tanganyika and for the killifish, particularly of the genus *Notobranchius*.

The River Zaire has a turbulent stretch which harbours a quite distinct biotype. For over 150 km (93 miles) the river crosses the Crysta

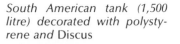

South American tank (1,500 litre) decorated with polystyrene and Discus

Mountains before draining into the Atlantic. Species in this area have adapted to their environment and show morphological and physiological mutations, such as atrophy of the air-bladder and microphthalmia.

Arranging West African tanks

Generally the water should be somewhere between soft and semi-hard with a pH varying between 5.8 and 7. Crude polyurethane decoration reminiscent of lava, is recommended for forest versions.

West African tank

Lacustrine regional tank (Malawi) for petricolour (rock-loving) M'buna *species*

Water: pH	6,0 à 7
dGH	2 à 5°
Temp	25 à 30 °C
Filtering	intense
Light climate	intense
Substratum	gravel
Decoration	rocks
Plants	Otellia alismoides
	Ammannia sp.
	Limnophila indica
	Myriophyllum spicatum
Fish	Alestes chaperi
	Barbus sp.
	Epiplatys sp.
	Hermichromis sp.

Savanna-type aquarium.

Water: pH	5,5 à 6,8
dGH	0 à 5°
Temp	22 à 26 °C
Filtering	medium on turf
Light climate	diffused
Substratum	powdered lava
Decoration	wood
	dark rocks
Plants	Anubias sp.
	Crinum natans
	Nymphaea lotus
Fish	Pantodon buchholzi
	Pelvicachromis sp.
	Aphyosemion sp.
	Gnathonemus petersii

Forest-type aquarium.

Gnathonemus petersii

For savanna tanks, use reddish-brown coloured polystyrene, to represent laterite.

Arranging a Congolese tank

This tank is distinguished by its lack of plants, which do not exist in the rapid stretches of the River Congo. Only floating species, such as *Eichhhornia* and *Pistia* cross the rapids. The tank's most striking ornament is an artificial decoration designed to represent large granite blocks which have been eroded smooth, huge pebbles and pieces of wood. Fish are from the• rheophilous species, which inhabit currents. In a tank as turbulent as this one, Cichlids will take cover among the pebbles, and fish territory will be more limited than in a calmer tank. Dissolved oxygen content should be near to saturation point.

Water: pH	6,5 à 7
dGH	2 à 5°
uS/cm²	80 à 200
Temp	22 à 25 °C
Filtering	very intense,
	turbulent normal
Light climate	normal
Substratum	large gravel
Decoration	large pebbles, wood
Plants	some surface plants
Fish	Mormyrops deliciosus
	Petrocephalus simus
	Alestes imberi
	Micralestes humilis
	Labeo sp.
	Synodontis notatus et
	brichardi
	Lamprologus congoensis
	Steatocranus cassuarius
	Nannochromis sp.
	Teleogramma brichardi
	Mastacembelus sp.
	Tetraodon mbu

Arrangement for Congolese tank.

Arranging East African tanks (Lake Malawi and Lake Tanganyika)

These two lakes have been known since 1962 thanks to huge imports of Cichlids, but they only contain this family of fish. The two lakes are quite similar in appearance: sandy and rocky zones alternate on their

	Malawi	Tanganyika
Water: pH dGH uS/cm^2 Temp Filtering	7,5 à 7,9 7 à 15° 300 à 500 24 à 26 °C normal	7,5 à 8,2 12 à 18° 600 à 1 000 25 à 28 °C normal
Light climate	intense	intense
Substratum	fine sand	fine sand
Decoration	some rocks and bamboo shoots	
Plants	among bamboo shoots *Vallisneria sp.* covering background	
Fish	*Barbus johnstonii* *Marcusenius nyasensis* *Synodontus nyassae* *Labeo altivelis* *Lethriop sp.* «*Haplochromis*» *compressiceps*	*Distichodus sexfasciatus* *Hippopotamyrus discorhynchus* *Synodontus granulosus* *Labeo kibimbi* *Xenotilapia* *Oreochromis tanganicae* *Cyprichromis*

Sandy-zone-type aquarium.
Water conductivity in the natural environment is 210 uS/cm^2 in Lake Malawi and 610 uS/cm^2 in Lake Tanganyika. It is difficult to maintain a highly alkaline pH level in semi-hard water, so harder water is recommended.

	Malawi	Tanganyika
Water: filtering	intense	
Substratum	powdered lava	
Decoration	rocks, polystyrene, polyurethane	
Plants	possibly: *Bolbitis heudelotii* and *Microsorium pteropus*	
Fish Cichlides	*M'buna* *Aulonocara sp.* *Trematrocranus sp.*	*Tropheus sp.* *Neolamprologus sp.* *Julidochromis sp.*

Rocky-zone-type aquarium.

circumference and the very clear water has a sub-lacustrine visibility of 20 m (22 yd). On rocky coasts rough waves favour oxygen saturation from 100 to 110%, which in turn eliminates carbon dioxide and prevents plant colonization. Only a film of yellow-green algae, *Cladophora sp.*, called Aufwuchs, covers the rocky substratum. Fish obtain food from these plants and plankton fauna (ostracods-copepods). Only the sandy or transitional zones contain some stunted plants and reedbeds. Two types of tank should be arranged for each lake, divided according to where species originate. In most cases it is disastrous to put species from different environments together and the same applies to a composite population from the two lakes even if they arise from the same biotype. The two lakes differ mainly in the chemical composition of their water; water in Lake Malawi is softer than in Lake Tanganyika.

Asia

This is the easiest kind of regional tank to create. There are so many fish and plants from India, Sri Lanka and South East Asia imported into Europe, that it is easy to recreate the environment, and it will always look attractive.

The tank can be a regional one in the broad sense of the term, or very local, specializing in species from Borneo, Sumatra or Malaya, etc.

Original biotypes, such as Madagascan, can also be created. You should use endemic plants and fish like *Bedotia geayi*, some Cichlids and aquatic plants of the genus *Aponogeton* to ornament the tank.

A neo-Guinean tank can be achieved with the use of Melanotaennids of the genera

Asiatic tank

Melanotaenia and *Glossolepis*, and possibly *Telmatherina*, *Iriatherina* (Atherinids) and aquatic plants like *Vallisneria gigantea*, *Marsilea crenata*, *Blyxa aubertii*, *Ceratopteris cornuta*, *C.thalictroïdes*.

Water:	pH	6,0 à 6,8
	dGH	3 à 10°
	uS/cm²	100 à 400
	Temp	25 à 30°C
Light climate		normal to intense
Substratum		fine gravel or powdered lava
Decoration		rocks from Thailand, bamboo, peat-bog roots
Plants		*Aponogeton crispus* *Aponegeton natans* *Blyxa echinosperma* *Cryptocoryne sp.* *Nymphaea lotus* *Rotala sp.* *Vallisneria asiatica ; V. spiralis*

Arrangement for Asiatic Aquarium.

Europe

The Ecological niches and biotypes of our rivers and streams are mainly sub-divided according to their degree of oxygenation (DBO and oxygen saturation) and their temperature. Upper streams are characterized by fast currents, highly oxygenated water, very little pollution and low temperatures. The river bed is covered by large pebbles or simply rocks. This is the natural habitat of Salmonids (trout, spring salmon) and also the following fish: chub, minnow, umber and dace. It is extremely difficult to care for these species correctly in captivity. You would need to cool the aquarium to stabilize the temperature below a critical level of 16°C (61°F).

A cold-water regional aquarium is usually designed for species from lower-mid streams, and certainly for species from the lower parts of the

Water:	pH	7,0 à 7,5
	dGH	6 à 20°
	uS/cm²	500 à 1 500
	Temp	maximum 23°C
	Filtering	average to strong plus ventilation
Light climate		normal to intense
Substratum		coarse sand, gravel, pebbles
Decoration		dead wood
Plants		*Potamogeton pectinatus* *Potamogeton crispus* *Callitriche obtusangula* *Ceratophyllum demersum* *Elodea nuttalii* *Elodea ernstae* *Lemma minor*
Fish		*Tinca tinca* (tench) *Carassius* (goldfish) *Rhodeus sericeus* (bitterling) *Gasteroteus aculeatus* (stickleback) *Lepomis gibbosus* (sun perch)

Arrangement for European aquarium.

streams. Water in these river sections is usually warmer and less oxygenated. Fish and plant life from these areas will easily adapt to warmer temperatures in the first instance, and so it is easier to look after them. Calm stretches of river, coves and bends are covered with sand, silt and mud. These areas are the home of burrowing species and their predators, particularly pike.

Depending on the water quality, there are many plant species which can be used to decorate a cold-water tank. American in origin and cousins of the Cichlids, the Centrarchids are suitable and thrive in aquariums of this type, although they should not be put with very small species.

A number of plant species found in well-nourished zones grow well in the aquarium and also look decorative.

Sometimes you come across subtropical plants in their natural environment. If you do, don't hesitate to select them and put them into the cold-water aquarium. Look out for *Azolla filiculoïdes, Trapa natans, Salvinia natans* and other surface plants.

Plants and fauna mentioned above are, of course, only examples. It is up to the aquarium owner to become familiar with the subject.

European river biotope

The aquarium at home

Many people regard the aquarium as a decorative piece while some use it to conduct experiments. Visually it has the power to soothe and relax the spectator as well as providing an open door at home to an exotic world, which can be entered without leaving the armchair. There is no reason why your aquarium should not be problem-free, and provided it blends well with the general decoration in your home and has been installed with due thought to its maintenance, you will not regret your choice. If you decide to construct it yourself, you can design it to fit perfectly into its appointed place.

In this way it can be modified to your own specification.

■ Constructing the aquarium

Choosing material

Glass is the obvious choice for constructing the tank, but when using second-hand glass from shop windows, for example, do be sure that it is not scratched—especially when used for the tank front. Once the glass is cut, various sections are stuck together with silicone glue.

Some typical glass sections for constructing a 450 l (99 gal)

aquarium (length 1.5 m [5 ft]; height 0.5m [1½ ft]; width: 0.6 m [2 ft]) are as follows:

For this height, glass should be 8 mm (½ in) thick.

- 2 sheets 150 x 50 cm (60 x 20 in) [front and back]
- 1 sheet 150 x 60 cm (60 x 24 in) [base]
- 2 sheets 58.3 x 50 cm (23 x 20 in) [sides]

Side widths of 58.3 cm (23 in) include combined thickness of front and back glass, i.e. 1.6 cm (½ in), to which is added 1 mm (⅟₃₂ in) thickness for glue.

Possible option: a 3 mm (⅛ in) thick glass tank cover: 3 sheets of 58 x 46 cm (23 x 18 in).

Two glass reinforcements must be provided for the front and back of the tank, measuring 148 x 5 cm (58 x 2 in), and two measuring 58 x 5 cm (23 x 2 in) spread over two-thirds of the centre section of the aquarium.

For tanks longer than 1.50 m (5 ft), put two longitudinal supports of 148 x 5 cm (58 x 2 in) over the bottom, along the front and back glass, so that they will not bend.

Glueing the tank

Sand down all the glass sections so that they are quite smooth—this will prevent you from being cut; then remove all traces of grease with trichlorethylene or acetone, before

Aquarium parts and order of installation.

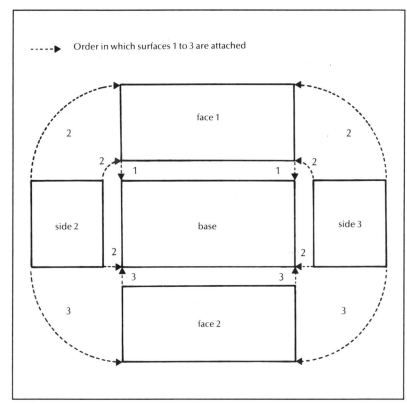

Order in which surfaces 1 to 3 are attached

face 1

2   2

2   2
1   1

side 2   base   side 3

2   2
3   3

3   3

face 2

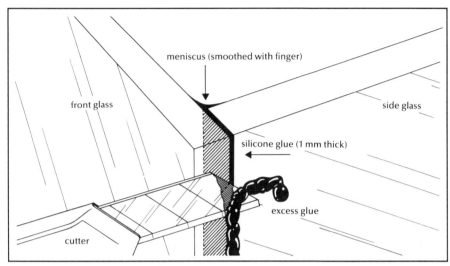

Trimming off excess glue with cutter.

you start to glue the sections. Using a spray-gun, spread the glue in a continuous line along the circumference of the base section and the two side pieces of the first large sheet of glass (section 1—see diagram). The latter should then be positioned on the base section, followed by the two side sections (sides 2 and 3) which should be adjusted until they are perfectly square.

Then the last sheet (section 2) is glued into place, thus completing the parallelepiped. When positioning this last section, be very careful that the three others don't move under the pressure. When all the

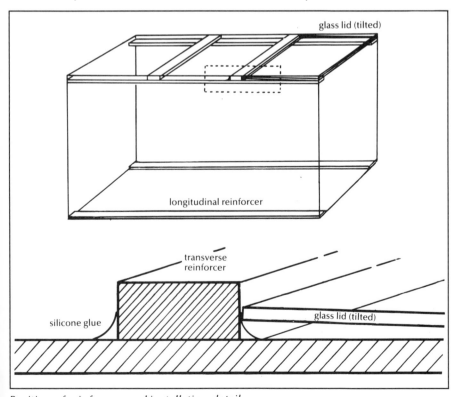

Position of reinforcers and installation detail.

The aquarium at home

glass is in place, secure the tank with adhesive tape until the glue dries. Using your finger, quickly smooth down the rolls of glue which appear on the internal angles of the tank. If necessary, base reinforcements are now put into place against the two large glass sections, and glued together. Allow twelve hours for the glue to dry, then remove the adhesive tape and cut away any excess glue.

Fix the upper reinforcements into place with clamps, or you can do this later after arranging the polystyrene or polyurethane decoration (p 52–5).

You must take adequate precautions before installing the aquarium in its proper place. The supporting structure must be strong enough to take the full load of the aquarium, which can be several hundred kilograms. The surface of this structure should be completely flat and covered by a compressed sheet of glass 10 to 22 mm (½ to 1 in) thick, plus a second layer of the same size in polystyrene. The second sheet is very important, as it will absorb the irregularities in the surface of the supporting structure. It is important to use a new sheet of glass (with its compression strength intact) as this will guarantee uniform weight distribution over the base of the tank. This precaution will avoid any risk of accidents, should the supporting structure or floor need altering in any way.

Covering showing feeding trap-door.
A. General view of cover.
B. Detail showing feeding trap-door.

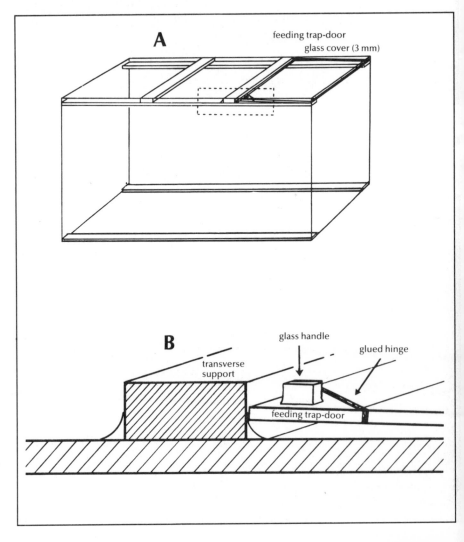

A · feeding trap-door · glass cover (3 mm)

B · glass handle · glued hinge · transverse support · feeding trap-door

Two examples of tanks which have been incorporated perfectly into a room

■ The aquarium: aesthetics and application

Installing your aquarium in one of the rooms at home will give rise to problems of aesthetics, technicalities and practicalities, all of which are worth considering in detail.

The most restful aquarium is the fresh-water one, because of its dominant green plant-life. A sea-water tank which often contains bright or white colours is more lively. The tank should be as large as possible and it should be put where it looks best with its surroundings. An aquarium will look good in the kitchen, hallway or bedroom, but you will also have to accommodate its accessories, which can be quite a problem when you are installing it. Remember that accessories like automatic time-switches and automatic feed distributors are seldom needed, only when you go away on holiday, for example.

Generally, an aquarium is a parallelepipedal vat made up of sheets of glass stuck together, adorned with pipes, electric wiring and sundry noisy pumps. All this unsightly paraphernalia has to be somehow fitted into your room. To fit such a large showcase in, you may consider knocking down an adjoining wall, but in most cases a corner or recess in a room will provide the ideal spot.

Tank housed in country-style furniture

■ Choice of tanks

Tanks with direct frontal access

This type of aquarium is available from specialist outlets. Furniture-aquariums, as they are called, are framed by silver or gold anodized metal and topped with a lighting rail. The latest models are cased in PVC with accessories fitted into the lighting rail, although this arrangement is far from ideal.

Some craftsmen will be able to offer you personalized tanks, but it is far better to make one yourself, that way you will get more enjoyment out of it as well as saving money.

Shop-bought tanks have frontal access, either by removing the lighting rail or via a flap-door. The filter is separate, often located underneath the aquarium.

If you intend to construct this type of tank yourself, put the lighting over the top in a separate case. Accessories like the water pump, decantation filters and air pump should be stored in a side compartment where access is either through the base of the tank or via a side door. The tank can be placed on top of an exisiting piece of furniture, but beware of antiques which may be warped. Two sheets, one in Novopan and one in polystyrene, are placed between the supporting structure and the aquarium. This

Front-access aquarium, showing detail of flap-door and lighting box

arrangement will absorb any irregularity in the furniture and distribute weight and pressure on the glass floor. Don't worry about the external appearance of your tank at this stage, but concentrate on the interior.

Rear access tank

For mainly technical, but also aesthetic reasons, rear access is certainly the most rational solution. The deciding factor will be the location of the tank: ideally, no-one should be aware of the presence of an aquatic refinery behind the aquarium—this can sometimes necessitate additional room.

There are many ways of achieving this sort of design. The simplest is to build a wooden housing, completely partitioned right up to the ceiling, comprising the aquarium section and a space behind it at least 50 cm (20 in) wide. Access would be via a discreet side door, hung on piano hinges, perhaps. The upper section would reach the ceiling which, for deep tanks, would provide housing for discharge lamps. There are more refined solutions, however. A broom cupboard, a garage next to the living room, a balcony off the living room, or a niche in shelving space would all provide the aquarium owner with rear access. Certain fittings would be needed to achieve this, but the problem is not insurmountable. A dividing wall can be removed with

the minimum of nuisance. There are two ways of doing this:

- keep the tank in the room and surround it with a wooden housing;
- or, fit the aquarium into the available space, so that it is recessed and the front glass is level with the wall.

The second solution means that the wall need only be opened up to the water level height. The additional space around the basin will leave room for technical apparatus, like a larger decantation tank on the same level as the aquarium, or air pumps fixed to the ceiling with a rubber spring, to cut out noise from their vibrations. Sea-water tank enthusiasts have the perfect place here for their foam injectors and U.V. lamps, etc. This sort of

Rear access tank

The aquarium at home

Cylindrical aquarium

Aquarium with three viewing sides

arrangement means that the aquarium can operate very discreetly, as electrical wiring, time-switches and lights can all be fitted to the internal partition wall, away from the water. Any fluorescent lighting tubes can be hung from a slatted frame, which would pivot against the partition by means of a piano hinge, or simply suspended by string and pulleys from the ceiling. In this way, lighting can be directed from the ceiling, rather than from the top of the tank.

The integrated aquarium is certainly the most adaptable to all kinds of interiors as well as being the most functional.

Four-sided vision tanks

This is definitely the most difficult kind of aquarium to create. There are problems with positioning accessories and with designing the tank's interior decoration. You will need a lot of ingenuity to solve this one and the standard-sized aquarium will not fit the bill. In most cases a cube 1.20 x 1.20 x 0.60 m (4 x 4 x 2 ft) high will provide the desired external volume and will give ample space inside (850 litres [187 gal]). The trick is not to be able to see the opposite side of the tank.

In the first instance you will need to pierce a 60 to 70 mm (2 to 3 in) hole in the middle of the aquarium floor. This will be used to thread through both electrical wiring for lighting situated in the cover and suction and back-flow tubes which are connected to the filter.

Wires and tubes pass through the middle of the tank in a water-tight glass column and emerge above the aquarium cover, well out of sight. The equipment is installed in a kind of plinth under the tank.

A more sophisticated method would be to install the tank on a slim, tulip-shaped plinth, in brushed or polished stainless steel, which will only take the electric conduit. Here again the aquarium floor is pierced with a 30 mm (1 in) hole to accommodate a water-tight glass column. A decantation tank encloses the column, where water circulates through compartments arranged around the central axis. The tank is dressed in a circular polystyrene decoration, which encircles the filter right up to the surface.

All accessories can be housed in the filter, i.e. heating, under-water pumps and turbines. The air pump itself is suspended from the lighting cover, the whole of which is preferably covered with stainless steel strips. It is quite difficult to arrange a fresh-water tank in this way, as you have to bear in mind its appearance all the time. This sort of aquarium, designed to house invertebrates exclusively, would go very well in a large, modern room.

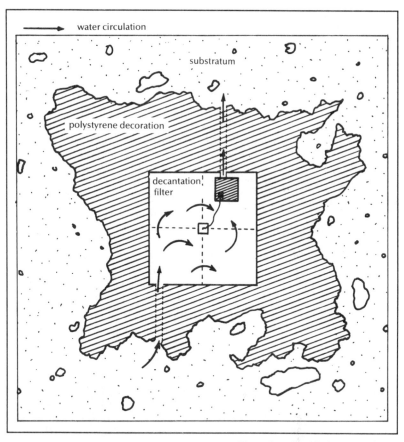

Plan of tank with four viewing sides.

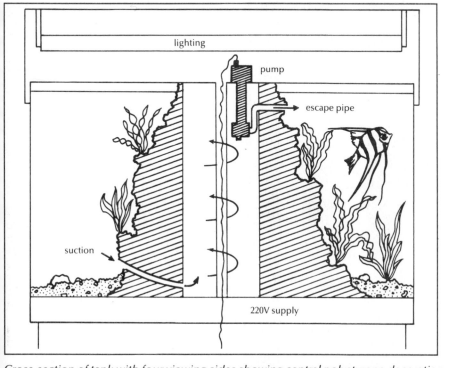

Cross-section of tank with four viewing sides showing central polystyrene decoration.

■ The Aquarium in the room: a marriage of styles

Choosing the prime position for your fish and plants is a matter of personal preference. Situated in the bedroom, you will be able to enjoy them day and night but the kitchen and sitting-room also have their advantages.

Above all, try to make the aquarium blend with the interior decoration of the room in question, whether it is modern, designer-style, country-style, contemporary, or reproduction.

to furniture copied from styles such as Louis XVI, Directoire, Chippendale or Regency, etc. It is actually quite difficult to match an aquarium to this style of furniture, so it is best not to attempt it and opt for an alternative solution, which would be to recess the tank and have its frame covered with wall paper to match the walls. If possible it is best to position the tank in an adjacent room.

Country-style

This term country-style is used for fashioned, wooden furniture copied from various regions or centuries, e.g. Regency, Louis XIII, Louis XIV. The best kind are recent copies made by craftsmen; it should be possible for a craftsman to build the housing for your aquarium along the lines of your furniture. A wooden chest, covered with tapestry or material such as jute in very dark brown colours, would be an economic solution. A coarse coating of white pebble-dash might also be suitable.

Reproduction

The word 'reproduction' is applied

Contemporary

The description 'contemporary' is applied to furniture designed in the post-war period, particularly to modern furniture made of glass, stainless steel, plastic, rattan or bamboo. An aquarium fits in very well with this style, and even one bought from a shop with an aluminium frame will not clash with leather furniture. A light, wallpaper-covered frame as a base for smoked-glass shelves, is the perfect accessory to darker, modern furniture. Scandinavian-style furniture is a very good match for an aquarium housed in a rough, light-wood frame; but only use light or dark, lacquered wood as a last resort, as it will look out of place in this setting.

Aquarium incorporated into a country-style dining-room

Aquariums and aquaterrarium housed in reproduction furniture

The collector's room

A room in which period furniture rubs shoulders with assorted curios is one of the most difficult styles in which to house an aquarium. If you make the aquarium the focal point of the room, keep the tank sober — painted matt-black or white with perhaps room for some books in the base.

■ A final word

Don't give house room to the following:

- a television-type aquarium
- bottle-shaped aquariums
- the aquarium 'bar'

Whenever possible, seek advice from designer friends.

Look for ideas in specialist aquarium and interior-design magazines and don't forget that often the simplest ideas are by far the best.

Aquarium in a contemporary room setting

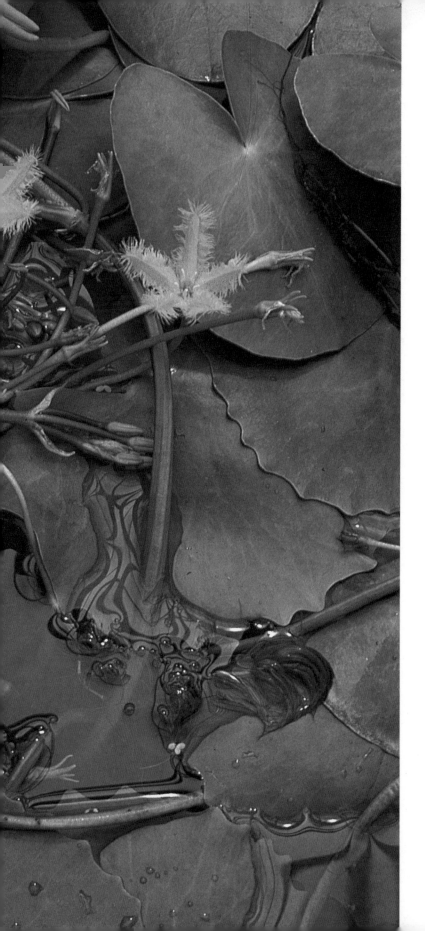

PLANTS

To choose the right plants for your aquarium, you need to be able to recognize and make use of them, as well as look after them properly.

Plants for the aquarium

Of the 8,000 species of non-microscopic fresh-water plants which are divided into more than 400 genera, there are roughly 250 species commonly available for sale. In Europe, only about 100 can generally be bought.

The system used to name aquatic plants, their taxonomy, is a subject of some dispute. In this book, we will use the names most commonly accepted by aquarium owners.

How plants get their names

The name of a plant normally has two parts: its genus and its species. The latter may be an adjective or a noun; it may describe the geographical area where the plant is found or it may be named after a person. If the name of the species is an adjective, it agrees in gender with the name of the genus. For example, *cornuta* is the species in the name of the plant *Ceratopteris cornuta*. As *ceratopteris* is feminine, the word *cornuta* (meaning 'horned') agrees with it. If the genus of the plant were masculine, it would be *cornutus*; if neuter, *cornutum*. Nouns do not change. Geographical adjectives end in *-ae, -ense* or *-ensis,* or use a latinized version of the place they are named after, such as *matogrossense* in the plant *Myriophyllum matogrossense,* found in the Mato Grosso in Brazil.

Species named after a person end in *-ae* for a woman, and *-i* for a man. So, for example, *Cryptocoryne korthausae* is named after Edith Korthause, while *Cryptocoryne nevilli* was named after the botanist Mr H. Nevill.

The name of the species is followed by the name of the person first describing it and by the name of any person

revising the data: hence, *Hygrophila strica* (Nees) Lindau.

Other abbreviations may follow the name of the plant, such as:

- *var.,* a natural variation of a species;
- *hort.,* a horticulturally bred variation of a species;
- *f.,* form, a different version of a species which is not so different as to constitute a separate variety;
- *foliis variegatis,* a species with variegated or partly-coloured leaves.

Some aquarium plants and how to look after them

The descriptions of plants which follow are in alphabetical order of genus and species. For each plant we have given details of the conditions it requires.

In the example below, pH = 6.0–7.0 indicates the minimum and maximum pH of the water.

°dH = 5–15 is the hardness of the water using the German system of measurement.

20°C (68°F) is the temperature in degrees Centigrade, with the Fahrenheit equivalent in brackets.

40 cm (15 in) is the minimum depth of water in

centimetres, with the depth in inches shown in brackets.

pH: 6.0–7.0	Temp.: 20°C (68°F)
°dH: 5–15	Water depth: 40 cm (16 in)

Example

ACORUS •

The Acoruses are part of the Araceae family. They are found in cold temperate zones, but they also appear in sub-tropical areas in the form of *A. calamus var. angustifolius.* There are two species, described below, which are found in several geographical and horticultural varieties.

The rhizome is horizontal and the plant has thin tapering leaves, varying in size from one variety to another, which spread out in a fan.

■ *A.calamus*

pH: 6.5–7.5	Temp.: 10–22°C (50–72°F)
°dH: 5–25	Water depth: 40 cm (15 in)

Family: *Araceae.*
Scientific name: *Acorus calamus* Linnaeus.
Synonyms: A.americanus, A.aromaticus, A.odoratus.

Common names: True acorus, Sweet Flag.

Geographical area: there are three separate geographical varieties. *A.c. var. angustifolius* is the most southerly, being found as far south as Java and Sulawesi in Indonesia; *A.c.var. verus* is found in Bengal, Sri Lanka, China and Japan; *A.c.var.vulgaris* is the north European *Calamus* and is common in north-eastern France, Belgium, West Germany and throughout Central Europe. *Acorus calamus* is a large cold or temperate water plant which can reach a height of 150 cm (5 ft). It is therefore not suited to aquariums, but goes well in a regional aquascape, placed in the background. It is also an excellent plant for garden ponds. The plant is reproduced by splitting the rhizome.

■ *A.gramineus*

pH: 6.5–7.5	Temp.: 10–22°C (50–72°F)
°dH: 5–25	Water depth: 20 cm (8 in)

Family: *Araceae*.
Scientific name: *Acorus gramineus* Solander.

A.gramineus

Synonyms: *A.humilis, A.intermedius, A.tartarinowii*.
Common name: Japanese Rush.
Geographical area: Central Asia, colder parts of south-east Asia, Japan.
This species has bright-green leaves spread out in a fan shape and reaches a height of 30 cm (12 in). It

and its horticultural variety, *foliis variegatis*, are often recommended to the aquarium owner. Unfortunately, they do not thrive in a tropical type of environment; they soon go yellow, the leaves become transparent and the plant eventually dies. On the other hand, in a temperate aquarium between 15 and 22°C (59 and 72°F), or in an aquaterrarium or paludarium with poor soil they grow well, if slowly. The dwarf variety, *A.g.var.pusillus*, is no more than 10 cm (4 in) high and makes a good foreground plant in a temperate aquarium. Acoruses do not like being uprooted so those sold in pots are the best buy. When planting, the earth in the pot should be left around the roots to avoid disturbing them.

ALTERNANTHERA

The Alternantherae are part of the Amaranthaceae family. There are about 170 species, most of which are marsh-dwelling. The majority come from America, but some of them are more widespread and can be found in Africa and Asia. Since 1970 there have been three or four species imported for aquarium enthusiasts under imaginative names such as *Telanthera*. One species, *A. variegata*, is found in Mediterranean countries and makes an attractive marginal plant.

■ *A.reineckii*

pH: 6.2–7.0	Temp.: 24–30°C (75–86°F)
°dH: 3–12	Water depth: 40 cm (16 in)

Family: *Amaranthaceae*.
Scientific name: *Alternanthera reineckii* Briquet.
Synonyms: *Telanthera osiris*.
Common name: Reineck's Alternanthera.
Geographical area: Southern Brazil and Paraguay.

This plant grows mainly above water, but does not mind being underwater for short periods. It is the most hardy, but also the least attractive species of the genus. It grows best in a fairly shallow aquarium around 30 cm (12 in) deep. If the leaves grow above the surface of the water they will die. The main stems should be trimmed regularly. The upper part of the leaves is a very bright-green colour under normal light and will turn a dark-brown colour if placed in a shady spot. It is an excellent plant for a paludarium or aquaterrarium, where it flourishes easily and will multiply fairly rapidly above water.

■ *A.sessilis*

pH: 5.8–7.0	Temp.: 24–30°C (75–86°F)
°dH: 3–15	Water depth: 40 cm (16 in)

A.sessilis

Family: *Amaranthaceae*
Scientific name: *Althenanthera sessilis* (Linnaeus), de Candolle.
Synonyms: *Achyranthes villosa, Adenogramma oppositifolia, Telantherarubra, T.lilacina*.
Common name: Sessile alternanthera.
Geographic area: Tropical and subtropical areas of America.

There are two main varieties found in aquariums, both with reddish leaves. These are *A.s.var.lilacina* and *A.s. var.rubra*. The former is distinguished by the greenish-brown colour of the upper part of the leaf and purplish-red undersides. The latter is red on both sides of the leaf. Unfortunately, this species does not last long when submerged (two to six months) and should be immersed as often as possible. The species does not have floating flowers above it. The stems should be planted at least ten or fifteen to a tank, far enough apart not to keep the light off each other. The plant should be brightly lit and the addition of carbon dioxide is essential. The plant multiplies by producing runners which grow into separate plants.

AMMANIA

Although there are not many species of Ammanias, they are found in large areas of the world. There are around thirty spread across the tropical and sub-tropical zones and in southern Europe. There are three species which are particularly suitable for aquariums: Ammania gracilis, A.latifolia, and A.senegalensis. When they grow in rice plantations they are regarded as weeds, and they also grow in stagnant or slow-flowing water. They thrive in sunny places.

■ A.senegalensis

pH: 6.5–7.2	Temp.: 25–30°C (77–86°F)
°dH: 3–10	Water depth:40 cm (16 in)

Family: Lythraceae.
Scientific name: Ammania senegalensis Lamarck.
Synonyms: Rotala senegalensis.
Common name: Red Ammania.
Geographical area: Senegal, Senegambia.
This grassy amphibious plant has a fine brown colour. This plant likes heat (up to 30°C or 86°F) and needs bright light, so it should not be grown in the same tank as any floating plants. When the topmost leaves appear above the surface of the water, they should be cut off; this stimulates the growth of the

parent plant's lateral stems. Runners can be planted out at a depth of 3–4 cm (1½ in) when they have reached 15 cm (6 in) in length; they can also be obtained by trimming the parent plant to a height of 15 cm (6 in). The plant then develops another stem which grows will in aquaterrariums and paludariums, where the leaves become a pale-green colour. Sexual reproduction is possible at this stage. The flowers appear on the axils of the leaves, which are sessile and opposite.

A.senegalensis

ANUBIAS

This genus is named after Anubis, the Egyptian God of the shadows. It is one of the Araceae family which consists of about 100 genera and 1,800 species, including the very popular genus of the Cryptocorynes. In Wim Crusio's revision of 1979 the genus Anubias was reduced to eight species. The genus is endemic to Africa, mainly in the tropical west of the continent. Depending on the species, the height can be less than 10 cm (4 in) in the case of A.barteri var.nana or over 1 m (40

in), as manifested by A.afzelii and A.gigantea. They grow in the savanna, in forests, and in hot, humid areas, as well as along major rivers such as the Zaire and the Ogowe (A.heterophylla, A.pynaertii). There are several varieties, particularly within the species A.barteri. All the species tend to be plants which prefer shady, dimly-lit places. They are tough plants, and this discourages plant-eating fish from nibbling at them. They grow slowly in weak light; the growth of harmful algae around them can be controlled using an algae-eating fish such as Gyrinocheilus aymonieri in a community tank or one of the Garra genus in a regional aquarium. Sexual reproduction is always difficult when the plants have been artificially cultivated; instead, asexual reproduction can be brought about by dividing the rhizome, or by separating the young plants from the parent plant. The rhizome should never be buried, as this would cause it to rot.

■ A.afzelii

pH: 6.5–7.2	Temp.: 24–28°C (75–82°F)
°dH: 3–10	Water depth: 40 cm (16 in)

Family: Araceae.
Scientific name: Anubias afzelii Schott.
Synonyms: none.
Common name: Afzel's Anubias.
Geographical area: this is the most northerly species of the genus. It is found in the Sima river in Senegal, in Guinea and Sierra Leone, along the banks of small streams, sandbanks and even treetrunks which have fallen into the water.
This species is only suitable for large paludariums where it can be grown immersed. It has bright-green leaves

which can be 35 cm (14 in) long and 13 cm (5 in) wide. The rhizome is sometimes more than a centimetre (½ in) thick.

■ *A.barteri*

pH: 6.0–7.5	Temp.: 22–25°C (72–77°F)
°dH: 3–15	Water depth: 30 cm (12 in)

Family: *Araceae.*
Scientific name: *Anubias barteri* Engler.
Synonyms: none.
Common name: Barter's Anubias.
Geographical area: Nigeria, Ivory Coast, Cameroon, Gabon.
Varieties: *A.b.var.barteri, A.b.var. caladiifolia, A.b.var.glabra = Anubias minima, A.b.var.lanceolata = Anubias lanceolata f.angustifolia, A.b.var.nana = Anubias nana.*
The smallest varieties, *nana* (Dwarf Anubias) and *glabra*, are the most popular amongst aquarium owners. The leaf of the Dwarf Anubias is up to 6 cm (2½ in) long and elliptical to heart-shaped; the stem is extremely short at 5 to 6 cm (2–2½ in). The form

A.b.var.glabra

glabra has larger, wider leaves (18 by 7 cm, or 7 by 3 in). The variety *lanceolata* has lance-shaped leaves between 10 and 16 cm (4 and 5 in) long on a stem 15 cm (6 in) long. The latter variety is much rarer in aquariums. These small plants function particularly well as a foreground decoration, or will form a very attractive carpet of foliage given time and suitable conditions. The rhizome should never be buried, and the fine roots soon stabilize the plant. They will happily attach themselves to

A.b.var.nana

pieces of rock or wood. If the temperature falls below 20°C (68°F) their growth, which is slow at the best of times, will stop completely. In an aquaterrarium the plants can be slightly polymorphous and they flower quite frequently. The spathe is situated at the end of a spur, and the floral spike, or spadix, bears male and female plants which can be fertilized using a small brush. Unfortunately, it is rare to find fertile seeds when the plants have been grown artificially. A medium- or even poorly-lit aquarium or aquaterrarium is sufficient for this plant. Asexual reproduction is comparatively easy: the young plants are separated from the parent using a razor blade or cutter. The piece of rhizome is held down on the substratum using a small weight, such as a pebble.

■ *A.gilletii*

pH: 6.0–7.2	Temp.: 22–25°C (72–77°F)
°dH: 3–10	Water depth: 40 cm (16 in)

Family: *Araceae.*
Scientific name: *Anubias gilletii* De Wild & Dur.
Synonym: *Amauriella gilletii.*
Common names Gill's Anubias.
Geographical area: Nigeria, Cameroon, Gabon, Congo, Zaire (along the main rivers).
This is a species of average height, reaching 25–30 cm (10–12 in). The leaves are 10–12 cm (4–5 in) long, lanceolate and oval, and are a deli-

cate-green colour. Because of its height, the plant can be planted on its own or in a clump of two or three stems in the middle of the tank. This species will live permanently underwater, but is only seen at its best in an aquaterrarium when it flowers. The plant can be reproduced by splitting the rhizome or by separation of the young plants.

■ *A.heterophylla*

pH: 6.2–7.2	Temp.: 22–25°C (72–77°F)
°dH: 2–8	Water depth: 50 cm (20 in)

Family: *Araceae.*
Scientific name: *Anubias heterophylla* Engler.
Synonyms: *Anubias affinis, A.bequaerti, A.congensis, A.engleri, A. undulata.*
Common name: Congolese Anubias.
Geographical area: spread over wide areas of tropical rain forest in the Congo, Zaire and Angola.
The leaves of this species are very polymorphic and can be oval, elliptical or lanceolate. The leaf can be up to 35 cm (14 in) long by 13 cm (5 in) wide. This plant is suited only to very large aquariums where it will not grow to such a great height. In a paludarium it may reach 80–100 cm (32–40 in).

APONOGETON

The species of this Afro-Asiatic genus imported for aquariums come mainly from Madagascar and south-east Asia. The African species are too large and are dormant for several months a year. One species, *A.distachyon*, was introduced to South America and the south of France. These species grow in rice fields and other stagnant water, but are also found in fast-flowing rivers, sometimes up to 2,000 metres (7,000 feet) above sea level. Most of the species are fresh-water ones, though some, such as *A.appendiculatus,* will live in brackish water for short periods. The rhizome can be spherical, cylindrical or ramified and in some species can be split. *Aponogeton* commonly produces flowers. The spike is protected by a spathe when submerged but is open to the air when growing out of the water. Asian and Australian species have a single spike; in Africa they have two, and in Madagascar they may have more than two. There are exceptions to this, namely *A.distachyus* and *A.hexapetalus.* In some species, such as *A.undulatus,* there is a floral spike which produces new plants. Some species develop embryo plants without fertilization (apomixis).

A.boivinianus

■ *A.boivinianus*

pH: 6.5–7.3	Temp.: 22–25°C (72–77°F)
°dH: 5–15	Water depth: 60 cm (24 in)

Family: *Aponogetonaceae.*
Scientific name: *Aponogeton boivinianus* Baillon ex Jumelle.
Synonyms: none. .
Common name: Boivin's Aponogeton.
Geographical area: the far north-west of Madagascar and the islands of Nossi-Be and Mayotte in the Comoro Islands off the north-west coast of Madagascar. Restricted to small areas and grows in running water up to 1.5 m (60 in) deep. Likes either shady or well-lit environment. The tuber is disc-shaped and up to 5 cm (2 in) in diameter by 2 cm (¼ in) thick. This should be half-buried in the soil and rooted in place. The large, slender, dark-green leaves have an indented, wavy surface and may reach 70 cm (30 in) in length in weak light. The petiole is short, at 5

to 7 cm (2–3 in). This is a fine plant which should go in the centre of the tank; it is easy to maintain because of its adaptation to fairly hard water. The spike is about 10 cm (4 in) long and made up of two to three branches. The flowers are white and self-fertilizing; the process can be carried out artificially using a brush. After two months of fructification the seeds should be covered with a layer of fine sand of the same thickness as the diameter of the seeds. The depth of water should be gradually increased as the plant grows. This species is often confused with *A.bernieranus,* which has smaller leaves and a spike with three to ten branches.

■ *A.crispus*

pH: 6.5–7.3	Temp.: 23–28°C (73–82°F)
°dH: 5–15	Water depth: 50 cm (20 in)

Family: *Aponogetonaceae.*
Scientific name: *Aponogeton crispus* Thunberg.
Synonyms: none.
Common name: Wavy-edged Swordplant.
Geographical area: Sri Lanka.
This plant's adaptation to fairly hard water has made it a popular species with aquarium enthusiasts. The light-green to reddish leaves grow very quickly and are narrow with crinkled edges. The plant is therefore best suited to a fairly large aquarium and

should be grown on its own or in a bunch of three or four stems in the centre of the tank. The leaves vary in size from 25 to 40 cm (10 to 15 in) in length and are between 1.5 and 4 cm (½ and 1½ in) wide. Under diffuse light the petiole will grow towards the surface of the water. This plant flowers easily if properly looked after. The spike has one branch and bears white flowers. The species is self-fertilizing and can be fertilized using a soft brush. The seeds mature after two months and can be grown easily in sand; the level of water should be gradually increased and the plants should be grown under bright light.

■ *A.longiplumulosus*

pH: 6.5–7.0	Temp.: 24–26°C (75–79°F)
°dH: 3–8	Water depth: 45 cm (18 in)

Family: *Aponogetonaceae.*
Scientific name: *Aponogeton longiplumulosus* Van Bruggen.
Synonyms: none.
Common name: Long-plumed Aponogeton.
Geographical area: Around Maromandia in the tributaries of the Sambirano in north-west Madagascar.
There are two different forms of this species which have been imported in recent years: one has a slightly wavy leaf and pink flowers, and the other has strongly undulating leaves and mauve flowers. Both forms have a spike with two branches. The tuber is a slightly elongated sphere about 2 cm (¾ in) in diameter. The leaves range in colour from brownish-green to bright-green and have one to three conspicuous longitudinal veins branching off either side of the broad central one. The leaf can be up to 30 or 40 cm (12–15 in) in length and the stem up to 10 cm (4 in). This species is easily confused with *A.ulvaceus;* however the latter has slightly curled leaves. It is maintained in the same way as other species of this genus, but requires more light. The plant frequently flowers and the spike produces many seeds which can be transplanted each time the plantlet stops growing.

A.madagascariensis

slightly curled. There are many large leaves, 30 to 40 cm (12–15 in) long and 4–6 cm (1½–2½ in) wide, so a single example of the species makes an attractive centrepiece. It should be placed in the middleground of the tank, in front of some fast-growing plants. If the light is insufficient the leaves will quickly reach the surface. After rapid growth of the leaves, and flowering, there is a period of dormancy. When this happens, the leaves and roots should be cut off the rhizome and the latter should be placed in a glass of water at 12 to 15°C (54–59°F) for two to three months. The inflorescence has two branches of yellowish, self-fertilizing flowers.

AZOLLA

This is the only genus belonging to the family *Azollaceae*, and consists of some half-dozen species. They are floating ferns which tend to overrun an aquarium. *Azolla filiculoïdes* is found in stagnant water throughout Europe and in Autumn can be recognized by the red carpet it forms on stagnant water.

■ *A.madagascariensis*

pH: 6.5–7.2	Temp.: 22–24°C (72–75°F)
°dH: 3–10	Water depth: 50 cm (20 in)

Family: *Aponogetonaceae*.
Scientific name: *Aponogeton madagascariensis* (Mirbel) Van Bruggen.
Synonyms: *Hydrogeton fenestralis, Aponogeton guillotii, A.henkelianus, A.fenestralis.*
Common names: Laceleaf plant; Madagascar Laceplant.
Geographical area: Central, western and eastern Madagascar. Has also been introduced to Mauritius, where it is thriving.
This plant is something of a botanical curiosity because of its skeletonized structure, with hardly any cellular tissue and a network of longitudinal and transverse veins. There are at least two known forms, one with long, tapering leaves and the other with short, broad leaves, both sold under the name *enkelianus*. Heat, bright light and particles suspended in the water are all harmful to this plant; ideally, it should be shaded by surface plants in a temperature of 21–23°C (70–73°F), and the water should be well filtered to ensure clarity. The rhizome is polymorphous, and can be spherical or very elongated and up to 10 cm (4 in) in length. When the rhizome appears healthy (being firm and good-sized) it may be split for asexual reproduction. A root taken out of the soil may produce a plantlet. Sexual reproduction is difficult to achieve. The spike has three to six branches. The flowers are white, but turn red after fertilization. The species is self-fertilizing.

■ *A.ulvaceus*

pH: 6.5–7.2	Temp.: 23–25°C (73–77°F)
°dH: 3–10	Water depth: 50 cm (20 in)

Family: *Aponogetonaceae*.
Scientific name: *Aponogeton ulvaceus* Baker.
Synonyms: none.
Common name: Ulvaceus Aponogeton.
Geographical area: Madagascar.
The tuber of this plant is smooth and spherical and the bright-green leaves grow rapidly. They are very wavy and

■ *A.caroliniana*

ph: 6,2–7,5	Temp: 20-30°C (68–86°F)
°dH: 2–20	Surface plant

Family: *Azollaceae*.
Scientific name: *Azolla caroliniana* Willdenow.
Other names: *A.bonariensis, A.densa, A.mexicana, A.microphylla.*
Common name: *Fairy Moss.*
Geographical area: Originally the USA, Mexico and South America; introduced to Europe in the 1870s in Rennes and Bordeaux and later found in Strasbourg, West Germany and Czechoslovakia. This plant reaches no more than 3 cm (1 in) in height when in its natural habitat. The leaves are arranged in two alternate overlapping rows like roof tiles.

In the aquarium, they will grow to only 1–1½ cm (½ in).

Asexual reproduction is very rapid and a few plants will soon take over the whole surface of the tank; it is therefore necessary to remove most of them in order to maintain enough light for submerged plants. They will spread even faster if there is a strong overhead light.

■ A.filiculoides

ph: 6.2–7.5	Temp: 15-30°C (59–86°F)
°dH: 2–20	Surface plant

Family: *Azollaceae*.
Scientific name: *Azolla filiculoïdes* Lamarck.
Synonyms: *A.arbuscula*, *A.magellanica*.
Common name: Fern Azolla..
Geographical area: originally South America; introduced to Europe around 1890, where it spread rapidly. In some countries it was introduced to combat malaria, as it forms a carpet on the surface of water which prevents mosquito larvae from breathing. This plant is very slightly bigger than *A.caroliniana*. Like the other species in the genus, it spreads very rapidly in the aquarium, but many plant-eating fish like it and it is very useful in breeding tanks where

it acts as a support for the bubble-nests made by the Belontiids (*Betta, Colisa, Trichogaster*, etc.) and as a refuge for fry produced by surface fish. Also, large numbers of various infusoria congregate between the submerged roots of this plant and provide useful extra food for very small fry.

■ A.pinnata

ph: 6.2–7.5	Temp: 15-30°C (59–86°F),
°dH: 2–20	Surface plant

Family: *Azollaceae*.
Scientific name: *Azolla pinnata Brown*.
Synonyms: none.
Common name: Pennate Azolla.
Geographical area: Tropical regions of Australia, Asia and Africa.
This species has many branches and reaches between 1 and 3 cm (½ and 1½ in) in length. The upper side is pale-green to brownish in colour. It is without doubt the species most suited to aquariums, but unfortunately is rarely found in them.

B

BACOPA

The Bacopa are widespread throughout the world, though most come originally from the tropics of South America. They include terrestrial, marsh-dwelling and aquatic plants with stems and opposite leaves. In some species the stem and leaf have hairs on them.

■ B.caroliniana

ph: 6.4–7.0	Temp: 20–24°C (68–75°F)
°dH: 3–8	Water depth: 30 cm (12 in)

Family: *Scrophulariaceae*.

Scientific name: *Bacopa caroliniana* (Walter) Robinson.
Synonyms: *Obolaria caroliniana, Septilia caroliniana, Bacopa amplexicaulis*, or part of the *Monniera* and *Herpestris* genera.

B.amplexicaulis

B.caroliniana variegata

Common name: Giant Red Bacopa.
Geographical area: Southern United States, Northern Mexico.
This plant has leaves which are directly attached by their bases to the axis of the plant; they are therefore sessile (i.e. they have no leaf-stalk). They are fleshy, bright-green and have a smooth, upper surface. The size of the leaf is about 25 mm by 15 mm (1 in by ½ in). The flower appears on the axil of the uppermost leaves; it is light-blue in colour and about 10 mm (½ in) long. There is a horticultural variety, 'variegata', which has yellow veins. This is a very

A.filiculoides

hardy species but it is important to add carbon dioxide carefully into hard water. This is also the case at high temperatures, where the amount of light should be increased. The plant should be arranged in a group towards the back of the aquarium. It reproduces by growing runners, which are separated from the parent plant by cutting it back to a length of 20 cm (8 in) and planting them out in the substratum at intervals of 3-4 cm (1½ in).

■ B.crenata

ph: 6.4–7.0	Temp: 23–27°C (73–81°F)
°dH: 3–8	Water depth: 30 cm (12 in)

Family: *Scrophulariaceae*.
Scientific name: *Bacopa crenata* (Beauvois) Hepper.
Synonyms: *Herpestris crenata*.
Common name: Bacopa.
Geographical area: Senegal to Angola, and in East Africa, Tanzania and Madagascar.
The leaves are ovoid to lanceolate and have slightly serrated edges; the median vein is fairly conspicuous. Some stems have unusually placed leaves, in whorls rather than opposite, and with three or four leaves to each node. The plant varies between 20 and 30 cm (8 and 12 in) in height when submerged, where it grows slowly. It can be grown in medium-hard water under bright light. This species should be arranged as a group of five to eight stems either at the front of the tank and slightly to one side, or in the middleground. The plant is much easier to maintain immersed in a paludarium or aquaterrarium, and here the white or pink flowers will appear. When the plant reproduces by producing runners, great care should be taken; the parent plant should be strong and firmly rooted.

■ B.lanigera

ph: 6.4–6.8	Temp: 22–26°C (72–79°F)
°dH: 2–6	Water depth: 30 cm (12 in)

Family: *Scrophulariaceae*.
Synonym: *Herpestris lanigera*.

Scientific name: *Bacopa lanigera* (Chamisso & Sclechtendahl) Werrstein.
Common name: Bacopa.
Geographical area: Brazil.
This species is easily recognized by the conspicuous hairs on the stem and the underside of the leaf. The leaves are almost round and about 20 mm (⅒ in) in diameter. There are two leaf-types within this species, one a plain green colour and the other with marked yellow veins. The species is very sensitive to the surrounding conditions and grows slowly. In fact, the yellow-veined form is difficult to maintain and is better off immersed in a paludarium. In both forms, when the plant is below the water the leaves become smaller towards the top of the plant and then rot away. It is possible to maintain the plants under bright light, with carbon dioxide added to the water.

■ B.monnieri

ph: 6.6–7.3	Temp: 22–26°C (72–79°F)
°dH: 4–15	Water depth: 35 cm (14 in)

Family: *Scrophulariaceae*.
Scientific name: *Bacopa monnieri* (Linnaeus) Wettstein.
Synonyms: *Lysimachia monnieri, Herpestris africana, H.brownei, H.moranensis, Bacopa gracilis, B.minor, B.baccata*, etc.
Common name: Monnier's Bacopa.
Geographical area: Southern United States, Central America (Mexico) and Madagascar.
This species is similar to *B.caroliniana*, but the internode is larger and makes the plant look taller and more slender. It is around 30 cm (12 in) high with smooth stem and leaves and a bright-green colour. Of all the species of this genus which are commonly imported, this is undoub-

B.monnieri

tedly the one which is easiest to maintain submerged. It should be arranged as a group of stems in the middle of the tank or to one side of it, and should be strongly lit. The plant grows slowly and its appearance changes little with the passing of time. When the top of the plant reaches the surface of the water, shoots are put out. If properly maintained, this is a good plant for the aquarium.

■ B.myriophylloides

ph: 6.6–7.2	Temp: 22–25°C (72–77°F)
°dH: 2–8	Water depth: 30 cm (12 in)

Family: *Scrophulariaceae.*
Scientific name: *Bacopa myriophylloides* (Bentham) Wettstein.
Synonyms: *Herpestris myriophylloides.*
Geographical area: Brazil.
This species is very rarely imported and is difficult to maintain. It appears to grow faster in an aquaterrarium and plants appear bearing short, fine, bright-green leaves. If planted underwater, the water should be soft, acid and fairly temperate at about 22°C (75°F). The plant should be brightly lit and placed in a group in the middleground. It reaches 35 to 40 cm (14 to 16 in) in height.

BARCLAYA

The three species belonging to this genus belong to the Waterlily family, which is widely distributed throughout the world. However, this particular genus is confined to South-East Asia.

■ B.longifolia

ph: 6.6–7.2	Temp: 25–28°C (77–82°F)
°dH: 5–12	Water depth: 40 cm (16 in)

Family: *Nymphaeaceae.*
Scientific name: *Barclaya longifolia* Wallich.
Synonyms: none.
Common name: Orchid Lily.

Geographical area: Southern Thailand and Burma, Malaysia.
This very attractive plant, whose leaves are olive-green to brownish on the upper surface and reddish-purple underneath, could be given pride of place in a Dutch tank or a South-East Asian aquarium. It reaches a height of 20 to 30 cm (8 to 12 in) and its distinctive colouring makes it contrast with other bright-green plants placed behind it. It also grows quickly, and under weak light the leaves darken and become shorter and wider. It multiplies both

B.longifolia

sexually and asexually. The flower is green outside and red inside, and is carried on a flower spike. It is self-fertilizing, but will not reproduce sexually unless underwater. Asexual reproduction takes place when the rhizome divides and small plantlets appear on it. This species is quite fragile and its leaves tear easily, so great care should be taken when transplanting it.

BLYXA

The genus *Blyxa* comprises ten species spread throughout Africa, Madagascar, South-East Asia, New Guinea and northern Australia.

They generally live in very fresh, stagnant or slow-moving water. The genus is divided into two groups, those with leaves arranged in rosettes from the rhizome (gr.

Blyxa), including *B.aubertii*, *B.echinosperma*, *B.leiosperma*, *B.senegalensis*, and those with alternate leaves on a stem (gr. Caulescentes), including *B.japonica*, *B.novoguineensis*, and *B.radicans*. The main distinguishing feature of this genus is the appearance of the lamina of the leaf, which is fine, narrow, tapering and pointed. There is little variation between the species.

■ B.aubertii

ph: 6.4–6.8	Temp: 24–26°C (75–79°F)
°dH: 3–8	Water depth: 40 cm (16 in)

Family: *Hydrocharitaceae.*
Scientific name: *Blyxa aubertii* Richemond.
Synonyms: *Blyxa oryzetorum.*
Common name: Aubert's Blyxa.
Geographical area: India, South-East Asia and Madagascar.
This species can be recognized by its leaves, which have a triangular base and sharp edges; the ends of the leaves are pointed and slightly spiral-shaped. Under strong light they acquire a reddish hue. The plant is about 30 cm (16 in) high in the aquarium, but can reach twice that height in its natural habitat. It is fairly difficult to maintain. The hardness of the water should be below 5°dKH, with an acid pH and strong to very strong light. Carbon dioxide diffusion is essential, particularly when the water has a high mineral content. Sexual reproduction is very unlikely, but asexual reproduction may take place by the growth of lateral shoots from the rhizome. These can be separated from the parent plant and planted out.

■ B.echinosperma

ph: 6.4–6.8	Temp: 24–26°C (75–79°F)
°dH: 3–8	Water depth: 40 cm (16 in)

Family: *Hydrocharitaceae.*
Scientific name: *Blyxa echinosperma* (Clarke) Hooker.

Synonyms: none.
Common name: Hedgehog Blyxa.
Geographical area: India and Indonesia.
This species differs from the previous one in that its leaves have a rounder base. They are fine, 3 to 6 mm (⅛ to ¼ in) across, and are pointed but not spiral in shape. The leaves can be up to 50 cm (20 in) long and are bright-green in colour. The fruit is a small, cylindrical object covered in spines and 2 to 3 mm long (up to ¼ in). The conditions this species requires are the same as those for *B.aubertii*.

BOLBITIS

This genus consists of aquatic and marsh-dwelling ferns from Africa and Asia. The best known is *B.heudelotii*, but another, *B.heteroclita*, is sometimes imported from Malaysia and New Guinea.

It is somewhat similar to *Microsorium pteropus*, but unlike this plant it has plantlets which develop above, not below, the frond. Also the apex is slightly longer, which distinguishes it from the Java Fern.

■ B.heudelotii

ph: 6.5–7.6	Temp: 22–25°C (72–77°F)
°dH: 5–12	Water depth: 50 cm (20 in)

Family: *Lomariopsidaceae*.
Scientific name: *Bolbitis heudelotii*.
Synonyms: *Campium angustifolium* Alston, *B.felixii*.
Common names: Heudelot's Bolbitis, Congo Fern.
Geographical area: Tropical West Africa from Senegal to Angola; found in fast-flowing water and waterfalls, where it is attached to the substratum by its rhizome.
The rhizome produces a number of fronds on a stem. This stem attaches itself equally firmly to a rock or a growing medium such as peat. The fern can reach 50 cm (20 in) after several years of growth. The plant

grows very slowly in hard, alkaline water and medium to strong lighting. The fern is particularly suitable for Cichlids; because even the plant-eating species will completely ignore it. It is a tough, fibrous plant which appears to taste unpleasant to the fish. The rhizome should never be buried; instead the plant should be fixed in place using a paper clip or by attaching it to a root or a stone using an elastic band or nylon thread. The

B.heudelotti

plant reproduces by growing fronds from the rhizome, which may then be divided. In a humid atmosphere and out of the water in a paludarium it is easier to cultivate; more branches grow and the colour darkens.

C

CABOMBA

This genus was formerly part of the Waterlily family, but a separate family has subsequently been created for it, the Cobombaceae. There are seven species spread across the American continent in warm temperate and tropical waters. It is difficult to tell one species from another by looking at the leaves, which are all

very similar; in fact, they can only be told apart when there are flowers present. Plants belonging to this genus are solely aquatic, living in stagnant water in marshes and ditches.

■ C.aquatica

ph: 6.2–6.8	Temp: 24–28°C (75–82°F)
°dH: 2–8	Water depth: 40 cm (16 in)

Family: *Cabombaceae*.
Scientific name: *Cabomba aquatica* Aublet.
Synonyms: *Nectris aquatica, Villarsia aquatica*.
Common name: Water cabomba.
Geographical area: Southern Mexico to Brazil.
In its natural habitat, this plant grows to 1.3 m (4 ft 4 in), while in the aquarium about half this depth appears to be the maximum in which it is possible to maintain sufficiently strong lighting for this species. The laminae are highly ramified with 200 to 300 segments. The yellow flower grows above water. If the light is inadequate, the plant will grow up to the surface and go yellow. The conditions for the plant's maintenance need to be very strictly adhered to: the water needs to be acid and slightly hard, and extra carbon dioxide is essential. An air diffuser will inhibit the growth of any *Cabomba*. This is why a great number of aquarium owners meet with failure where these beautiful aquatic plants are concerned. Reproduction occurs via lateral runners and cuttings from the parent plant.

■ C.caroliniana

ph: 6.5–7.2	Temp: 23–26°C (73–79°F)
°dH: 5–10	Water depth: 40 cm (16 in)

Family: *Cabombaceae*.
Scientific name: *Cabomba caroliniana* Gray.
Synonyms: *C.aubletii, C.pinnata, C.viridiflora*.
Common name: Green Cabomba.
Geographical area: From the southeastern United States, along the At-

C.aquatica

C.caroliniana

lantic slopes of Central America, to Argentina.

This is a more resistant species than the previous one and has a less segmented lamina (150 to 200 segments). Its bright-green colour, height and faster growth all make it suitable as a background plant, particularly in a Dutch tank. The flower is pink or white. If the water is at all hard this should be compensated for by the addition of carbon dioxide. The plant dislikes air diffusers and alkaline water. The parent plants produce lateral shoots which can be planted out in the soil after carefully trimming the very ends of each shoot. The stems are arranged in groups 2 to 3 cm (about an inch) apart with some empty space around the group. The plants take up more space than their frail appearance suggests. There are three varieties and one horticultural form: *C.c.var. caroliniana*, *C.c.multipartita*, *C.c.paucipartita* and *C.c.var torta hort.*

■ *C.piauhyensis*

ph: 6.4–6.8	Temp: 23–26°C (73–79°F)
°dH: 2–8	Water depth: 30 cm (12 in)

C.piauhyensis

Family: *Cabombaceae.*
Scientific name: *Cabomba piauhyensis* Gardener.
Synonyms: none.
Common name: Red Cabomba.
Geographical area: South America: El Salvador, Northern Brazil, Bolivia, Caribbean: Cuba, Puerto Rico, Trinidad and other islands.

This reddish species is less bushy and there are only a hundred or so segments per lamina. The reddish colour is particularly noticeable on the internodes and the forks of the leaves. The flower of *C.piauhyensis* is reddish-purple. If the water is too hard the plant will die in a few days; the ends of the segments turn transparent and then decompose. The species requires soft, acid water. The whole of the plant should be strongly lit; this means that it needs to be planted some way away from its neighbours. No more than 40 cm (16 in) of water should be used to ensure that the plant is sufficiently well-lit. The colour of this plant makes it suitable for a Dutch tank, but its special needs probably make it too demanding a plant to look after properly.

CALLITRICHE

The genus *Callitriche* is made up of around 25 species of cold-water plants which are characterized by leaves with hooked ends. These species are extremely well suited to cold-water tanks and species such as *C.hamulata*, *C.obtusangula*, *C.palustris* or *C.platycarpa* are not difficult to find in streams and gravel pits. Most of the species are European, but the genus as a whole is spread widely throughout the world.

■ *C.hamulata*

ph: 6.7–7.3	Temp: 10–22°C (50–72°F)
°dH: 5–20	Water depth: 50 cm (20 in)

Family: *Callitrichaceae.*

Scientific name: *Callitriche hamulata* Küntzing.
Synonyms: *C.intermedia, C.autumnalis.*
Common name: Hooked callitriche.
Geographical area: All of Europe below 1,500 m (4,500 feet).

This species is distinguished by its leaves, both sides of which are an identical shade of green. The plant is up to 80 cm (32 in) high with a space of 3 cm (1¼ in) between nodes. This

C.aquatica

species dislikes heat, and temperature of the water should not exceed 22°C (72°F). From spring to autumn the plant should be brightly lit for 14 to 16 hours a day. If the temperature is reduced to 10°C (50°F) during the winter, the plant will become dormant and last for several years.

CERATOPHYLLUM

The hornworts are found throughout the world. There are about ten known species, of which two are sometimes found in aquariums. These plants will happily live in a wide variety of environments, and *C.demersum* is found both in the cold regions of Europe, in warm Mediterra-

nean areas and even Mexico. If the environment is a particularly favourable one, the plant may reach 2 m (6 ft) in length and large floating clumps are sometimes found.

■ *C.demersum*

ph: 6.8–7.5	Temp: 15–30°C (59–86°F)
°dH: 5–20	Water depth: 30 cm (12 in)

Family: *Ceratophyllaceae.*
Scientific name: *Ceratophyllum demersum* Linnaeus.
Synonyms: *C.asperum, C.cornutum, C.cristatum, C.gibbum* etc.
Common name: Immersed hornwort.
Geographical area: Worldwide.

This is a lively perennial plant with a fragile rootless stem. Depending on the area, the leaves range from bright-green to yellowish but may also be pale-green. This species is particularly suited to a cold or temperate aquarium, and medium to hard water. There is a much less common, red form found near Veracruz in Mexico, but this appears to be *C.echinatum*. The plant may be gradually adapted to warm water up to 28°C (82°F), increasing the intensity of light at the same time. As there are no roots, it is difficult to fix the stems in one place. Multiplication takes place frequently by throwing out runners, and this gives the plant its bushy appearance.

CERATOPTERIS

The taxonomy of this genus of ferns has been a subject of some disagreement in the past, but the matter appears to have been settled now. There are currently six known species, but different authors sometimes confuse them one with another. There are two floating species and one underwater cultivated species found in aquariums. The genus is found in tropical and sub-tropical countries.

■ *C.cornuta*

ph: 6.5–7.2	Temp: 22–30°C (72–86°F)
°dH: 3–15	Surface plant

Family: *Parkeriaceae*.
Scientific name: *Ceratopteris cornuta* (Beauvois) Le Prieur.
Synonyms: *C.thalictroides*.
Common name: Floating horned fern.
Geographical area: worldwide.
The fronds of this species are very large and are divided into three lobes which are more or less lanceolate. In strong light, this plant will quickly cover the whole surface of the aquarium. If grown submerged, the fronds ramify and the bright-green colour of the surface-growing plant becomes a yellowish green. This species is particularly popular with

C.cornuta   C.thalictroides ▶

surface-dwelling fish, such as the Belontiids, in breeding tanks. It is also liked by ovoviviparous species of fish, whose fry can take refuge amongst its roots and floating leaves. The plant multiplies rapidly by producing plantlets on the lower surfaces of the fronds, *C.pteridioides* (Hooker) Hieronymus is a very similar species but has less divided fronds. It requires exactly the same conditions as *C.cornuta*.

■ *C.thalictroides*

ph: 6.5–7.2	Temp: 22–30°C (72–86°F)
°dH: 3–15	Water depth: 40 cm (16 in)

Family: *Parkericeae*.
Scientific name: *Ceratopteris thalictroides (Linnaeus) Brongniart*.
Synonyms: *Acrostichum thalictroides, A.siliquosum, Crytogenis*

ferulacea, C.parkeri.
Common name: Indian fern.
Geographical area: tropical zones.
This is a non-floating fern, varying little in shape and bright-green in colour. The leaves are finely divided when the plant grows underwater and the roots are strongly developed. The plant needs bright light and should be planted in an uncluttered area of the tank so that the light is not obstructed. It can be used as a floating plant if desired, but if this is done the shape of the leaves changes and the plant is less attractive. The height of the plant under optimum conditions varies between 50 and 60 cm (20 and 24 in). The plant is an annual which tends to wither easily. It reproduces asexually, with plantlets growing on the leaf edges.

CRINUM

This genus contains over a hundred species, all of them native to tropical and sub-

tropical Asia, Africa and South America. It belongs to the same family as the Daffodil and the Snowdrop. The plants have a large onion-like bulb. Some are strictly aquatic and other, such as the Purple Crinum *(C.purpurascens)* are paludinous. Few of the species are imported for use in aquariums, but those that are are highly resistant both to unfavourable conditions and to plant-eating fish.

■ *C.natans*

ph: 6.8–7.5	Temp: 20–30°C (68–86°F)
°dH: 5–20	Water depth: 1 m (39 in)

Family: *Amaryllidaceae*.
Scientific name: *Crinum natans* Baker.
Synonyms: none.
Common name: Water Crinum.

Geographical area: Tropical West Africa.

This species has attractive, white, lily-like flowers which grow above the surface of the water. It is an aquatic plant and its height, resistance to hard water and tough fibres make it an ideal background plant for very large tanks. Sometimes it grows to more than 150 cm (60 in) and its leaves will spread out across the surface of the water. The leaves are crinkled with very undulating edges. They should be brightly lit or they will start to become yellowish. It is rare for the plant to multiply either sexually or asexually in an aquarium, but it should nevertheless last several years.

■ C.thaianum

ph: 6.8–7.5	Temp: 24–28°C (75–82°F)
°dH: 5–20	Water depth: 1 m (39 in)

Family: *Amaryllidaceae*.
Scientific name: *Crinum thaianum Schultz*.
Synonyms: none.
Common name: Onion Plant.
Geographical area: southern Thailand.

The leaves of this plant have smooth edges and their ribbon-like, non-undulating shape makes it look very like *Vallisneria gigantea*, though the latter is much more fragile. It grows up to 150 cm (60 in) in height and the leaves can be up to 2 or 3 cm (about an inch) wide. A few clumps of the plant arranged along the rear glass of the tank will form a long-lasting green backcloth. The bulb should be buried up to its middle in a fairly heavy medium such as round gravel. It makes an excellent plant for a large tank of Cichlids and other herbivorous fish; its leaves should be trimmed from time to time. The plant never reproduces sexually in an aquarium, and it is rare for it to reproduce asexually, which it does by growing offsets on the bulb.

CRYPTOCORYNE

This genus contains more than sixty known species, some aquatic and some amphibious. Some species are extremely polymorphous (*C.wendtii*), and others vary in colour depending on whether they are growing immersed or submerged (*C.schultzei*). In most species it is very hard to identify the exact species if there are no flowers, so it is not surprising that the names given to these members of the *Araceae* family have been changed and revised many times since the genus was first described by Fischer in 1828. Even now, botanists are divided in their opinions as to which species is which. The genus is found in an area extending from western India to Indo-China, Malaysia and Indonesia, as well as southern China, the Philippines and New Guinea. Sri Lanka itself has eleven native species. About thirty species are, or have in the past been imported for aquariums. The most common are those which are least fragile and difficult to grow. The inflorescence of the Cryptocorynes is used to trap insects. It consists of a spathe with a usually coloured upper part which has a tube or horn-shaped part above it which protects the reproductive organs of the plant. The flowers themselves have no petals.

■ C.affinis

pH: 6.5–7.5	Temp.: 20–28°C (68–82°F)
°dH: 3–15	Water depth: 30 cm (12 in)

Family: *Araceae*.
Scientific name: *Cryptocoryne affinis* Brown ex Hooker.
Synonym: *C.haerteliana*.
Common name: Haertel's Cryptocoryne.
Geographical area: Malaysian peninsula.

This is the species of plant most commonly found in aquariums. It varies in height between 10 and 30 cm (4 and 12 in) depending on the lighting and how densely it is planted. It goes well almost anywhere in a tank, either at the front or along the sides. It is a very decorative plant with satiny, green foliage, and can live in a variety of environments, though like other species in the genus it is sensitive to sudden changes in the chemical or physical composition of the tank. It will quickly cover the whole floor of an aquarium if the stolons are not removed, and under these conditions the plants will not thrive. However, if one parent plant is separated and the stolons are systematically removed, it may reach a height of 40 to 50 cm (16 to 20 in), with twenty or so leaves. The tube of the inflorescence reaches 25 to 30 cm (10 to 12 in) and the spathe curves round to the left. It is brownish outside and violet or purple on the inside, whilst closer to the opening of the tube it becomes red. The spathe unrolls after eight or ten days, but retains two twists permanently. The lighting should not be too bright. In an aquaterrarium, half submerged, the plant will flower fairly regularly after two to three years of growth.

■ C.albida

pH: 6.5–7.0	Temp.: 20–25°C (68–77°F)
°dH: 3–5	Water depth: 30 cm (12 in)

Family: *Araceae*.
Scientific name: *Cryptocoryne albida*.
Synonym: *C.korthausae*.
Common name: Cryptocoryne.

C.albida

Geographical area: Thailand.
The leaves reach 15 cm (6 in) in length, with an elliptical shape and fairly wavy edges; they range from green to brown in colour. This is a land-growing Cryptocoryne which should be grown in a hot, humid paludarium. In the aquarium, it grows extremely slowly. The white lamina of the inflorescence is covered in red spots and has a horizontal twist at the end.

■ C.balansae

pH: 6.5–7	Temp.: 25–28°C (77–82°F)
°dH: 3–8	Water depth: 40 cm (16 in)

Family: *Araceae*.
Scientific name: *Cryptocoryne crispatula*.
Synonyms: *C.longispatha, C.somphongsii*.
Common name: Balansa's Cryptocoryne.
Geographical area: Thailand, Vietnam, Southern China.
This is a very elegant plant with long, tapering leaves, growing up to 30 or 40 cm (12 or 16 in) in the aquarium and 80 cm (32 in) in deep water in its natural habitat. The leaf has a crinkly surface on either side of the conspicuous central vein. There are several conditions which should be observed: a light growing medium, such as round gravel, the correct temperature, medium to strong lighting and average water hardness. The species can be used as a centrepiece or in a line along the back of the tank. The plant reproduces asexually by growing stolons from the rhizome, which initially is a slow process but which accelerates with time. In a paludarium, the aerial leaves remain short and narrow at only 1 cm (½ in).

■ C.becketii

pH: 6.8–7.5	Temp.: 24–28°C (75–82°F)
°dH: 5–15	Water depth: 40 cm (16 in)

Family: *Araceae*.
Scientific name: *Cryptocoryne becketii* Thwaites ex. Trimen.
Synonyms: none.
Common name: Beckett's Cryptocoryne.

Geographical area: Sri Lanka.
This is a very resilient species with an unusual colour—brown to olive green on the upper half of the leaf and purple to red on the underside. It therefore provides an attractive contrast to other plants in an aquarium. Other reddish-brown species (*C.petchii, C.siamensis*) are also available in shops, although they are less easy to obtain. The leaves reach 10 to 20 cm (4 to 8 in) in length and 2 to 4 cm (¾ to 1½ in) in width. This species goes well in the middle of a communal or Dutch tank or in the corners at the front. Ideally it requires medium-hard water, a pH of

C.balansae

C.beckettii

7.5 and a temperature of 25–27°C (77–81°F). Asexual reproduction takes place when stolons grow from the rhizome: the young plants should be separated and planted out in a part of the tank where there is plenty of space.

■ C.ciliata

pH: 6.8–7.8	Temp.: 24–28°C (75–82°F)
°dH: 6–20	Water depth: 40 cm (16 in)

Family: *Araceae*.
Scientific name: *Cryptocoryne ciliata* (Roxburgh) Fisher.
Synonyms: *C.elata, C.drymorrhiza*.
Common name: Ciliated Cryptocoryne.
Geographical area: Widespread in Asia from India to New Guinea.
The species is so called because of the cilia, or fine hairs, on the outer edge of the spathe. The plant grows to about 40 cm (16 in) in height; the leaves are white, lanceolate and pointed. The outer edge of the leaf is sometimes slightly wavy. The stem is about 10 cm (4 in) long when fully grown.

The botanist Rataj also describes a second form, *C.c.var.latifolia*, which has shorter, wider leaves and a brighter underside to the leaf. This variety does not produce stolons from the rhizome; instead, plantlets grow straight from the rhizome itself.

C.ciliata is well known for its ability to survive in hard or brackish water. It needs bright lighting and dislikes being transplanted. In an aquaterrarium, half submerged, the plant produces a reddish-purple inflorescence up to 7 cm (3 in) long.

■ C.cordata

pH: 6.5–7.5	Temp.: 24–26°C (75–79°F)
°dH: 5–20	Water depth: 30 cm (12 in)

Family: *Araceae*.
Scientific name: *Cryptocoryne cordata* Griff.
Synonyms: *Cryptocoryne blassii, C.kerri, C.siamensis*.
Common name: Siamese Cryptocoryne.
Geographical area: Borneo, Sumatra, Thailand.
There are several known varieties of this species, which can be distinguished from one another by the shape of their leaves. In the form *siamensis* the lamina is oval, whilst in *kerri* it is heart-shaped and in *ewansii* it has notched edges.

The elliptical form, with reddish leaves and pale red veins, is the one most commonly found in aquariums. Its maximum height is around 15 to 20 cm (6 to 8 in) and it is a hardy plant which does not mind hard water. It makes an attractive contrast with other green plants in the

C.cordata

background. The best way of heating the water is to use a cable buried in the substratum as the plant is very sensitive to a cold, growing medium. The plant requires average lighting and water no harder than 5 to 8 dKH. The plant multiplies by growing stolons from the rhizome, but it is not a very productive species.

■ C.spiralis

pH: 6.5–7.2	Temp.: 22–25°C (72–77°F)
°dH: 5–12	Water depth: 40 cm (16 in)

Family: Araceae.
Scientific name: Cryptocoryne spiralis (Retzius) Fischer.
Synonyms: Arum spirale, Ambrosinia spiralis, Cryptocoryne huegelii, C.unolicularis, C.tortuosa.
Common name: Spiral Cryptocoryne.
Geographical area: Widespread in India, Gulf of Bengal, Bangladesh.
This is an amphibious, marsh-dwelling species which will live underwater for very short periods. Compared to other species of this genus, C.spiralis in its land-dwelling form, is a very robust species and not difficult to grow underwater either. The leaves are slender and pointed, with slightly undulating edges; when grown in an aquarium the stem is

shorter than when in its natural habitat. The plant grows to 30 cm (12 in) in height. The water may be soft and acid, but alkaline water and medium-hard water will not harm the plant. It requires medium illumination. In an aquaterrarium, the plant is much more spectacular, with narrower leaves only 15 mm (½ in) wide, flowers and a spathe characteristic of a land-dwelling species. The plant reproduced by growing stolons from the rhizome; reproduction is more rapid in an aquaterrarium.

■ C.wendtii

pH: 6.8–7.5	Temp.: 24–27°C (75–81°F)
°dH: 5–20	Water depth: 30 cm (12 in)

Family: Araceae.
Scientific name: Cryptocoryne wendtii de Wendt.
Synonyms: none.
Common name: Wendt's Cryptocoryne.
Geographical area: Sri Lanka.
This species takes more different leaf forms than any other of the species. Although the inflorescence varies little, there are at least ten different types of leaf which grow above and below the surface of the water. Rataj described five varieties:

var.wendtii: the aerial leaves are oblong with a round or heart-shaped base 8 to 10 cm (3 to 4 in) long and 2 to 3 cm (¾ to 1¼ in) wide. Below water, the leaves are narrower (15 cm by 3 cm or 6 in by 1 in) and taper regularly towards a pointed end. The edges of the leaves are slightly wavy and their upper surfaces are olive green with beige spots and stripes. The underside of the leaf is green for the most part with additional tinges of red.

var.jahnelii: Underwater, the leaves are up to 12 cm (5 in) by 8 cm (3 in). The upper face of the leaf is reddish brown in strong light, whilst the underside is red. The edges are slightly wavy but under weaker light become smooth and the red colour becomes paler. The plant generally reaches a length of about 20 cm (8 in) in height.

var.krauteri: leaves growing underwater resemble those of var. wendtii, though the latter is darker in colour and does not change colour in weak light. The plant is about 15 cm (6 in) high, but if growing in a thick group the petiole is longer and the plant can be twice as tall.

var.nana (also known as var.minima): the leaves are 4 to 6 cm (1½–2½ in) long by 5 to 10 mm (¼ to ½ in). They are lanceolate with a round or slightly heart-shaped base, a very narrow, tapered point and wavy edges. The leaves are olive-green to reddish-brown on the top surface, depending on the amount of light, while the veins are reddish or pink. This is an excellent foreground plant for an aquarium.

var.rubella: submerged leaves are lanceolate, 6 cm by 1 cm (2½ by 1½ in). The base and point of the leaf are short, while the edges are slightly undulating; the upper half of the leaf is olive-green with a dark stripe across it, whilst the underside is brown with green veins. This variety is very well suited to a foreground position in an aquarium. The plant is prolific and a few groups arranged properly will soon produce a whole carpet of Cryptocorynes by producing stolons from the rhizome.

C.wendtii requires no special conditions, though it can be risky to make sudden changes in the chemical or physical composition of the water or the amount of light the plants receive.

■ C.willisii

pH: 6.5–7.0	Temp.: 24–26°C (75–79°F)
°dH: 5–12	Water depth: 20 cm (8 in)

Family: *Araceae*.
Scientific name: *Cryptocoryne willisii* Reitz.
Synonym: *Cryptocoryne nevillii*.
Common name: Willis's Cryptocoryne.
Geographical area: Sri Lanka.
This species should not be confused with *C.willisii* Engler ex. Braum, which is the same as *C.axelrodii* Rataj. This is a small foreground plant with lanceolate leaves 3 to 5 cm (1½–2 in) long and 8 to 10 mm (½ in) wide, arranged on a long, fine petiole. The leaves are bright-green. The species should be planted in groups of ten to twenty stems; in the right conditions, the plant multiplies rapidly. The hardness of the water is not important and the plant can cope with a lower temperature. This species is also easily mistaken for *C.parva*.

E

ECHINODORUS

The genus *Echinodorus* is found in the southern United States and down as far as Argentina, but it is absent in Africa and Asia. About fifty species have been described, most of them marsh-dwelling and amphibious. Few will spend an entire year underwater. About thirty species have been imported for aquarium owners. Like the Cryptocorynes, there is a high degree of polymorphism in the leaves, depending very much on where and how the plant is grown. Generally speaking, members of the species like slightly acid to slightly alkaline water, medium hardness, a temperature of 23 to 27°C (73–81°F) and medium lighting.

The genus is divided into several groups, depending on the height of each species. The *Tenellii* group consists of six dwarf species, most notably *E.tenellus*, *E.bolivianus*, and *E.quadricostatus*. Another consists of 'Swordplants' with long, tapering leaves; *E.amazonicus*, *E.bleheri* and *E.parviflorus* are the best known. The last group contains tall species with oval, heart-shaped or lanceolate leaves. When these grow underwater they also produce leaves growing above the surface or floating on it: these are *E.cordifolius*, *E.grandiflorus*, *E.macrophyllus* and *E.scaber*.

Asexual reproduction takes place in four ways:

- Production of plantlets on the floral spike;
- Runners growing from the rhizome;
- Plantlets growing from the rhizome;
- Division of the rhizome.

■ E.amazonicus

pH: 6.0–7.2	Temp.: 22–26°C (72–79°F)
°dH: 3–12	Water depth: 40 cm (16 in)

Family: *Alismataceae*.
Scientific name: *Echinodorus amazonicus* Rataj.
Synonym: *E.brevipedicellatus*.
Common name: Amazon Swordplant.
Geographical area: Lower Amazon, Brazil.
This aquatic species is very popular amonst aquarium owners. It has linear, lanceolate leaves up to 40 cm (16 in) long by 2–3 cm (about an inch) wide. There are three veins running from the base to the tip of the leaf. The species is often confused with *E.bleheri*, which has broader leaves. The plant makes a very good main centrepiece, though in hard water it does not grow very much. It requires medium to strong illumination. The plant will reproduce asexually very easily: if the water level is slightly

E.amazonicus

lowered, the floral spike produces plantlets which should be planted out in a growing tank as soon as they have formed a few roots, and the water level should be raised as they grow larger.

■ E.bolivianus

pH: 6.0–7.0	Temp.: 20–28°C (68–82°F)
°dH: 3–8	Water depth: 20 cm (8 in)

Family: *Alismataceae*.
Scientific name: *Echinodorus bolivianus* (Rusby) Holm Nielsen.
Synonyms: *Alisma boliviana*, *E.austroamericanus*.
Common name: Dwarf Bolivian Amazon Swordplant.
Geographical area: This is the most southerly South American species, being found in Southern Brazil, Argentina, Uruguay and in the foothills of the Peruvian Andes.
The specimens which are imported are easily recognized by the reddish area on the petiole, which distinguishes them from *E.quadricostatus var.xinguensis*. This is an excellent foreground plant for an aquarium. It grows to no more than 12 cm (5 in) and has a short stem with leaves 5 to 8 mm (¼ to ⅓ in) broad. It is an

adaptable plant and will survive in temperatures anywhere between 20 and 28°C (68 and 82°F). In hard water, it is essential that the water has carbon dioxide and nutrients added, because otherwise the leaves will turn yellow and then transparent. The plant multiplies very quickly by producing stolons from the rhizome. A handful of plants spread around the tank will soon produce a bright-green carpet of young plants. If this layer of foliage becomes too dense, growth will come to a near standstill and at this point the plants should be cut back at regular intervals. The flowers are white and arranged in a crown at the top of a floral spike.

■ E.cordifolius

pH: 6.2–7.0	Temp.: 22–28°C (72–82°F)
°dH: 3–10	Water depth: 40–80 cm (16–32h13 in)

E.cordifolius

Family: Alismataceae.
Scientific name: Echinodorus cordifolius (Linnaeus) Grisebach.
Synonym: Echinodorus radicans.
Common names: Radicans Sword; Spade-leaf Plant.
Geographical area: Southern United States, Mexico.
This is an amphibious species which will live permanently submerged if required. The morphology of the plant is different when grown under-water: the petiole is shorter, about the same length as the lamina and the leaf is rounder and has four veins on either side of the central vein. The base of the lamina is heart-shaped. The leaves are very attractive when grown underwater, but they need plenty of space and any floating leaves should be cut back. If the

plant continues producing floating leaves, the number of central leaves should be reduced to four or five and the petioles should be lightly pulled on to release 15 to 20 cm (6–8 in) of roots. This magnificent plant sometimes reaches 40 to 60 cm (16–24 in) in height, and in an aquaterrarium it can reach 1.5 m (57 in), where flowering and the intensive production of adventitious plantlets on the floral spike is continuous. The floral spike stretches out sideways and bears large white self-fertilizing flowers. The plantlets develop more quickly when the plant is immersed with only its roots below the surface.

■ E.horizontalis

pH: 6.2–7.4	Temp.: 22–25°C (72–77°F)
°dH: 3–12	Water depth: 40 cm (16 in)

Family: Alismataceae.
Scientific name: Echinodorus horizontalis Rataj.
Synonyms: E.guianensis, E.muricatus.
Common name: Horizontal Echinodorus.
Geographical area: Amazon basin from Peru to Belem in Brazil, as well as northern parts of South America. The unusual feature of this plant is the fact that the leaf grows out from the petiole at an angle of almost 90°. The leaf is elliptical, 15 to 20 cm (6 to 8 in) by 6 to 10 cm (2½–4 in). The medial vein is very pronounced and has three other veins on either side. This is a plant of medium height which can be placed in the centre of a tank containing 500 litres (100 gallons) to a depth of 50 cm (20 in). The species can be distinguished from E.cordifolius by the finer and longer apex of the leaf. It produces no surface leaves. New leaves are reddish and gradually change colour. The plant takes a long time to acclimatize and requires strong lighting, but it is a very adaptable plant. When the plant is grown immersed, its leaves span 30 to 40 cm (12 to 16 in) and the floral spike produces large numbers of plantlets and white flowers. The plantlets can be planted out underwater when their roots are strong enough.

■ E.maior

pH: 6.2–7.2	Temp.: 22–25°C (72–77°F)
°dH: 3–10	Water depth: 30 cm (12 in)

Family: Alismataceae.
Scientific name: Echinodorus maior (Micheli) Rataj.
Synonyms: E.martii, E.leopoldina.
Common name: Ruffled Amazon Sword.
Geographical area: Brazil (Goias, Gerais and Minas States).
This is a purely aquatic plant which produces no leaves on or above the surface. The leaves are long, tapering and bright-green, growing wider towards the apex. The petiole is sometimes twisted and gives the plant an elegant appearance. The plant may grow up to 35 or 40 cm (17 to 18 in) with leaves 2 to 6 cm (1 to 2½ in) wide. This species will survive in slightly alkaline water, but not at too great a temperature: the maximum is 25°C (77°F). The addition of carbon

E.maior

dioxide and nutrients will make the plant grow much better. The floral spike never grows very far above the surface of the water, and the adventitious plantlets it bears appear below the surface. Asexual reproduction may also take place by the production of shoots on the rhizome. Sexual reproduction is also easy: the white flowers are self-fertilizing and the seeds should not be collected until they have turned brown.

■ E.osiris

pH: 6.2–7.2	Temp.: 22–25°C (72–77°F)
°dH: 3–10	Water depth: 40 cm (16 in)

Family: *Alismataceae*.
Scientific name: *Echinodorus osiris* Rataj.
Synonyms: *E.osiris rubra, E.aureobrunneus, E.aureobrunata*.
Common name: Swedish Echinodorus.
Geographical area: Southern Brazil.
This marsh-dwelling *Echinodorus* is a very resistant species. It does not mind alkaline, slightly hard water and may reach 40 to 50 cm (16 to 20 in) in height. It has abundant foliage consisting of leaves 30 to 40 cm (12 to 16 in) long by 4 to 6 cm (1½–2½ in) wide, with many veins. The lamina has wavy edges. This is a very attractive species for a communal or South American aquarium; the young central leaves are reddish or brownish in colour. Bright lighting, carbon dioxide diffusion and the addition of nutrients are all essential. It is rare for there to be an inflorescence when the plant is grown in an aquarium, but the floral spike produces adventitious plantlets. Asexual reproduction also takes place with the production of stolons from the rhizome. This species dislikes heat and is not suitable for a paludarium.

■ *E.parviflorus*

pH: 6.2–7.2	Temp.: 22–27°C (72–81°F)
°dH: 3–15	Water depth: 40 cm (16 in)

Family: *Alismataceae*.
Scientific name: *Echinodorus parviflorus* Rataj.
Synonyms: *E.peruensis, E.peruense, E.tocantinus*.
Common names: Black Echinodorus or Black Amazon Swordplant.
Geographical area: Uncertain, probably western South America, Pacific Peru.
This species is very similar to *E.aschersonianus*, with dark-grey leaves and deep-brown veins. There are large numbers of leaves (about fifty), which take two different forms. One is lanceolate, whilst the other is shorter and broader, being elliptical to slightly heart-shaped. The first of these is very like *E.amazonicus*. *E.parviflorus* is resistant to extremes of environment and makes a good centrepiece for a tank. It multiplies frequently and rapidly by producing large numbers of plantlets from the

E.palaefolius

spike. When these have developed sufficiently strong roots, the floral spike should be bent downwards under the water while its end and middle should be attached to the growing medium, without separating it from the parent plant. When these have taken, the spike may be detached from the parent plant. However, if the plant produces very large numbers of offspring it may indicate that it is about to die.

■ *E.tenellus*

pH: 6.2–7.0	Temp.: 22–25°C (72–77°F)
°dH: 3–8	Water depth: 20 cm (8 in)

Family: *Alismataceae*.
Scientific name: *Echinodorus tenellus* Buchenau.
Common name: Pigmy Chain Swordplant.
Geographical area: Southern United States and southern Brazil.
This species used to be very popular. Today, the 'false tenellus' (*Lilaeopsis novae-zelandiae*) tends to be preferred as a foreground plant. About ten plants equally spaced in a tank will rapidly produce stolons and create a carpet of bright green. These should be controlled by removing all the plants, choosing those of medium height and replanting them. This will also make their growth and reproduction more vigorous. The *parvulus* variety prefers slightly harder water and less light. *E.t.var.tenellus* has leaves 5 to 6 cm (2–2½ in) long by a few millimetres wide. This species is fairly sensitive to excessively hard water but is suited to a South American tank.

EGERIA

This genus differs from the *Elodea* in the structure of its flowers, which are fertilized by insects above the surface of the water.

E.tenellus

▪ E.densa

E.densa

pH: 6.5–7.5	Temp.: 15–23°C (59–73°F)
°dH: 5–15	Water depth: 50 cm (20 in)

Family: *Hydrocharitaceae*.
Scientific name: *Egeria densa* Planchon.
Synonyms: *Elodea densa, Anacharis densa, Philotria densa*.
Common name: Giant Elodea.
Geographical area: South America (Argentina, Uruguay, Paraguay, Brazil) and elsewhere.
This species has many branches and is suitable only for temperate tanks up to 23°C (73°F). it does not mind hard, alkaline water but requires bright lighting. This species is often sold as an excellent purifier of tanks, but its cleaning abilities should not be relied upon too much; too many plants would be required to do the job properly. In its natural habitat, the plant can reach more than 3 m (10 feet) in length. It should be placed in small groups in the middle of the tank or at the sides. It produces large numbers of lateral shoots, which should be regularly removed and planted out. The stem of the parent plant can be cut back above the beginning of the shoot.

EICHHORNIA

This genus is part of the Pontederiaceae family, and consists of seven tropical or subtropical species. The family includes eight other genera besides this one, including *Heteranthera, Monochoria* and *Reussia*, some species of which are sometimes imported for use in aquariums. The *Eichhornia*, or 'Water Hyacinth', forms semi-spherical leaves above water which catch the wind and help the plant to propagate. Some species grow submerged, such as *E.azurea* and *E.diversifolia*. *E.crassipes*, as we will see, is suitable only for a brightly lit aquaterrarium or an aquarium with no lid which is lit by fluorescent lamps.

▪ E.azuera

pH: 6.2–7.0	Temp.: 22–26°C (72–79°F)
°dH: 3–10	Water depth: 40 cm (16 in)

Family: *Pontederiaceae*.
Scientific name: *Eichhornia azurea* (Sw.) Kunth.
Synonym: *Pontederia azurea*.
Common name: Blue Water Hyacinth.
Geographical area: Tropical and subtropical America.
This marsh-dwelling plant can be grown in an aquaterrarium, where it

E.azurea

develops broad spoon-shaped leaves. The petiole is quite long and does not have the spongy swelling of *E.crassipes*. The flowers are deep violet and are arranged in a raceme. This species must spend a certain amount of time submerged when grown in an aquaterrarium. In an aquarium, it has fine, tapering ribbon-shaped leaves with blunt ends situated alternately along the slender stem. The lower leaves have a tendency to rot away. The plant should be well lit in an aquarium and very well lit if grown in an aquaterrarium. The plant frequently reproduces, by division of the stem.

▪ E.crassipes

pH: 6.5–7.5	Temp.: 22–30°C (72–86°F)
°dH: 5–15	Surface plant

Family: *Pontederiaceae*.
Scientific name: *Eichhornia crassipes* (Martuis) Solms.
Synonyms: *Pontederia crassipes, P.elongata, Eichhornia speciosa, Heteranthera formosa*.

E.crassipes

Common name: Water Hyacinth.
Geographical area: Worldwide. The very rapid growth of this floating plant is a serious problem on navigable waterways in tropical and subtropical areas.
E.crassipes is an aquatic plant which cannot be grown properly in a glass-covered aquarium, as the amount of space available constricts its growth; they are therefore only suited to very

E.crassipes

ELEOCHARIS

These are aquatic, marsh-dwelling plants. They are slender and grassy and require intense sunlight. They are found throughout the world.

■ *E.minima*

pH: 6.5–7.2	Temp: 22–26°C (72–79°F)
°dH: 3–10	Water depth: 20 cm (8 in)

Family: *Cyperaceae*.
Scientific name: *Eleocharis minima*.
Synonyms: none.
Common names: Hairgrass, Scirpa.
Geographical area: Widespread in tropical and sub-tropical areas. When grown underwater, this plant looks very like a tuft of grass. The bright-green leaves are in fact stems which grow to 40 or 60 cm (16 to 24 in) in the aquarium and 5 to 20 cm (2 to 8 in) in an aquaterrarium. The chemical content and temperature of the water are fairly unimportant as far as this species is concerned, though the depth of water should not exceed 40 cm (16 in) or there will not be enough light for it. It is primarily a paludarium plant and it is here that it flowers most easily. The plant multiplies by producing short stolons. When the stems become too dense they can be separated.

large tanks or aquaterrariums. Apart from their decorative value, they have the effect of softening a bright light, and the fine roots serve as a refuge for fry and a support for eggs near the surface of the water. The plant develops a spongy swelling at the base of the petiole which makes it unsinkable, while the spoon-shaped leaves catch the slightest of breezes which propels them across the water. In its natural habitat the plant reaches 1 m (39 in) in length, but it is considerably smaller when cultivated. The lighting should be strong, preferably in the form of fluorescent tubes. The plant flowers frequently in the aquaterrarium or in outdoor ponds and asexual reproduction is by stolons growing from the parent plant.

ELATINE

There are twenty or so species in this genus, all aquatic or riparian. Some of them are suitable for the decoration of cold or temperate aquariums; some form a grass-like carpet of foliage, such as *Elatine hydropiper* and *Elatine macropoda*.

■ *E.macropoda*

pH: 6.6–7.4	Temp: 12–25°C (61–77°F)
°dH: 5–15	Water depth: 20 cm (8 in)

Family: *Elatinaceae*.
Scientific name: *Elatina macropoda Gussone*.
Synonym: *Elatine fabri*.
Common name: Large-rooted Waterwort.
Geographical area: Southern France, Spain, Morocco, Algeria; usually in isolated outcrops.
This is a small but very fast-growing species which grows many stolons in strong light. The leaves are 5 to 15 mm (¼–½ in) long by 2 to 4 mm (⅛–¼ in), and opposite. The roots grow to 4 cm (1½ in). A few plants spread around the bottom of the tank, towards the back, will take it over in a few months. Young plants should be protected from fish and burrowing snails (*Melanoides tuberculata*) until they have taken root. The plants do not flower in the aquarium, but will support temperatures of up to 25°C (77°F) and hard water. Unfortunately, the species belonging to this genus are no longer available commercially, which is regrettable because they are very useful plants, especially in breeding tanks where they make a good support for eggs.

E.vivipara

■ E.vivipara

pH: 6.5–7.2	Temp: 20–25°C (68–77°F)
°dH: 3–8	Water depth: 30 cm (12 in)

Family: *Cyperaceae*.
Scientific name: *Eleocharis vivipara* Link.
Synonym: *Eleocharis prolifera*.
Common name: Viviparous Eleocharis or Hairgrass.
Geographical area: Southern United States.
This plant has short roots and long fine stems 40 to 60 cm (16 to 24 in) long and 5 mm (¼ in) in diameter. In fresh water and fairly bright light this species should grow well. If grown in small groups and surrounded by other small species it is particularly attractive. The plant reproduces asexually by growing adventitious plantlets which can be planted out in the bottom of the tank. The plantlets should be given plenty of space until they have reached 15 or 20 cm (6–8 in).

FONTINALIS

This genus belongs to the Fontinalaceae, and numbers around sixty species. They are mostly aquatic mosses from cold or mountainous areas of the world. Formerly, only *F.antipyretica*, sometimes confused with F.hypnoides, was available to the aquarium owner, but it has now been overtaken in popularity by the Bogor Moss from South-East Asia, which is better suited to the warm-water aquarium.

■ F.antipyretica

pH: 6.2–7.5	Temp: 0–20°C (32–68°F)
°dH: 3–15	Water depth: 10 cm

Family: *Cyperaceae*.
Scientific name: *fontinalis antipyretica Linnaeus*.
Synonyms: *Hypnum antipyreticum, Fontinalis trifaria, Pilotrichum antipyreticum*.
Geographical area: Europe, Asia, North America, Algeria.

F.antipyretica

This moss is extremely useful in breeding tanks, though unfortunately it cannot withstand temperatures over 20°C (68°F). Several forms have been described, each living in different environments and temperatures. The leaves grow directly from the stem and overlap like scales. The species is suitable for cold-water aquariums and is much easier to maintain than species such as *F.gracilis* and *F.tenuis*. The forms growing in stagnant water such as *F.vulgaris* and *F.gigantea*, are more resistant to heat. The common form has oval leaves 4 to 6 mm by 3 to 4 mm (½ by ¼ in) which are pale-green to brownish in colour. It is rough to the touch, which makes it easy to recognize. It does not like fresh, acid water but will reproduce quickly in hard water and makes a good decoration for a rock or piece of wood.

GYMNOCORONIS

This genus forms part of the Asteraceae family (=*Compositae)* which contains 50,000 species as diverse as the daisy, chrysanthemum and dandelion. There is one single species, *G.spilanthoides*, which has been imported for aquariums since the 1960s.

■ G.spilanthoides

pH: 6.5–7.5	Temp.: 20–26°C (68–79°F)
°dH: 5–15	Water depth: 40 cm (16 in)

Family: *Asteraceae*.
Scientific name: *Gymnocoronis spilanthoides* de Candolle.
Synonyms: none.
Common name: Spade-leaf Plant.
Geographical area: Tropical South America.

G.spilantoides

This species has elliptical or lance-olate leaves with slightly notched edges, which is how it can be distinguished from the Hygrophilas, which have smooth leaves. The leaves are pale-green and opposite. The stem produces many adventitious roots and the very rapid growth of the plant is accompanied by an increase in the length of the internode. It needs plenty of space to grow upwards and the minimum depth of water it requires is 40 cm (16 in); in shallower tanks the stems are shortened and this can have an adverse effect on the plant. Its rapid growth can be slowed down by lowering the temperature of the water to about 23°C (73°F) and increasing the light. The plant is very resistant to hard or alkaline water. This species can easily be grown in an aquaterrarium and then moved out to a garden pond. When the plant grows above surface level, an aerial shoot can be removed and transplanted to the aquaterrarium. After a month or so, to acclimatize the leaves to the comparative lack of moisture, they can be planted out beside a pond or even a balcony if they are kept in water.

HEMIANTHUS

Opinions vary amongst botanists as to how exactly species belonging to the genera *Hemianthus* and *Micranthemum* should be classified. About ten species have been described, but only four species are recognized. Since 1974 they have been separated out into two distinct genera again. They are primarily amphibious marsh-dwelling plants living in the south-eastern United States, the larger Caribbean islands and other tropical areas of America.

■ *H.micranthemoides*

pH: 6.2–7.0	Temp.: 22–27°C (72–81°F)
°dH: 2–10	Water depth: 40 cm (16 in)

Family: *Scrofulariaceae*.
Scientific name: *Hemianthus micranthemoides* Nuttall.
Synonym: *Micranthemum micranthemoides*.
Common name: none.
Geographical area: South-eastern United States, Cuba.
This species can easily be confused with others unless it is grown above water. Underwater, it is a slender, fine-stemmed plant with small leaves growing in whorls of three. Often in an aquarium four leaves will appear on the stem, which makes it easily confused with another species. It is a fairly fragile plant with stems that break easily and both snails and chemicals such as algicides will damage it. The hardness of the water should not exceed 10 °dH. It goes well in a strongly lit Dutch tank; planted in compact groups. Asexual reproduction occurs by the production of lateral runners, which can be planted out.

HETERANTHERA

This genus includes ten or so species and forms part of the Pontederiaceae family. They adapt very well to hard water and bright light and produce floating leaves, though they should not be grown in a paludarium as they tend to become weak and spindly. They live primarily in marshes and shallow stagnant water.

■ *H.dubia*

pH: 6.5–7.5	Temp.: 22–27°C (72–81°F)
°dH: 5–15	Water depth: 40 cm (16 in)

Family: *Pontederiaceae*.
Scientific name: *Heteranthera dubia* (Jacquin) MacMillian.
Synonyms: *Schollera graminea, S.graminifolia, Heteranthera graminea, Zosterella dubia*.
Common name: Yellow-flowered Heteranthera.
Geographical area: Southern United States, Mexico, Cuba.
The stem reaches 70 to 80 cm (28 to 32 in) in length and makes a good screen against the back of the tank if there is no artificial decoration. The leaves themselves are smaller at about 10 cm (4 in) long and are pale- to bright-green in colour. Hard water, carbon dioxide diffusion and the addition of nutrients are necessary if this plant is to be grown properly. Sexual reproduction is difficult to achieve, but can occur if the depth of water in the tank is decreased. Asexual reproduction is by the production of runners which can be cut off beneath one of the nodes protecting the adventitious roots or by laying the plant down flat against the bottom of the tank. In the latter case, the stem will produce roots at different points along its length.

■ *H.reniformis*

pH: 6.5–7.4	Temp.: 22–25°C (72–77°F)
°dH: 5–15	Water depth: 30 cm (12 in)

Family: *Pontederiaceae*.
Scientific name: *Heteranthera reniformis* Ruiz et Pavon.
Synonyms: *Heteranthera acuta, H.pubescens, Leptanthus reniformis*.
Common name: Reniform Heteranthera.
Geographical area: From the southern United States to Argentina; has also been introduced to the Caribbean islands.
The heart-shaped to oval leaves are usually arranged on a creeping stalk on which adventitious roots appear. The plant is suited to hard water, needs bright light and will grow to an average of 20 cm (8 in). The plant may

H.reniformis

flower in an aquaterrarium, though it is difficult to get the seeds to mature properly. Asexual reproduction occurs fairly continuously for a few months each year and takes place through the growth of stolons.

■ *H.zosterifolia*

pH: 6.2–7.0	Temp.: 22–26°C (72–79°F)
°dH: 3–10	Water depth: 22–25 cm (9–11 in)

Family: *Pontederiaceae*.

H.zosterifolia

Scientific name: *Heteranthera zosterifolia* Martius.
Synonym: *Heteranthera zosteraefolia*.
Common name: Water Stargrass.
Geographical area: South America.
This is a very bushy species which can be used in groups to decorate the back and sides of an aquarium. The slender stem bears alternate, distichous leaves which are straight and tapering, about 3 to 5 cm (1–2 in) long by 5 mm (¼ in) wide. The plant grows up to about 50 or 60 cm (20 or 24 in). It grows very fast and produces runners on a frequent basis. When it reaches the surface it flowers and a number of lateral runners appear, which should be planted in the rooting medium. It is not a difficult species to grow and is suited to all types of tank, in particular Dutch tanks where it should be planted in the background under fairly strong light. Before planting the shoots, they should be allowed to float on the surface of the tank for a few days. The floral stem appears on a leaf axil, near the surface of the water, and bears two bright-blue flowers with yellow spots which gradually fade away.

HOTTONIA

The Hottonias, like the Marsh Marigolds (*Lysimachia*) and the Samolas, belong to the Primulaceae family. They are found in cold and temperate regions of the northern hemisphere and have leaves which are divided and grow either alternate or in rosettes.

■ *H.inflata*

pH: 6.5–7.0	Temp.: 12–20°C (54–68°F)
°dH: 5–15	Water depth: 30 cm (12 in)

Family: *Primulaceae*.
Scientific name: *Hottonia inflata* Linnaeus.
Synonyms: some botanists believe this plant has been wrongly classified and call it *Proserpinaca pectinata*

H.inflata

instead.
Common name: Tropical Water Violet.
Geographical area: South-eastern United States, Venezuela.
This plant looks like a larger version of a *Myriophyllum*. It has a thick stem, with the space between the nodes being swollen, and has finely divided leaves. The thinness of the leaves varies with the amount of light they receive. The upper surface of the leaf is bright-green, while the lower half has silvery tints. This species should be planted in small, compact groups; the height of the plant should be kept down to a maximum of 30 cm (12 in) by pinching out the end of the stem, otherwise leaves will tend not to grow

further down the stem. Sexual reproduction is difficult, if not impossible in the aquarium; asexual reproduction occurs by shooting and selected shoots should be cut off at the level of a node which has adventitious roots.

■ H.palustris

pH: 6.5–7.5	Temp.: 12–20°C (54–68°F)
°dH: 5–15	Water depth: 40 cm (16 in)

Family: *Primulaceae.*
Scientific name: *Hottonia palustris* Linnaeus.
Synonyms: *Hottonia millefolium, Breviglandium palustre.*
Common name: Marsh Hottonia.
Geographical area: Europe, Siberia.
This species will grow only in a temperate aquarium or paludarium under bright light. The stem and leaves are very fragile; the leaves are finely divided between ten and forty leaf segments. The plant's height may be over 1 m (39 in) and the floral stem reaches up to 40 cm (16 in), well above the surface of the water. The flowers, of which there are three to six per stem, are pink with a yellowish base. The plant is particularly suited to a cold-water tank or outdoor pond, where sexual reproduction is quite possible. The plant may also reproduce by shooting.

HYDROCHARIS

The genus *Hydrocharis* belongs to the Hydrocharitaceae family, which includes both floating and submerged species. This genus is one of plants with floating leaves, slightly reminiscent of the Water-lilies.

■ H.morsus-ranae

pH: 6.5–7.5	Temp.: 10–20°C (50–68°F)
°dH: 5–15	Surface plant

Family: *Hydrocharitaceae.*
Scientific name: *Hydrocharis morsus-ranae* Linnaeus.

Synonyms: *Hydrocharis asarifolia, H.batrachyodegma, H.cellulosa, H.cordifolia, H.rotundifolia.*
Common name: Frog-bit; so-called because the floating leaves are bitten by frogs when insects land on them.
Geographical area: Worldwide, except America, though it was introduced to Canada by mistake in 1932 and colonized the lower reaches of the Ottawa River up to Quebec.
This is a very resilient species with bright-green, heart-shaped leaves growing on the surface of the water. The nodes of the horizontal stem grow from finely divided roots. In a

H.morsus-ranae

cold or temperate aquarium the tank should be brightly lit, as otherwise the leaves will remain in dwarf form. The plant is only likely to flower in an outdoor pond, and in an aquarium it requires an annual period of dormancy when the temperature and lighting should be turned down.

HYDROCOTYLE

The Hydrocotyles, or Marsh Pennyworts, belong to the Apiaceae family, or Umbelliferae, the same family as the carrot and the parsley. This genus includes a hundred or so species, but only three or four are grown in aquariums. Two are American (*H.leu-copetala* and *H.verticillata*), while *H.vulgaris* comes from Europe and North Africa. These species will tolerate heat and the quality of the water is not important.

H.leucopetala

■ H.leucopetala

pH: 6.2–7.0	Temp.: 22–28°C (72–82°F)
°dH: 3–10	Water depth: 30 cm (16 in)

Family: *Apiaceae.*
Scientific name: *Hydrocotyle leucopetala* Chamisso & Schlechtendahl.
Synonym: *Hydrocotyle leucocephala.*
Common name: White-petalled Hydrocotyle.
Geographical area: South America (Brazil).
The kidney-shaped leaves, fresh-green colour and adaptability to almost any situation of this species make it one of the most attractive to the aquarium enthusiast. It serves several functions: as a floating plant if allowed to develop on the surface; as a vertical one if attached by one end to the rooting medium; or even as a plant growing on the bottom of the tank if weighed down at regular intervals by small pebbles. The rapid growth of the plant can be slowed down by trimming the stems frequently, while unwanted surface leaves should also be removed regularly. The species needs a great deal of strong light. Sexual reproduction sometimes takes place in the aquarium, though multiplication by the production of shoots is very straightforward.

■ H.vulgaris

pH: 6.5–7.5	Temp.: 15–30°C (59–86°F)
°dH: 5–15	Water depth: 40 cm (16 in)

Family: *Apiaceae.*
Scientific name: *Hydrocotyle vulgaris* Linnaeus.
Synonyms: none.

Common name: Pennywort or Umbrella Plant.

Geographical area: Europe, Corsica, Sicily, Crete, Algeria.

This cold-water species has round leaves and reaches a length of between 40 and 100 cm (16 and 40 in). The distance between the nodes varies depending on the amount of light from 4 to 10 cm (1½–4 in). If the

H.verticillata

water is more than 40 cm (16 in) deep, the submerged leaves tend to stay dwarf, while floating leaves develop normally and reach about 4 cm (1½ in) in diameter. The plant does not mind high temperatures, despite its geographical origins, but if the water is very warm the lighting should be very bright. This species can also be grown in an aquaterrarium or paludarium.

HYGROPHILA

The genus *Hygrophila* belongs to the Acanthaceae family and includes some eighty to ninety species, not all of which have been definitively described and classified. Some have several varieties, and in total there are eighteen different forms known. The species with reddish or brownish leaves have not yet been described. Although the genus is found in many parts of the world, most of the species are from Asia.

H.corymbosa

■ *H.corymbosa*

pH: 6.2–7.2	Temp.: 22–27°C (72–81°F)
°dH: 3–15	Water depth: 30 cm (12 in)

Family: *Acanthaceae*.

Scientific name: *Hygrophila corymbosa* (Blume) Lindau.

Synonym: *Nomaphila stricta*.

Common names: Hygrophila, Stricta.

Geographical area: India, Malaysia, Indonesia.

This is a popular aquatic species with aquarium owners. It grows very quickly and is very adaptable. It can be planted as part of a group or on its own. The brownish stalk bears opposite lanceolate leaves 8 to 12 cm (3 to 5 in) long by 3 to 5 cm (1 to 2 in) wide. The plant will tolerate most conditions, though a pH below 6.0 may lead to dwarf leaves with brown spots. This is an excellent plant for the background or sides of a tank. The plant should be regularly trimmed and planted out. The plant reproduces by growing shoots which are obtained by cutting the top off the plant. The shoots appear laterally on the stem, which grows to about 20 cm (8 in) in height.

■ *H.difformis*

pH: 6.2–7.2	Temp.: 22–27°C (72–81°F)
°dH: 3–15	Water depth: 30 cm (12 in)

Family: *Acanthaceae*.

Scientific name: *Hygrophila difformis* (Linnaeus) Blume.

Synonyms: *Synnema triflorum, Cardanthera triflora, Ruella triflora*.

Common names: Indian Hygrophile, Synnema, False Fern, Water Wisteria.

Geographical area: Burma, Thailand, Malaysia.

This plant grows in rice fields and is very readily available to aquarium owners. Underwater leaves are finely notched and pale-green in colour. The species can be placed in a group in the middle of the tank where the water is fairly deep (over 40 cm [16 in]). It should be kept at a temperature above 24°C (75°F) or the leaves will remain dwarf. The physical and chemical conditions in which the plant is kept are relatively unimportant, but the plant should be more brightly lit than other members of the genus. If there is not enough light, the lower part of the stem loses its leaves, the length between the nodes increases and the leaves become less divided. Asexual reproduction is by the growth of lateral shoots. Leaves above the surface are dark green and the flower is dark-violet.

■ *H.polysperma*

pH: 6.5–7.5	Temp.: 16–30°C (61–86°F)
°dH: 5–15	Water depth: 35–40 cm (14–16 in)

Family: *Acanthaceae*.

Scientific name: *Hygrophila polysperma* Anders.

Synonyms: *Justica polysperma, Hemiadelphis polysperma*.

Common name: Dwarf Hygrophila.

Geographical area: India.

This is one of the easiest of all plants to keep in an aquarium. It will live in almost any degree of water hardness and any temperature from 16 to 30°C (61 to 86°F). The leaves are lanceolate and about 5 cm by 1 cm (2 in by ½ in), with a fairly short petiole; they are a soft-green colour with brownish tinges. A few plants spread over a

H.difformis

H.polysperma

small area will soon produce a dense group by growing lateral stems. These plants should be regularly cut back and thinned out. They grow quickly and are very useful for creating a curtain of greenery across the back of the tank. The only definite way of distinguishing the species from other similar ones is by the flower which appears on the leaf aerial axil. Asexual reproduction occurs with the growth of shoots. This plant tends to make the water in the aquarium acid.

■ *H.salicifolia*

pH: 6.2–7.2	Temp.: 22–25°C (72–77°F)
°dH: 3–10	Water depth: 40 cm (16 in)

Family: *Acanthaceae.*
Scientific name: *Hygrophila salicifolia* (Vahl) Nees.
Synonyms: *Ruellia salicifolia, Hygrophila angustifolia, H.assurgens, H.ciliaris, H.dimidiata, H.malabarica, H.obovata, H.radicans, H.stricta* (non Vahl).
Common name: Willow-leaf Hygrophila.
Geographical area: From southern China to Sri Lanka, plus Australia and New Zealand.
This species was known for a long time by one of its many synonyms: *H.angustifolia.* The reason for this large number of different names is the fact that it is spread over a large area of the globe and is very polymorphous. The leaves are opposed, long and thin—10 to 20 cm (4 to 8 in)

long and only 1 to 2 cm (½–¾ in) wide. They have a very short leaf-stalk and often are arched upwards. The young leaves are reddish and covered with a fine down, whilst older leaves are pale-green. Under bright light this colouring may become brown. The central vein on the upper surface of the leaf is reddish. The species reaches 80 to 100 cm (30 to 40 in) in height. The stem of the immersed form is slightly square in cross-section. In weak light and at a high temperature (over 25°C or 77°F) the distance between nodes increases considerably and the plant's decorative effect is lost. The plant should be planted on its own, not in groups, in the centre of the tank. It may also be grown in an aquaterrarium, where the aerial leaves take on an arched shape. The purple flowers appear in a crown on the axils of the aerial leaves. The plant reproduces by growing shoots.

Those which grow in cold areas will nevertheless live quite happily in temperatures over 20°C (68°F). The tropical species are rarely imported for aquarium owners.

■ *I.lacustris*

pH: 6.2–6.8	Temp.: 10–22°C (50–72°F)
°dH: 3–8	Water depth: 30 cm (12 in)

Family: *Isoetaceae.*
Scientific name: *Isoetes lacustris* Linnaeus.
Synonyms: *Isoetes macrospora, I.atrovirens, I.morei.*
Common name: Lake Isoetes.
Geographical area: Europe, western Siberia, North America.
This fern somewhat resembles a member of the *Acoraceae.* The leaves grow from a short, compact stem, varying in number with the age of the plant. A plant which is three or four years old is likely to have up to thirty leaves. These are fine and slender and grow up to 30 cm (12 in) in length. There are three known forms: *var.curvifolia,* with curved leaves, *var.rectifolia,* with straight leaves, and *var.morei,* found only in Ireland. The leaves of *I.lacustris* are pale-green and very fragile, so should be handled as little as possible. Ideally this plant should be grown in fresh water and in a shaded position in the tank. The temperature should not exceed 22°C (72°F). Reproduction is by small black spores produced by the leaf; these can be sown on damp peat.

ISOETES

This genus is represented throughout the world and consists of nearly eighty species. They are amphibious, terrestrial or aquatic ferns.

LAGAROSIPHON

This genus contains about fifteen species, all Elodea from Africa and Madagascar. These are true aquatic plants with their leaves arranged in a spiral around the stem. The best known species is *L.major*, but sometimes *L.cordofanus* from East Africa and *L.madagascariensis* are also sold here.

■ *L.major*

pH: 6.8–7.4	Temp.: 18–23°C (64–73°F)
°dH: 5–15	Water depth: 40 cm (16 in)

Family: *Hydrocharitaceae*.
Scientific name: *Lagarosiphon major* (Ridley) Moss.
Synonyms: *L.muscoides var.major, Elodea crispa*.
Common name: African Elodea, 'Crispa'.
Geographical area: Southern Africa; also naturalized in Europe.
This species is suitable for temperate, hard-water tanks. It has fine leaves, 1–2 cm by 2–3 mm (½–¼ in by ⅛ in) in a spiral around the stem. They are slightly rolled back on themselves and notched along the edges. The shape of this plant makes it slightly difficult to fit into the overall decoration of an aquarium. If the temperature goes above 22°C (72°F), the plant's growth slows down considerably and the leaves tend towards dwarfism. The plant is best grown in strong light and not very deep water. It reproduces by producing shoots.

LAGENANDRA

Species belonging to this genus are very similar to the *Cryptocorynes*, but there are differences in the morphology of the flower and leaf. The genus comes from Sri Lanka and south-west India. It is made up of twelve species, some of which can be grown submerged in an aquarium. It also includes some marsh and amphibious plants. There is one species which is very poisonous (*L.toxicaria*) and it

is possible that others, or at least their rhizomes, are also. It is therefore advisable not to grow these species in shallow water and to avoid cutting or damaging the rhizome and petioles.

■ *L.koenigii*

pH: 6.4–6.8	Temp.: 25°C (77°F)
°dH: 3–8	Water depth: 50 cm (20 in)

Family: *Araceae*.
Scientific name: *Lagenandra koenigii* (Schott) Thwaites.
Synonym: *Cryptocoryne koenigii*.
Common name: King's Lagenandra.
Geographical area: Sri Lanka and southern India.
This species is best suited to a humid paludarium or an aquaterrarium where the plant is partly submerged. The leaves are long, narrow and pale-green in colour. The plant reaches 40 to 50 cm (16 to 20 in) in height and the leaves 10 to 15 cm (4–6 in). It is quite hard to grow in an aquarium, and only flowers above water by producing a spathe. The water and growing medium should be slightly acid and the lighting of medium intensity.

L.koenigii

■ *L.lancifolia*

pH: 6.4–6.9	Temp.: 22–28°C (77–82°F)
°dH: 3–10	Water depth: 50 cm (20 in)

Family: *Araceae*.
Scientific name: *Lagenandra lancifolia* (Schott) Thwaites.
Synonyms: *Cryptocoryne lancifolia, Arum minutum*.
Common name: Spearhead Lagenandra.
Geographical area: Sri Lanka.
This marsh plant reaches a height of 50 cm (20 in) when grown underwater. The leaves are lanceolate and pale-green, 5 to 7 cm (2–3 in) long and situated on a fairly sizeable petiole which grows straight from the rhizome. This species is easily confused with some of the species belonging to the genus *Cryptocoryne*. It is best grown in an earthenware pot, as this makes it easier to change the plant's environment by moving in from the aquarium to the paludarium and vice versa. These changes should be made gradually by raising or lowering the depth of water. The water itself should be soft and acid. This species dislikes direct sunlight and if the light is too bright the leaves become reddish and grow smaller. When grown in the rooting medium of a paludarium, the plant particularly likes heating by means of a buried cable. It will only flower in a paludarium, and reproduces by growing stolons and suckers from the rhizome. The rhizome can also be split, as it should create plantlets. This means of propagation should be carried out when the plant is in a tank on its own, for the species is believed to give off a poisonous substance.

■ *L.ovata*

pH: 6.4–6.8	Temp.: 25–28°C (77–82°F)
°dH: 3–8	Water depth: 40 cm (16 in)

Family: *Araceae*.
Scientific name: *Lagenandra ovata* (Linnaeus) Thwaites.
Synonyms: *Arum ovatum, Caladium ovatum, Cryptocoryne ovata*.
Common name: Oval-spathed Lagenandra.

Geographical area: Sri Lanka, western India.

This is a very hardy marsh-growing plant with a rhizome 5 cm (2 in) thick. In a paludarium it grows to a height of 1 m (39 in). When grown underwater the leaves reach between 20 and 40 cm (8 and 16 in) in length by 7 to 12 cm (3 to 5 in) in width. The leaf is lanceolate to oval and slightly wavy. The leaf is pale- or bright-green, sometimes with tinges of reddish-brown on the upper surface; the underside is always brighter in colour. The central vein is 7 mm (½ in) wide, with many veins running off it diagonally all across the leaf. In the aquarium, only the first leaves are interesting. When the plant grows larger, the new leaves rapidly reach the surface and start growing above it. The petiole is protected by a sheath for about a third of its length. The plant reproduces spontaneously via stolons, and also often by fragmenting of the rhizome. The latter is very poisonous and should be grown in a separate tank. The plant may flower in an aquaterrarium or paludarium, but fructification can be difficult to achieve.

■ L.thwaitesii

pH: 6.4–6.8	Temp.: 24–26°C (75–79°F)
°dH: 3–8	Water depth: 50 cm (20 in)

Family: Araceae.
Scientific name: Lagenandra thwitesii Engler.
Synonyms: none.

L.thwaitesii

Common name: Thwaite's lagenandra.
Geographical area: Sri Lanka.
This species is best suited to a humid paludarium. There are two forms of leaf, one slender with crinkled edges and the other oval and slightly undulating. Both have silvery edges and a reddish petiole the same length as the leaf. In the paludarium this species of Lagenandra, which dislikes dry conditions, reaches a height of up to 45 cm (18 in). In the aquarium, however, it will grow to only half this size. The plant will live in comparatively low light, though it should not be placed in the shade.

As a rule, Lagenandras differ from Cryptocorynes partly in their flower structure, but there is also a difference in their leaves. In Lagenandra, the lower edges of the leaf meet the central vein at the stem, which is not the case with Cryptocoryne. It is worth noting that these two genera both belong to the same family.

LEMNA

The Duckweed family, or Lemnaceae, consists of six genera and about thirty species covering the whole world. The genus Lemna is widespread and consists of nine species. Unlike exotic species belonging to the genera Wolffiella, Wolffiopsis or Pseudowolffia, the Duckweeds are often unwanted 'squatters' introduced into a tank by accident via other plants or live fish-food. It is a difficult plant to get rid of and these floating plants very soon get in the way. However, they do have a number of uses, including acting as a shade against the light and a refuge for the fry of surface-dwelling fish. Plant-eating fish are fond of it and will consume it in large quantities. It reproduces mainly by producing 'discs'.

■ L.gibba

pH: 6.4–7.5	Temp.: 5–30°C (41–86°F)
°dH: 3–15	Water depth: 5 cm (2 in)

Family: Lemnaceae.
Scientific name: Lemna gibba Linnaeus.
Synonyms: Lemna trichorrhiza, Telmatophace gibba, Lenticula gibba.
Common name: Thick Duckweed.
Geographical area: Europe, Asia, America.
This is a floating plant which may be round, oval or ovoid, with a conspicuously bulging underside. The upper surface is a pale shiny green, and the whole plant is between 2 and 5 cm (1 and 2 in) high. This species has only one root and can be grown quite easily if desired. The lighting should be bright and the air beneath the lid of the tank should be humid. It is very hard to tell this species apart from L.minor when grown outside its natural habitat. It will live in virtually any conditions though it seems that a high level of nitrates helps the plant's growth. It is rare for them to flower in an aquarium although this is a species which flowers easily.

■ L.minor

pH: 6.4–7.2	Temp.: 5–30°C (41–86°F)
°dH: 3–15	Water depth: 5 cm (2 in)

Family: Lemnaceae.
Scientific name: Lemna minor Linnaeus.
Synonyms: Lemna minuta, L.cyclostasa, Lenticula vulgaris.
Common name: Lesser Duckweed.

L.minor

.minor

the surface of the water. It reproduces in a tangle of plants where several generations of Duckweed are joined together. The tiny 'leaves' are 10 to 12 mm (½ in) long and thin down into a stem joining them to another leaf. The plant reproduces more slowly than other species. The optimum temperature is 22°C (72°F), under not very bright lighting, but the plant will tolerate up to 28°C (82°F) under stronger lighting. It is particularly useful in breeding tanks or where fry are growing, and will also create a decorative carpet about a third of the way down from the surface to the bottom of the tank, as it is not a surface plant.

LILAEOPSIS

This genus contains eighteen species from South America, Australia and New Zealand. They cover substantial areas of marsh or soil, but some grow totally or partly submerged. Unfortunately, the species that are imported from New Zealand and Australia, notably *Lilaeopsis-brownii, L.gunnii, L.fistulosa, L.polyantha* and *L.novae-zelandiae* are difficult to tell apart. The latter two species are fairly common in the aquarium and *Eichinodorus tenellus* is losing ground to them as a foreground plant.

■ *L.novae-zelandiae*

pH: 6.4–7.0	Temp.: 22–26°C (72–79°F)
°dH: 3–6	Water depth: 20 cm (8 in)

Family: *Apiaceae.*
Scientific name: *Lilaeopsis novae-zelandiae* Hill.
Synonyms: *None.*
Common name: False Tennellus.
Geographical area: New Zealand, Australia.
This species is less commonly found on sale than *L.polyantha,* and is often confused with *Echinodorus tenellus.*

Geographical area: Worldwide, with the exception of the polar regions. This is the most commonly found species in aquariums. It reproduces extremely rapidly and a few plants will soon cover the entire surface of the tank. If there are any other plants in the aquarium they will not get enough light unless most of the Duckweed is removed. The plant is bright-green in colour and the disc is flat, unlike that of *L.gibba.*

Many cold water varieties are known, including *var.latiuscula,* which has a larger, pale green lanceolate lobe, and *var.leptophylla* which is light-green, oval and translucent.

■ *L.trisulca*

pH: 6.4–7.5	Temp.: 15–28°C (59–82°F)
°dH: 3–15	Water depth: 5 cm (2 in)

Family: *Lemnaceae.*
Scientific name: *Lemna trisulca* Linnaeus.
Synonyms: *Lemna cruciata, Lenticula trisulca.*
Common name: Trilobate Duckweed or Ivy-leaved Duckweed.
Geographical area: Worldwide, except Africa.
This water lentil differs from other species in that it will grow beneath

L.novae-zelandiae

L.laevigatum

It is particularly useful as a foreground decoration, reaching a height of 3 to 5 cm (1½–2 in); it also has the advantage of being comfortable in almost any type of water. In aquarium shops it is often sold in bunches of around ten plants held together with a nylon thread. The thread should be removed and the bunch split into four; this will allow the plants to cover a fairly sizeable area in a short space of time. It reproduces rapidly, using stolons, and forms a carpet of greenery. This should be thinned occasionally; the surplus can be used to start another tank. The species thrives in a paludarium. At a temperature of 20°C (68°F), the plant grows much more slowly, and at 28°C (82°F) it will grow well provided there is very bright lighting. The ideal temperature is around 25°C (77°F).

LIMNOBIUM

This genus belongs to the Hydrocharitaceae family and is found mainly in northern temperate regions.

■ L.laevigatum

pH: 6.5–7.5	Temp.: 20–30°C (68–86°F)
°dH: 3–15	Water depth: 5 cm (2 in)

Family: *Hydrocharitaceae.*
Scientific name: *Limnobium laevigatum* (Humboldt and Bonpllandt) Heine.
Synonyms: *Salvinia laevigata, Limnobium stoloniferum, Hydromistria stolonifera.*
Common name: Amazon Frogbit.
Geographical area: South and Central America, from Mexico southwards.
This is a free-floating plant though in its natural habitat it will develop roots if the water is very shallow. The leaves are arranged in a rosette and are round with a diameter of 2 to 5 cm (1–2 in). The leaves are spongy and ensure that the plant stays afloat. The upper surface of the leaves can be any colour from pale- to bright-green and it is convex, while the underside is bright green. As with most floating plants, the light and humidity below the lid of the tank should be high, though 10 cm (4 in) should be left between the plants and the light source to prevent them from burning. The plant reproduces by growing stolons. The plant often flowers in an aquarium, but produces only female flowers. *L.laevigatum* can also be grown in a paludarium provided the soil is very wet.

LIMNOPHILA

The genus *Limnophila* includes about thirty-five species, mostly from Southeast Asia, but also from Africa and Australia. In its natural habitat, the plant is amphibious and it is regarded as a weed in rice fields. About a dozen species are commonly found in aquariums, where they have great decorative value. They contrast attractively with other plants because of the distinctive shape of their submerged leaves, which are finely divided. Their rapid growth makes them more suited to medium to deep tanks, where they may be left to float on the surface for a while before taking cuttings and planting them out.

■ *L.aquatica*

pH: 6.5–7.0	Temp.: 24–26°C (75–79°F)
°dH: 5–12	Water depth: 30 cm (12 in)

Family: *Scrofulariceae*.
Scientific name: *Limnophila aquatica* Roxburgh.
Synonyms: none.
Common name: Giant Ambulia.
Geographical area: Sri Lanka, India.
The leaf crown of this plant can be up to 10 or 12 cm (4 to 5 in) in diameter. It is made up of eighteen to twenty-two finely divided leaves. The leaf segments are fine and thread-like with no conspicuous central veins. The plants do not always grow particularly well, especially those picked from the wild. Water with a low mineral content combined with bright illumination will reduce the distance between the nodes and make the plant more compact and attractive. Asexual reproduction is by lateral shoots which can be obtained by removing the head from the plant.

■ *L.aromatica*

pH: 6.4–6.8	Temp.: 20–24°C (68–75°F)
°dH: 3–8	Water depth: 30 cm (12 in)

Family: *Scofulariaceae*.
Scientific name: *Limnophila aromatica* (Lamarck) Merrill.
Synonyms: *Ambulia aromatica, Limnophila gratissima*.
Common name: Aromatic Ambulia.
Geographical area: Tropical South-East Asia.
This is a marsh-dwelling and amphibious species common in rice fields. The leaves are in opposite pairs, lanceolate and finely toothed. The stem reaches up to 50 cm (20 in) in length. This species is best suited to an aquaterrarium, where it will grow pink or purple flowers on a peduncle growing out from the leaf axils. The water should be slightly acid and the lighting kept high to preserve the attractive compactness of this plant. Sexual reproduction sometimes takes place via the flow-

L.aquatica

ers in an aquaterrarium, though it is rather more difficult to get the seeds to germinate. The stem may produce shoots if it is cut at the level of a node with adventitious roots. This species should be planted in separate groups at the back of the aquarium, or semi-submerged in the water section of an aquaterrarium.

■ *L.heterophylla*

pH: 6.5–7.0	Temp.: 22–26°C (72–79°F)
°dH: 3–8	Water depth: 30 cm (12 in)

Family: *Scofulariaceae*.
Scientific name: *Limnophila heterophylla* (Roxburgh) Bentham.
Synonyms: *Limnophila roxburghii var.tenuior, L.reflexa, Columnae heterophylla*.
Common name: Heterophyllous Ambulia.
Geographical area: India, Pakistan, Sri Lanka, southern China, Japan.
This species is recommended for the background of an aquarium, but should be grown in a single group in Dutch tanks. The leaf crown is 5 to 6 cm (2½–2¾ in) across and has between five and thirteen leaves. The ends of the segments, which are forked, are sometimes reddish in colour. The plant itself is bright-green, though the leaves of the aerial

form of the plant are darker. This aerial form has leaves 2 cm (¾ in) long with markedly toothed edges. The flower is white with purple-edged petals and grows on the axils of the leaves. In a paludarium the plant has creeping stems which produce adventitious roots. In weak light the temperature should not go above 22°C (72°F). In these conditions, the morphology of the plant remains unchanged. Asexual reproduction takes place by the growth of lateral shoots after the head has been removed from the parent plant. The *reflexa* form has leaf segments with tendrils and the underside of the leaf is a brighter colour.

■ *L.indica*

pH: 6.4–6.9	Temp.: 24–26°C (75–79°F)
°dH: 3–8	Water depth: 40 cm (16 in)

Family: *Scrofulariaceae*.
Scientific name: *Limnophila indica* (Linnaeus) Druce.
Synonyms: *Limnophila trifida, L.gratioloides, L.myriophylloides, L.elongata, Hottonia indica*.
Common name: Indian Ambulia.
Geographical area: Tropical Africa, Australia and South East Asia.
There are several varieties of this species, of which the best known

L.heterophilla

L.sessiliflora

are: var.indica, with a leaf crown 5 cm (2 in) in diameter, with six to twelve leaves, and var.elongata, whose leaf crown is about 7 cm (3 in) in diameter and has eight to ten leaves. The end of each segment is forked. The shape of aerial leaves varies considerably, being lanceolated and toothed, or feathery. The flower may be purple, pink, white or yellow. The species requires strong light and is best planted in groups. Cuttings of the plant's shoots should be taken with care, particularly when the tank is fairly shallow, as the plant appears to give off a substance which is poisonous to fish. The cutting should therefore preferably be carried out outside the aquarium and the shoot should be rinsed before planting. This precaution will ensure that there is no danger to any fish in the tank.

■ L.sessiflora

pH: 6.5–7.2	Temp.: 20–26°C (68–79°F)
°dH: 3–12	Water depth: 20 cm (8 in)

Family: Scrofulariaceae.
Scientific name: Limnophila sessiflora (Vahl) Blume.
Synonym: Hottonia sessiflora.
Common name: Sessile Ambulia.
Geographical area: India, Sri Lanka, Indonesia, Japan.
This species can be distinguished from others of the genus by the enlarged apex of the last segment of the leaf. The whorl grows to 8 or 10 cm (3 or 4 in) and the leaf is about 2 cm (¾ in) long. The species should be planted in small groups with each plant 2 or 3 cm (about an inch) away from its neighbours. L.sessiflora adapts fairly easily to most conditions. If the water is soft, the plant need only be lit to average brightness. The plant will also grow well in hard water provided the lighting is turned up. In good conditions, the distance between whorls is 2 or 3 cm (about an inch), but if the temperature is raised and the light not very strong, this distance will increase and make the plant less attractive. Reproduction is by the growth of lateral shoots, helped by removing the head of the parent plant.

LOBELIA

This genus contains more than 350 species, most of which are found in tropical and sub-tropical America. Some of the rarer and more northerly species found in the area between Florida and Mexico can be grown successfully in an aquarium. However, they are all marsh- or land-dwelling plants.

■ L.cardinalis

pH: 6.5–7.2	Temp.: 20–30°C (68–86°F)
°dH: 5–15	Water depth: 30 cm (12 in)

Family: Lobeliaceae.
Scientific name: Lobelia cardinalis Linnaeus.
Synonym: Rapuntium cardinale.
Common name: Cardinal Lobelia.
Geographical area: North America.
This is a land-dwelling species which can be grown in a pot, but will also live fairly happily in an aquarium or paludarium, where it reaches a height of 20 to 30 cm (8 to 12 in). The leaves are bright-green, spatulate and 4 to 6 cm (1½–2½ in) by 2 to 3 cm (1 in). The aerial form may reach 120 cm (48 in) in height with leaves 15 cm (6 in) long. In an aquarium, the plant should be kept in temperate water between 18 and 20°C (64 and 68°F), while in a tropical tank the higher temperature should be accompanied

L.cardinalis

by brighter light. Because the plant grows fairly slowly, it tends to get covered in algae such as Composopogon, Dedogonium or Audouinella. The species should be arranged in small groups of three to four stalks in the centre of the tank. Reproduction may take place by the production of seedlings from the red flower, which appears only when part of the flower is above the water, but also by growing shoots if the top of the stalk is pinched out to encourage adventitious roots.

LUDWIGIA

L.palustris has been the main species belonging to this genus to be found in aquariums since 1894. Although the genus is spread throughout the world, it is found mainly in America. The plants can only be distinguished from one another by their flowers, and this is made even more difficult by the presence of hybrids such as L.repens X L.palustris and L.repens X L.arcuata. Ludwigia are excellent plants for the tropical or temperate aquarium.

■ L.alternifolia

pH: 6.5–7.0	Temp.: 20–25°C (68–77°F)
°dH: 3–8	Water depth: 30 cm (12 in)

Family: *Onagraceae*.
Scientific name: *Ludwigia alternifolia* Linnaeus.
Synonyms: *Isnardia alternifolia, Ludwigia macrocarpa, L.microcarpa, L.ramosissima*.
Common name: Alternate-leaved Ludwigia.
Geographical area: East coast of the United States.
This is an amphibious species found in marshes. The leaves are alternate (not opposite, as many works on aquarium plants have stated), lanceolate, narrow and very pointed. They reach 3 to 5 cm (1 to 2 in) in length by 10 to 15 mm (½ to ¼ in) wide. The edges and undersides of the leaves are wrinkled. The upper surface is a brownish-green colour whilst the underside also has reddish tinges to it. The length of the internodes varies a great deal depending on how well the plant is lit. In the aquarium it should be arranged in small groups with enough space between them for the leaves not to shade each other from the light. The temperature of the water should not exceed 25°C (77°F). The plant cannot be kept in a paludarium. The flowers are very small and grow on the axils of the leaves. Reproduction takes place via shoots.

■ L.brevipes

pH: 6–7	Temp.: 20–25°C (68–77°F)
°dH: 3–15	Water depth: 40 cm (16 in)

L.brevipes

Family: *Onagraceae*.
Scientific name: *Ludwigia brevipes* (Long) Eames.
Synonym: *Ludwigiantha brevipes*.
Common name: False Lysimachia.
Geographical area: South-eastern United States.
This is a very difficult species to grow submerged. The leaves are bright-green on both sides and the stalk is brownish or red. The underwater leaves are long and thin, about 3 cm by ½ cm (1½ by ¼ in) but out of the water they are fairly short and heart-shaped. In both cases the leaves are opposite and decussate (arranged in pairs, each pair at right angles to those above and below it). The space between the internodes on the submerged part of the plant is large.

The plant is well suited to a paludarium, where it tends to creep. The flower is yellow and grows on the leaf axils. The temperature of the water should not be too high; 25°C (77°F) is the maximum.

From spring to autumn, this species makes a good decoration for the edges of garden ponds and will quickly take over that part of the bank which is above the water level. Sexual reproduction is possible, albeit difficult. Asexual reproduction will take place without any problems: once the top of the stalk has been pinched out, adventitious roots soon develop on the axils of the petioles. When the latter are cut off they can be planted in the growing medium as shoots.

■ L.palustris

pH: 6.5–7.4	Temp.: 18–25°C (64–77°F)
°dH: 3–15	Water depth: 30 cm (12 in)

Family: *Onagraceae*.
Scientific name: *Ludwigia palustris* (Linnaeus) Elliot.

Synonyms: *Isnardia palustris, Dantia palustris, Ludwigia petala, L.nitida, Quadricosta palustris*.
Common name: Marsh Ludwigia.
Geographical area: North America, North Africa, Asia, Europe (particularly Greece, near Corfu).
This is a marsh-dwelling species which forms a red carpet on the surface of the water. The leaves are attached directly to the stem by a very short petiole. The upper surface is a vivid-green colour, whilst the underside is darker and tends towards being reddish in low light. The leaves are 3 cm (1½ in) by 1.5 cm (¼ in) wide. Considerable numbers of adventitious roots are produced from the leaf axils. The species adapts well to being grown underwater and also to differing types of water and temperatures, though the water should not be more than 25°C (77°F). Strong lighting is recommended. This plant should be arranged in groups of four to six which should regularly have their tops pruned to retain their bushy appearance. Under these conditions, a fairly large number of lateral shoots should appear; when these have had a chance to develop, they can be cut off and planted out. L.palustris is recommended for a temperate paludarium, but they are not as attractive as some other species for aquariums.

■ L.repens

pH: 6.5–7.5	Temp.: 20–30°C (68–86°F)
°dH: 5–15	Water depth: 30 cm (12 in)

L.repens

Family: *Onagraceae*.
Scientific name: *Ludwigia repens* Forster.
Synonyms: *Ludwigia fluitans, L.mulertii, Isnardia natans, Ludwigia natans*.
Common name: Red Ludwigia.
Geographical area: Southern United States, Central America, parts of the Caribbean.

This species is very polymorphous from one area to another. No proper description has yet been made of the various sub-species and geographical varieties. To add to the confusion surrounding these different forms, there are a number of 'cross-breeds' on the market, which are self-fertilizing and almost disconcertingly easy to grow immersed. *L.repens* has two leaf forms: one with round leaves slightly longer than they are wide, and the other lanceolate and pointed and sometimes slightly wavy. These two forms also appear in different colours: sometimes they are green and sometimes red. This species dislikes very high temperatures, though it will tolerate up to 28 or 30°C (82 to 86°F). Sexual reproduction from the self-fertilizing flower can be helped using a brush to pollinate it. Asexual reproduction can be achieved by cutting the stalk at the level of an internode which has adventitious roots on its upper part.

LYSIMACHIA

This genus is widely represented throughout the globe, and consists of 200 or so species. Some of these are occasionally imported for aquarium use, such as *L:vul-*

L.nummularia

garis and *L.nummularia*. They belong to the Primula family and are often also known as or Loosestrife.

■ L.nummularia

pH: 6.5–7.5	Temp.: 15–22°C (59–72°F)
°dH: 5–15	Water depth: 30 cm (12 in)

Family: *Primulaceae*.
Scientific name: *Lysimachia nummularia* Linnaeus.
Synonyms: *Lysimachia nemorum, L.repens, L.rotundifolia, L.suaveolens, L.zavadeskii, Ephemerum nummularium, Nummularia centimorbia, N.officinalis, N. prostrata, N.repens*.
Common name: Moneywort, Creeping Jenny.
Geographical area: Europe, east coast United States, Japan.

This plant is found in ditches, on riverbanks and in marshes and wet grassland. The shoots can easily be transplanted from plants growing on land into an aquarium. The stalk bears opposite leaves on a short petiole. They are bright green, round and about 2 cm (¾ in) across. The temperature should not go above 22°C (72°F) and the plant should be kept in very bright light. It is best suited to a cold or temperate aquarium or to the banks of a garden pond. In a tropical aquarium with a temperature above 23°C (73°F) the plant will soon die. It is fairly hardy in a temperate paludarium and will quickly cover any space which is left free.

MARSILEA

This is a genus of amphibious ferns, similar to *Pillularia* and *Regnellidium*. There are about sixty-five species with creeping rhizomes which divide in the reproductive process. Very few of these species can

be kept in an aquarium; exceptions are *Marsilea crenata, M.drummondii, M.exarata* and, less frequently, *M.quadrifolia*, though none of these is easy to maintain. The leaves take various forms but are divided into four lobes; hence the common name of Marsh Trefoil or Clover. *M.quadrifolia* is unfortunately threatened with extinction in Europe.

These various species can only be told apart by their immersed form and their spores. When immersed, the leaves close up at night. The rhizome creeps along the ground and produces a number of fronds which, if there is sufficient light, will reach the surface of the water. Ideally, they should be grown in reasonably soft water which is slightly acid. Eventually, the plant will turn yellow and die soon afterwards. In a paludarium the fronds grow slightly longer.

MAYACA

This genus is the only member of the Mayacaceae family. It contains about ten species from tropical and sub-tropical South America and one from south-west Africa. They are all ground-rooted plants with linear leaves grouped in a spiral around the stalk.

■ M.fluviatilis

pH: 6.4–7.0	Temp.: 22–28°C (72–82°F)
°dH: 3–8	Water depth: 40 cm (16 in)

Family: *Mayacacae*.
Scientific name: *Mayaca fluviatilis* Aublet.

Synonym: *Mayaca vandellii.*
Common name: Marsh Moss.
Geographical area: Guyana, French Guiana, Brazil.
This species has a very fragile stalk with alternate leaves arranged in a spiral. The leaf is straight and pointed, 1 to 2 cm (½–¾ in) by 0.1 to 0.2 cm (¹⁄₁₆ in) and yellowish-green in colour. This plant should be arranged in groups (not too crowded) in the front or centre of the tank. Each group should be well away from all the others, as it is very important that they receive enough light. The best water for the plant is soft and acidic; carbon dioxide diffusion makes it easier to grow the plant in harder water. This species does not like medicinal substances added to the water for the fish. It reproduces by shooting.

MICROSORIUM

This genus is made up of nearly forty species, though only one is commonly kept in aquariums.

▪ *M.pteropus*

pH: 6.5–7.8	Temp.: 23–30°C (72–86°F)
°dH: 5–20	Water depth: 40 cm (16 in)

Family: *Polypodiaceae.*
Scientific name: *Microsorium pteropus* (Blume) Ching.
Synonym: *Polypdium pteropus.*
Common name: Java fern.
Geographical area: Widespread in South-East Asia and China.
This is a very useful plant for aquarium owners, particularly if plant-eating fish are kept, as it provides decoration for tanks in which other water plants would not be able to survive. The tough leaf tissue and probably also its unpleasant taste, mean that plant-eating fish will not touch it. The fronds are pale-green or brownish and grow from a creeping rhizome. They grow to 25 or 30 cm (10 or 12 in) in height and 5 or 7 cm (2 to 3 in) in width. The lamina is undivided, with undulating edges. The rhizome should never be buried; instead it should be attached to a root, a rock or part of the

M.pteropus

aquarium decorations using a nylon thread or paper clip. The fern will then attach itself using the roots which appear along the rhizome. It will survive in almost any kind of water, including water with a high pH and low carbon dioxide. It requires medium to strong lighting. It should also grow well in a paludarium provided the humidity is high enough. Asexual reproduction occurs via lateral stalks which grow from the rhizome and adventitious plantlets which grow on the undersides of the leaves.

MYRIOPHYLLUM

About forty species make up this genus; all are aquatic or amphibious and the genus is found throughout the world. Those species which are used in aquariums all have whorls of leaves with straight segments. They are delicate and have considerable decorative value, but should not be grown in tanks containing any fish which eat plants, as the young leaf shoots are very tender and fish like eating them. The water should be either soft and acidic or hard and alkaline, depending on where the species comes from. However, Myriophyllums adapt well to most conditions. They are best suited to the background of a Dutch tank but can also contrast attractively with other groups of plants as different species are different colours. They can be difficult to grow because strong lighting and carbon dioxide diffusion are a prerequisite. The choice of fish should also be made carefully. Although an air diffuser will usually kill them, gently-moving water, or fish which create currents in the water are actually good for them, as they help to keep them free of the microscopic parasites which lodge in their fine, ferny leaves.

■ *M.alterniflorum*

pH: 6.5–7.2	Temp.: 15–22°C (59–72°F)
°dH: 2–8	Water depth: 30 cm (12 in)

Family: *Haloragaceae*.
Scientific name: *Myriophyllum alterniflorum* de Candolle.
Synonyms: *Myriophyllum alternifolium, M.montanum*.
Common name: Alternate-flowered Milfoil.
Geographical area: Temperate and cold areas of Europe, North America and North Africa.
This species has widely-spaced whorls and jagged leaf segments. Each whorl consists of four (occasionally three) leaves, each about 25 mm (1 in) long. The stalk can be anything between 50 and 150 cm (20 and 60 in) long, though in an aquarium it is best to restrict this length to 30 cm (16 in) by pinching out the ends of the stalks. The flowers grow on an aerial spike; the lower ones are female and the upper ones male. The plant will flower in a European tank with soft cold water (8 °dH) and is particularly recommended for keeping and breeding sticklebacks (*Gasterosteus, Puntgitius*) which use it to build their nests. If the ends of the stems are pinched out regularly, there will be a considerable increase in the growth of lateral shoots, some of which can be used to reproduce the plant.

■ *M.aquaticum*

pH: 6.4–7.0	Temp.: 22–28°C (72–82°F)
°dH: 3–8	Water depth: 40 cm (16 in)

Family: *Haloragaceae*.
Scientific name: *Myriophyllum aquaticum* Verdcourt.
Synonyms: *Myriophyllum brasiliense, M.proserpinacoides*.

M.aquatica

Common name: Water Milfoil.
Geographical area: Brazil, Argentina, Uruguay, Chile; also introduced to the southern United States.
This is a very good species with which to decorate a tropical tank. It reaches anything between 50 and 150 cm (20 and 60 in) in height, with a whorl made up of four to six leaves, each divided into eight to ten bright-green segments. In strong light, the ends of the segments turn slightly reddish. The plant likes soft, acidic water and medium to strong lighting. The stems should not be planted too close together; nor should they be trimmed too often. When part of the plant reaches the surface, several lateral stalks appear and these can be planted out when they have reached a resonable length. Under the right lighting conditions, aerial leaves will grow above the surface.

■ *M.heterophyllum*

pH: 6.5–7.2	Temp.: 18–25°C (64–77°F)
°dH: 5–15	Water depth: 40 cm (16 in)

Family: *Haloragaceae*.
Scientific name: *Myriophyllum heterophyllum* Michaux.
Synonym: *Potamogeton verticillatum*.

Common name: Heterophyllous Milfoil.
Geographical area: South-eastern United States, northern Mexico.
Although this is a very hardy species, it is rarely imported for use in the aquarium. Each whorl consists of four to six leaves divided into anything between ten and twenty-six segments which can quite easily reach a height of 5 cm (2 in). There is also a second form, with leaves only 2 cm (¾ in) long. The aerial leaves can be either lanceolate or spatulate but are never finely divided. The flowers, which are very small, grow on the axils of the leaves. The male flowers are on the upper part and the female on the lower. The plant grows fairly slowly. The maximum temperature should be 25°C (77°F), though temperate aquariums of 18°C (64°F) and upwards are equally suitable. Vegetative reproduction using shoots is relatively difficult because both adult plants and shoots take a long time to grow roots.

■ *M.hippuroides*

pH: 6.5–7.2	Temp.: 20–25°C (68–77°F)
°dH: 5–15	Water depth: 40 cm (16 in)

Family: *Haloragaceae*.
Scientific name: *Myriophyllum hippuroides* Nuttal ex Torrey Gray.
Synonyms: *Myriophyllum scabatum* Cham et Schle, non Mich. et *M.mexicanum*.
Common name: Red Florida Milfoil.
Geographical area: Southern United States and Mexico.
This plant should be arranged in small groups in a temperate tank. The whorl consists of four to six leaves. The petioles of any one whorl are not necessarily at the same level on the stalk. The leaf is 5 cm (2 in) long and divided into six to ten closely-set segments. Under strong light the species turns reddish or brown, particularly at its tips. The leaves and their segments generally point upwards. Algae and particles suspended in the water can rapidly take over the whole plant; this can be avoided by strong filtration and the use of fish which keep the water moving. Asexual reproduction is by lateral shoots.

● *M.spicatum*

pH: 6.6–7.5	Temp.: 22–28°C (72–82°F)
°dH: 5–15	Water depth: 30 cm (12 in)

Family: *Haloragaceae*.
Scientific name: *Myriophyllum spicatum* Linnaeus.
Synonyms: *Pentapteris spicanuda, Potamogeton foliis-pennatis, Myriophyllum spicanuda*.
Common name: Spiked Milfoil.
Geographical area: Widespread in Central and South America, tropical Africa and Australia. Also introduced to North America (California, Texas, Florida).
This is a very robust species which grows up to 3 m (9 ft 9 in) in its natural habitat. On a stem 2 to 4 mm (⅛ to ¼ in) in diameter, the internode may be 5 cm (2 in). The whorl consists of four to five leaves (occasionally only three), each 3.5 cm (1½ in) long and divided into thirteen to thirty-six segments. The plant therefore looks as though it has a hairy, tangled stem. Tiny, pink inflorescences of four to six flowers grow on the immersed part of the stem. The leaf covering these flowers is not divided. The species will support high temperatures of between 24 and 28°C (75 and 82°F) and hard, alkaline water. The ends of the stems should be regularly trimmed so as to keep this plant small and compact. In common with the other species of the genus, reproduction is by cuttings from the lateral shoots.

● *M.verticillatum*

pH: 6.8–7.5	Temp.: 18–23°C (64–73°F)
°dH: 3–10	Water depth: 40 cm (16 in)

Family: *Haloragaceae*.
Scientific name: *Myriophyllum verticillatum* Linnaeus.
Synonyms: *Myriophyllum spicatum* Gmelin, *M.limosum, M.siculum*.
Common name: Whorled Milfoil.
Geographical area: Europe, Asia (from Iran to Japan), North America, North Africa.
This species only lives underwater and can reach 3 m (9 ft 9 in) in length. The whorls are very tightly-packed and consist of five leaves (occasional-

ly four or six) divided into twenty to thirty-five thread-like segments. The leaves covering the floral spike, which bears anything between ten and twenty-five flowers, are even more finely divided than the submerged ones. The upper flowers are male and the lower ones female. This Milfoil prefers cool, fairly soft water and bright light. Asexual reproduction can be started by removing the top of the stem; this will produce lateral shoots which can be planted as cuttings.

NAJAS

All fifty species making up this genus, which are widespread throughout the world, are aquatic. The flowers always remain submerged and the female flowers are pollinated beneath the surface. Only two or three species are commonly found in aquariums, most notably *N.indica* and *N.guadelupensis*. The latter is found only in America and the Caribbean islands. The species can only be distinguished by looking at the plants when they are fertilized, though there are some features such as the length of the leaf and the number and size of the denticles on the edges of the leaf which mean that they can be identified with a reasonable degree of confidence.

● *N.indica*

pH: 6.5–6.8	Temp.: 24–28°C (75–82°F)
°dH: 3–8	Water depth: 30 cm (12 in)

Family: *Najadaceae*.
Scientific name: *Najas indica* (Willedenow) Chamisso.
Synonyms: *Caulinia indica, Fluvialis indica, Najas minor var.indica, N.tenuis, N.kingii*.
Common name: Indian Najad.
Geographical area: Tropical Asia.
The stem of this and other species of the genus breaks very easily, which is why it is not often imported. The plant should never be taken home in newspaper, but in a plastic bag which has been blown up with air and had a little water placed in it. The leaves are bright-green and opposite (sometimes grouped in threes), and form a pseudo-whorl. The leaf is up to 2.5 or 3 cm (1 to 1¼ in) long and 0.2 to 0.3 mm (¹⁄₉₀ in) wide. The edge has ten to twenty denticles. Planting should be done extremely carefully because of the fragility of the stalk, and each one should be planted individually, not in a group. The internode will remain short provided it is brightly lit; if planted in a shady position or too close to other plants, the leaves will drop off the lower part of the stalk. In hard water, carbon dioxide diffusion is essential. The temperature should be kept between 24 and 28°C (75 and 82°F). The best shoots for planting out have reached a length of 10 to 15 cm (4 to 6 in).

NITELLA

A few rare species belonging to this genus are found in aquariums. The genera *Nitella* and *Chara* together form an intermediate stage between lower plants (algae and mosses) and higher ones. The genus is found throughout the world and contains approximately eighty species.

● *N.gracilis*

pH: 7.0–7.5	Temp.: 15–25°C (59–77°F)
°dH: 5–10	Water depth: 20 cm (8 in)

Family: *Characeae*.
Scientific name: *Nitella gracilis* (Smith) Agardh.

Synonyms: *Chara gracilis, Ch.exilis, Ch.capitata.*
Common name: Slender Nitella.
Geographical area: Worldwide, except Australia.
This is a fairly fragile, very decorative species which grows to a height of 20 cm (8 in). The leaves are very divided and joined to the stem by a fairly long petiole. The female sexual organs are at the level of each division of the leaf. The plant grows slowly and any sudden change in the environment could harm it severely. The water should therefore be no harder than 8–10 °dH, with the pH over 7. The plant has no particular requirements as to temperature, except that it should not exceed 25°C (77°F). When the light is bright, there is a risk of the plant becoming covered in algae and it is therefore a good idea to keep fish in the tank which will eat the algae. This species is particularly recommended as a decoration for shallow tanks. The plant can be reproduced by removing the spores from the aquarium, drying them out for a while, and then putting them back into an aquarium beneath 2 or 3 cm (about an inch) of water and away from direct light.

NYMPHEA

The Nymphaea, or Water-lilies, are particularly suitable for decorating garden ponds. They include a number of horticultural varieties.
In the aquarium, however, only those species which are tropical and which reach a reasonable size can be used. Of these, by far the most suitable is *Nymphea lotus*, of which there are several varieties. Another species, *N.stellata* (Indian Water lily) can be grown successfully.

■ *N.lotus*

pH: 6.5–7.2	Temp.: 22–28°C (72–82°F)
°dH: 2–8	Water depth: 40 cm (16 in)

Family: *Nymphaeaceae.*
Scientific name: *Nymphaea lotus* Linnaeus.
Synonyms: *Castalia thermalis, Nymphea dentata.*
Common names: Egyptian Lotus, Tiger Lotus (depending on variety).
Geographical area: Africa and Asia.
This Water-lily can be used as the main plant of the aquarium. When submerged, the leaves are dark-red to brownish for the *rubra* variety and green with brown stripes for *var. viridis*. Both varieties can be found on their own or together in their natural habitat. There are also different leaf-forms, which are 'cross-breeds' of different colours, the colour varying with the intensity of the light in which the plant is grown. The plant can also be used as the centrepiece of a Dutch tank. In the tank it should be placed slightly off-centre. It produces surface leaves which should be cut back, as otherwise the submerged leaves will not grow from the rhizome. If flowers are desired, the leaves should simply be allowed to grow to the surface. The flower is about 10 cm (4 in) across, has a very short lifespan and only opens at night. Asexual reproduction occurs with the production of stolons from the rhizome.

N.lotus

N.stellata

N.lotus

NYMPHOIDES

This genus, containing about twenty-five species, is represented mainly in tropical and sub-tropical areas of the world. They grow almost exclusively surface leaves and flowering takes place above the surface. The genus belongs to the Menyanthaceae family along with three other genera: *Menyanthes*, *Liparophyllum*, *Nephrophyllidium* and *Villarsia*. Several of these False Water-Lilies, as they are called, are currently grown by aquarium enthusiasts, including *N. aquatica*, the Banana Plant, which has tubers containing nutrition for the plant and is very similar to *N.cordata*. Sometimes species from New Guinea can be found on sale: these include *N.parviflora* and *N.hydriocharoides*, which have white or yellow flowers depending on their variety. These are some of the few plants where it is advisable to add extra nutriment to the growing medium, as the surface leaves cannot gain any from the water and it is therefore up to the roots to feed the plant.

■ *N.humboldtiana*

pH: 6.4–6.8	Temp.: 22–26°C (75–79°F)
°dH: 3–8	Water depth: 40 cm (16 in)

Family: *Menyanthaceae*.
Scientific name: *Nymphoides humboldtiana* (Kunth) O. Kuntz.
Synonyms: *Villarsia humboldtiana, V.communis, V.platyphylla, Limnanthemum humboldtianum, Menthanthes brasilica, M.Indica* Aublet, *M.meridionalis*.
Common name: Humboldt's False Water-lily.

Geographical area: Tropical America.
This plant is particularly good as surface cover for a medium-depth tank, as its leaves are 15 cm (6 in) in diameter and will considerably cut down the light in a South American tank. The leaf is round to heart-shaped, often wider than it is long. The upper side of the leaf is pale-green and shiny, whilst the underside is rough and reddish in colour. The petioles can reach 1 m (39 in) in length. This species is quite fragile and should be kept in soft water no harder than 3 to 8 °dH. In harder water the leaves will remain in dwarf form. Flowering takes place above the water and the white flower has five petals with fine hairs on them. The plant is sometimes found on sale with one leaf and a few roots. The roots should be buried in the bottom of the tank and the leaf should initially be given plenty of light if it is to reach its proper size.

N.humboldtiana

■ *N.indica*

pH: 6.5–7.2	Temp.: 20–28°C (68–82°F)
°dH: 3–15	Water depth: 40 cm (16 in)

Family: *Menyanthaceae*.
Scientific name: *Nymphoides indica* (Linnaeus) O. Kuntz.
Synonyms: many, including *Menyanthes indica, M.petioliflora, Villarsia eglandulosa, Nymphoides eckloniana, N.orbiculata, N.thunbergiana, Limnanthemum calycinum*.
Common name: False Indian Water-lily.

Geographical area: Throughout the tropics, with different sub-species from one continent to another.
This is a much hardier plant than the previous one. It is a perennial which may grow up to 1 m (39 in) in height, depending on the depth of water in the aquarium. The surface leaves can be anything between 5 and 20 cm (2 and 8 in) across, and are round or slightly lanceolate with a heart-shaped base. A flower or adventitious plantlet may develop on the axil of a surface leaf. The leaf has fine, dark veins. The plant may reproduce sexually via seeds, but it is very easy to obtain asexual reproduction. This is done by placing a surface leaf in a small terrarium with a damp substratum. The whole surface of the leaf should be in contact with the substratum. Roots will grow from the underside of the leaf, and then new leaves will develop. Both the growing medium and the air should always be humid. When two or three leaves have developed, the water level can be increased as the plant continues to grow.

■ *N.peltata*

pH: 6.5–7.2	Temp.: 18–24°C (64–75°F)
°dH: 3–10	Water depth: 40 cm (16 in)

Family: *Menyanthaceae*.
Scientific name: *Nymphoides peltata* (Gmelin) O. Kuntz.
Synonyms: many, including *Limnanthemum nymphaeoides, Nymphoides europae, N.orbiculata* Gilibert, *Waldschmidia nymphoides, Schweykerta nymphoides*.
Common name: Peltate False Water-lily or Water Fringe.
Geographical area: Europe, Asia, China, Japan.
This is a very hardy species which can be used to decorate garden ponds. The rhizome sometimes grows to 2 m (6 ft 6 in) in length, and the internodes are between 7 and 20 cm (3 to 8 in) long. This species grows submerged leaves which are small and heart-shaped and grow near the rhizome on stalks which are shorter than those of the surface leaves. The surface leaves are bright-green with blackish spots of different shapes and sizes on their upper surfaces. The underside is reddish with tinges

of violet. The flower is funnel-shaped, divided into five yellow, villous petals. The plant is particularly suited to cold or temperate tanks; as with the previous species, the growing medium should be slightly enriched by mixing in a few small granules of baked clay.

ORYZA

Unlikely though it may sound, rice actually makes a very good decoration for an aquarium or aquaterrarium. Because it is grown as a crop, it is widespread throughout the world and exists in several different forms. It is also possible to find a False Rice, *Leesia oryzoïdes*, spread across most of Europe although this is not common.

■ *O.sativa*

pH: 6.5–7.5	Temp.: 20–28°C (68–82°F)
°dH: 3–15	Water depth: 30 cm (12 in)

Family: *Gramineae*.
Scientific name: *Oryza sativa* Linnaeus.
Synonyms: *Oryza subulata, O.denudata, O.communissima*.
Common name: Rice.
Geographical area: Originally from tropical Asia: introduced to warm climates throughout the world, where it has reverted to the wild state.
This is an annual plant which can grow to 1.5 m (5 ft) in height with linear leaves 30 to 55 cm (12 to 22 in) long. There are many decorative forms, but some of these are infertile. The most unusual are those with red leaves, such as the *atropurpurea hort* and *rufibarbis* varieties. It is perfectly possible to grow good,

strong plants from seed, particularly paddy rice. The seeds are sown on the top of the substratum and covered with 1 or 2 cm (½ or 1 in) of water. This little 'greenhouse' should be heated to 25°C (77°F) and covered to ensure a high level of humidity. The seeds take a week to germinate. When the plants reach a height of 10 cm (4 in), which happens quickly if the light is strong enough, they can be transferred to a shallow aquarium 20 or 30 cm (8 to 12 in) deep or an Asian regional aquaterrarium. The plants make a good background decoration and the young plants can also be grown on the edges of an outdoor pond from June to September, but they will not flower in northern Europe.

OTTELIA

This genus is found throughout the tropics and includes about forty species. They live in slightly-shaded forest locations and open marshland and flower easily with self-fertilizing flowers. Unfortunately, they are sensitive to changes in conditions and are annual plants, so they do not live for very long.

■ *O.alismoides*

pH: 6.4–6.8	Temp.: 20–25°C (68–77°F)
°dH: 3–8	Water depth: 30 cm (12 in)

Family: *Hydrocharitaceae*.
Scientific name: *Otelia alismoides* (Linnaeus) Persoon.
Synonyms: *Stratiotes alismoides, Damasonium indicum, Hymentheca latifolia, Ottelia indica, O.lactucaefolia, O.lanceolata*.
Common name: Ottelia alisma.
Geographical area: Tropical and subtropical Asia and Australia; North Africa (Egypt); southern Italy.
Although it is less demanding than other species of this genus, *O.alismoides* is difficult to acclimatize and is impossible to grow in hard water. It is therefore only suited to a

specific soft-water aquarium. The leaves are 10 to 20 cm (4 to 8 in) long, round to heart-shaped with extremely undulating edges. The petiole is triangular and denticulate. In older plants, the leaf becomes trumpet- or funnel-shaped. Under perfect conditions (strong light and the addition of carbon dioxide) the plant will reach 35 cm (14 in) in height. Fish that create currents in the water should be avoided because it is so delicate; it is also much liked by snails as a source of food. The plant will only reproduce sexually but even this happens very rarely.

PILULARIA

The Pilularia are ferns belonging to the Pilulariaceae family. They are found in temperate and sub-tropical areas.

■ *P.globulifera*

pH: 6.5–6.9	Temp.: 20–25°C (68–77°F)
°dH: 3–8	Water depth: 20 cm (8 in)

Family: *Pilulariaceae*.
Scientific name: *Pilularia globulifera*.
Synonym: *Pilularia natans*.
Common name: Globular pilularia.
Geographical area: Europe and North Africa.
This is a very hardy marsh-dwelling fern. Despite its geographical origin, it can be kept in a warm-water aquarium or aquaterrarium up to a temperature of 25°C (77°F). The fronds are cylindrical and reach 30 cm (12 in) in length when underwater. The plant grows rapidly and forms a green carpet of fronds growing from a creeping rhizome. Asexual reproduction also takes place by the division of the rhizome, which means that it can be grown in groups spread around the tank. Strong lighting and carbon dioxide diffusion are essential. The water should be soft

and slightly acidic. In an aquaterrarium or humid terrarium, the leaves will not grow beyond 10 cm (4 in).

PISTIA

This genus belongs to the Araceae family. It contains only one species, which has been classified in different ways at different times. It is a floating plant spread across large areas of the world, though it does not expand as rapidly as the Water Hyacinth. Where the two plants grow together, *Pistia* will always come off worse.

■ *P.stratiotes*

pH: 6.5–7.5	Temp.: 20–30°C (68–86°F)
°dH: 5–15	Surface plant

Family: *Araceae*.
Synonyms: many, including *Pistia aegyptica, P.commutata, P.linguaeformis, P.brasiliensis, Apiospermum obcordatum, Limnonesis commutata, Kiamba kitsii*.
Common names: Water Lettuce, Pistia.
Geographical area: Tropical and subtropical regions.
This floating plant has a dense network of roots which are black in the adult state and white when young. The leaves are arranged in spirals and rosettes. They grow to a length of 25 cm (10 in) by 10 cm (4 in) wide. They take various forms: some are shell-shaped and some spoon-shaped. The surface of the leaf is downy, bright-green on the upper surface and whitish-green on the lower. There are five to fifteen convex veins arranged in parallel. It is a very attractive plant which requires strong light in the form either of direct sunlight or a fluorescent lamp. The plant multiplies very rapidly with

P.stratiotes

plantlets growing from a stolon. The flowers are very small and appear on the leaf axils. It is a surface plant which can be used, for example, on the surface of an Amazonian tank, although it will cut out much of the very bright light which submerged species need for growth.

PONTEDERIA

Species belonging to this genus are not often seen in aquariums. The most common is *P.cordata*, which has many different leaf forms. The genus belongs to the Pontederiaceae family along with the Heteranthera and Water Hyacinth.

■ *P.cordata*

pH: 6.5–7.5	Temp.: 20–28°C (68–82°F)
°dH: 5–15	Water depth: 40 cm (16 in)

Family: *Pontederiaceae*.
Scientific name: *Pontederia cordata* Linnaeus.
Synonym: *Pontederia sagittata*.
Common names: Pickerel Weed.
Geographical area: Shallow pools throughout North America.
This is a perennial, marsh-dwelling plant which is amphibious and grows up to 1.5 m (5 ft) in height. Many different leaf forms have been described, amongst them *angustifolia, ovalis, sagittata* and *brasiliensis*. Depending on the variety, the leaves may be lanceolate, heart-shaped, oval or with wavy edges. They vary between 10 and 40 cm (4 and 16 in) in length by 2 to 20 cm (1 to 8 in) wide. In all cases, the base of the blade is always more or less cordate. The leaves can be bright or pale-green and the central vein is very conspicu-

ous at the base of the leaf. It has violet flowers, though the uppermost ones are yellow. They are arranged on a spike, supported and protected by a leaf or bract, which is trumpet-shaped. This plant is best suited to aquaterrariums between 20 and 30 cm (8 and 12 in) deep. The humidity level should be kept high to ensure that the stems and the edges of the leaves do not dry out. The plant needs bright light. Specimens from North America can be kept outdoors in ponds. The plant reproduces by division of the rhizome.

POTAMOGETON

There are currently more than one hundred known species in this genus, which is found throughout the world. Some are wholly tropical while others are also found in Europe. They are often difficult to maintain. In the long-term, those which are solely tropical are easier to grow in an aquarium. This is the case, for example, with *P.gayi*, *P.malaianus* and *P.ortandrus*. The inflorescence grows above water and usually consists of a cylindrical spike.

■ *P.gayii*

pH: 6.5–7.2	Temp.: 22–26°C (72–79°F)
°dH: 3–15	Water depth: 50 cm (20 in)

Family: *Potamagetonaceae*.
Scientific name: *Potamogeton gayi* Bennet.
Synonym: *Potamogeton aschersonii*.
Common name: Gay's Potamogeton.
Geographical area: South America.
This is a slender, fast-growing plant, best suited to the background of a deep-water tank. The stem is thin and fragile with alternate, straight leaves and no petioles. They are bright-green in colour, 10 cm (4 in) long by 0.5 cm (¼ in) wide. A central

vein extends from the base of the leaf, with a lateral vein on either side which is often invisible to the naked eye. The young runners often take some time to take root and acclimatize. However, this is an undemanding plant which adapts well to

P.gayi

all situations and levels of lighting. Asexual reproduction is by the growth of stolons from the rhizome and by runners growing from the parent plant.

RICCIA

The genus *Riccia* belongs to the Liverworts, or Hepatica. It is widespread throughout the world, with more than 180 known species, though some have yet to be definitely identified. Some are land-growing, whilst others are amphibious or purely aquatic. Two or

three species are commonly found in aquariums; the most popular of these is *R.fluitans*.

■ *R.fluitans*

pH: 6.5–7.5	Temp.: 20–28°C (68–82°F)
°dH: 3–15	Surface plant

Family: *Ricciaceae*.
Scientific name: *Riccia fluitans* Linnaeus.
Synonyms: *Ricciella fluitans*, *Riccia frankoniae*.
Common name: Crystalwort or Riccia.
Geographical area: Europe, America, Asia.
This floating Liverwort can take up all the spare space at the top of the aquarium, but below the surface of the water. The plant is a thallus (a body with no distinction between stem, leaf and root) 1 to 2 mm (⅒ in) long. It is pale-green and divided into forks with their two ends separated. The plant spreads fairly swiftly and some of it should be removed so that light can get to the species

R.fluitans

below it in the tank. Soft water does not appear to suit the plant. It is a very good plant for breeding tanks as some fish like to lay their eggs in it. It also makes a good shelter for fry and also for infusoria which are often the main source of food for fry. The plant reproduces by dividing.

RORIPPA

About seventy species go to make up this genus; some botanists divide it into a number of genera, such as *Nasturtium*, *Neobeckia* and

Armoracea. Four species are aquatic but with strong amphibious traits and can be grown in an aquaterrarium or paludarium.

■ *R.aquatica*

pH: 7–7.5	Temp.: 20–25°C (68–77°F)
°dH: 8–15	Water depth: 20 cm (8 in)

Family: *Brassicaceae.*
Scientific name: *Rorippa aquatica* (Eaton) Palmer.
Synonyms: *Armoracea aquatica, Neobeckia aquatica.*
Common name: Water Rorippa.
Geographical area: United States.
Rorippa aquatica is the species of this genus best known to aquarium enthusiasts. The submerged leaves are bright-green with finely-toothed edges and they are ribbon-shaped —between 25 and 70 mm (1 and 3 in) long. The terrestrial form has very jagged-edged leaves, which are grouped in rosettes, as well as upper leaves are not jagged. The plant reaches about 15 cm (6 in) in height. It will not live in acidic or soft water and needs medium to strong lighting. The flower is white and sexual reproduction may take place using seeds; the plant also reproduces by cluster division.

ROTALA

This genus contains some very beautiful tropical aquarium plants. There are about fifty known species, some of which are regarded as parasites in rice fields. The leaves may be either opposed (*R.macrandra*) or whorled (*R.wallichii*), but are always sessile.

■ *R.macrandra*

pH: 6.5–6.9	Temp.: 22–26°C (72–79°F)
°dH: 3–8	Water depth: 20 cm (8 in)

Family: *Lythraceae.*

R.aquatica

R.macrandra

Scientific name: *Rotala macrandra* Koenne.
Synonym: *Rotala macrantha.*
Common name: Giant Red Rotala.
Geographical area: Asia, particularly India and Sri Lanka.
This is one of the most popular aquarium plants and is imported in large quantities from farms in South-East Asia and Sri Lanka. When planted in a small bunch it looks very attractive. The leaves are arranged in opposite pairs, and are ovoid in shape. Their colour depends very much on the type and intensity of lighting they receive. The distance between the leaves decreases towards the top of the stem as the plant grows towards the surface. The leaf is greenish on the upper face and pinkish or purple on the lower.

It is rare, but not impossible for the plant to flower in an aquarium. If it does so, it will be when the plant is floating on the surface, and a peduncle will grow on the axil of the leaf. The spike is reddish in colour. The best growing conditions are under bright light, and with added carbon dioxide. It is better grown in a Dutch tank than one with fish in it, as currents created by the fish and also snails, will both kill it. The plant reproduces by shooting; a number of lateral shoots can be replanted

and the parent plant can be pinched out at the level of a node to produce adventitious roots.

■ *R.rotundifolia*

pH: 6.5–7.0	Temp.: 22–26°C (72–79°F)
°dH: 3–8	Water depth: 20 cm (8 in)

Family: *Lythraceae.*

Scientific name: *Rotala rotundifolia* (Roxburgh) Koehne.

Synonyms: *Ammania latifolia, A.subspicata, Ameletia rotundifolia, Peplis diandra, Rotala indica* Koehne, non (Willednow) Koehne.

Common name: Round-leafed Rotala.

Geographical area: Widespread throughout South-East Asia.

This is an excellent plant for the background of an aquarium which is deeper than 40 cm (16 in). It has paired, opposite leaves which taper and, like the previous species, have different colours on either side of the leaf. The upper face is olive-green and the lower reddish to yellowish. Leaves growing above the surface are green on both sides. The water should be slightly acidic and not too hard. The shoots should be arranged in bunches and are about 20 cm (8 in) long. These will form an attractive contrast with other plants, particularly in a Dutch tank. Carbon dioxide diffusion is necessary if this plant is to grow as well as possible. The suckers should be cut level with an internode with adventitious roots. The adult plant should be pinched out when it reaches the surface to maintain its bushy appearance.

SAGITTARIA

The Sagittaria are species which come mainly from America. Few of them are suitable for aquariums. The morphology of the submerged parts of the plants is very varied and sometimes there is a strong resemblance to species of the *Vallisneria* genus. These are amphibious plants which will adapt to all conditions. The following species and their different varieties are those mainly found in aquariums: *S.graminea, S.latifolia, S.sagittifolia, S.subulata, S.lancifolia.*

■ *S.graminea*

pH: 6.5–7.6	Temp.: 18–25°C (64–77°F)
°dH: 3–15	Water depth: 40 cm (16 in)

Family: *Alismataceae.*
Scientific name: *Sagittaria graminea* Michaux.
Synonyms: *Sagittaria sinensis, S.chinensis.*
Common name: Graminaceous Sagittaria.
Geographical area: North America, Mexico, Caribbean islands.
The many varieties of this species can be identified mainly by the width of their underwater leaves or phyllodes (petioles resembling stems). All of these are ribbon-shaped with flat ends; different varieties grow to different heights.
S.g.var.graminea (synonym: *S.eatonii*) has leaves arranged in rosettes

S.graminea

15 to 25 cm (6 to 10 in) long by 1 cm (½ in) wide.
S.g.var.platyphylla Engelmann (synonym: *S.platyphylla*) has leaves 20 to 30 cm by 2.5 cm (8 to 12 in by 1 in).
S.g.var.weatherbiana (Fernald) Bogin (synonym: *S.weatherbiana*) has leaves 20 cm (8 in) long by 1.5–2.5 cm (½–1 in) wide, with very pointed ends.
S.g.var.teres (Waths) Bogin has lanceolate leaves measuring between 10 and 30 cm (4 and 12 in) depending on their age, on an oval

petiole. This is a very hardy species which can go either in the foreground or middleground of a tank depending on which variety is used. The water should always be more than 20 cm (8 in) deep or the plant will soon form aerial leaves. The plant is not difficult to look after and it will grow slowly but surely whether

S.lancifolia

the water is hard or soft, acid or alkaline. Asexual reproduction is by the production of stolons.

SALVINIA

This genus forms part of the Salviniaceae family, which in turn belongs to the aquatic ferns. All species of the genus have an axial stem with floating leaves arranged in pairs on either side. These may be round, oval or oblong. The surface of the floating leaf can be downy, verrucose or smooth depending on the species. Underneath each pair of floating leaves, there is a third submerged one resembling, and partly serving as, a root. These plants live in stagnant water, or slow-moving streams and rivers where there is plenty of sunlight.

■ S.auriculata

pH: 6.8–7.2	Temp.: 18–25°C (64–77°F)
°dH: 5–12	Surface plant

Family: *Salviniaceae*.
Scientific name: *Salvinia auriculata* Aublet.
Synonyms: *Salvinia hispida*, *S.biloba*.
Common name: Butterfly Fern.
Geographical area: Widespread in Central and South America from Mexico to Paraguay.
This species has floating leaves 2 cm long by 1 cm wide (1 in by ½ in) arranged on either side of a floating horizontal axis up to 20 cm (8 in) in length. There is a third leaf underneath each pair of floating ones which is thread-like, finely divided and resembles a root. This is a very useful plant for tanks where fish are bred and grown, as it offers shelter to fry as well as to the bacteria and infusoria on which they initially feed. The plant will rapidly take over the whole aquarium if there is sufficient light, so it should be regularly culled so as to allow light through to the plants below. If the tank has a glass cover, this should be slightly tilted so that drops of condensation do not fall back onto floating leaves. Reproduction is by stolons which appear at the base of the plant.

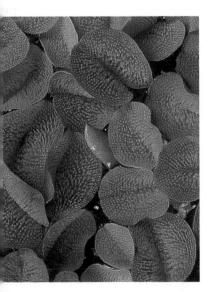

S.auriculata

■ S.minima

pH: 6.8–7.2	Temp.: 10–25°C (50–77°F)
°dH: 5–15	Surface plant

Family: *Salviniaceae*.
Scientific name: *Salvinia minima* Baker.
Synonyms: none.
Common name: Little Salvinia.
Geographical area: Southern Brazil.
This plant's height makes it the best suited of its genus to aquariums. It was imported only recently and has often been unnoticed or confused with another species. It has a fine stem with two opposite floating leaves. The leaf is bright-green, more or less round, and is 5 to 9 mm (¼–½ in) long with a short petiole. Its base is slightly heart-shaped. The upper side is not verrucose, but slightly downy with two sets of 'hairs'. It requires some care to grow: soft water, and an absence of condensation above the surface are both essential. It can also be grown on wet turf in a paludarium which is humid and brightly lit. In tanks used for breeding Labrynth fishes, which make their nests from bubbles, it makes a good support for eggs as they are laid. It is also useful for the

S.minima

fry of ovoviviparous species which often need shelter near the surface. The plant reproduces using stolons.

SAMOLUS

This genus contains more than a dozen amphibious species, commonly known as Water Roses. The genus is found throughout the world. Two or three species are currently sold for use in aquariums.

■ S.parviflorus

pH: 6.5–7.2	Temp.: 20–24°C (68–75°F)
°dH: 3–8	Water depth: 30 cm (12 in)

Family: *Primulaceae*.
Scientific name: *Samolus parviflorus* Rafinesque.
Synonyms: *Samolus floribundus*, *S.americanus*, *S.aquaticus*.
Common name: Water Cabbage.

S.parviflorus

Geographical area: All of America plus western India.
This small plant reaches 10 cm (4 in) in height and goes well in the foreground of an aquarium. It often produces a particularly nice contrast. Unfortunately, it is quite fragile and difficult to acclimatize. The leaves form a rosette at the base and are bright-green, spatulate and 6 to 10 cm (2½–4 in) long by 3 to 4 cm (1–1½ in). The plant will only grow under bright light at a temperature of 20 to 24°C (68 to 77°F) and with plenty of additional carbon dioxide. The group of plants should be sparsely planted in gravel in a part of the tank where there is plenty of room. It can also be grown immersed, when it will flower and produce seeds. These will germinate easily on a wet, growing medium. The plant also reproduces

via plantlets which appear on the stem and on the axils of leaves on the floral spike; the stem also produces runners between two groups of plantlets.

SAURURUS

These are herbaceous plants which grow to a maximum of 1 m (39 in). They have rhizomes and their leaves end in a tapering point.

■ S.cernuus

pH: 6.8–7.2	Temp.: 18–22°C (64–72°F)
°dH: 5–12	Water depth: 50 cm (20 in)

Family: Saururaceae.
Scientific name: Saururus cernuus Linnaeus.
Synonyms: Saururus lucidus, Serpentaria repens, Mattuschkia aquatica.
Common name: Lizard's Tail.
Geographical area: East coast of North America, from Florida to Canada.
This is a herbaceous, marsh-dwelling plant with a strong underground rhizome. The plant grows up to 1.5 m (5 ft) in length. The leaves are alternate with a petiole 8 to 12 cm (3 to 5 in) long, and they are downy when young. The lamina is heart-shaped at the base, smooth and shiny and 10 to 15 cm by 6 to 8 cm (4 to 6 in by 2½ to

3½ in). The veins are concave on the top side of the leaf and convex underneath. The leaf tissue between the veins is slightly swollen. The leaves are a satiny green and bent slightly downwards. This species can only be used in tanks deeper than 50 cm so that the plant can still reach the surface of the water and continue growing and flowering. The flowers are yellowish and arranged on a floral spike 15 to 20 cm (6 to 8 in) long. The species can also be planted around a garden pond, but it is important to note that the rhizomes will probably damage a pond with a nylon lining. The plant reproduces by growing shoots and by division of the rhizome. This is a very hardy plant.

SPATHIPHYLLUM

This genus comprises mainly amphibious species, mostly grown out of the water and in a pot. Some are sold for use in aquariums: these include S.grandifolium, S.patini and S.wallisii. Long-term immersion in water will harm these plants, though they are easy to grow in a paludarium.

■ S.wallisii

pH: 6.4–7.2	Temp.: 22–25°C (72–77°F)
°dH: 3–12	Water depth: 40 cm (16 in)

Family: Araceae.
Scientific name: Spathiphyllum wallisii Regel.
Synonyms: none.
Common name: Wallis's Spathyphyllum.
Geographical area: South America (Colombia).
This plant can be kept in an aquarium for up to about six or seven months. It is recommended mainly for tanks where the fish create plenty of movement in the water. It will last longer in an aquarium if the plant is placed on the growing medium while still inside its pot so that the roots are not exposed. The leaves are lanceolate and grow on the end of a very long

S.wallisii

petiole. The upper side of the leaf is pale-green and shiny, while the lower half is bright-green and matt. The veins are conspicuous and on the lower side of the leaf they are convex. The plant will not undergo asexual reproduction in the aquarium.

STRATIOTES

This genus comprises only one species, S.aloides, a perennial surface or semi-submerged plant. The leaves are denticulate and arranged in a rosette, not unlike the Aloe.

■ S.aloides

pH: 6.8–8.2	Temp.: 18–20°C (64–68°F)
°dH: 3–8	Surface plant

S.aloides

Family: Hydrocharitaceae.
Scientific name: Stratiotes aloides Linnaeus.

S.cernuus

Synonyms: *Stratiotes aculeatus, S. aquaticus, S.ensiformis, S.generalis.*
Common name: Water Aloe or Water Soldier.
Geographical area: Europe, northern Asia.
This species should preferably be grown in a cold tank in its submerged form. Here it will grow rosettes of ten to twenty-five ribbon-like leaves. The leaf grows to a maximum length of between 20 and 80 cm (8 and 32 in) and is bright-green. The temperature should not exceed 30°C (68°F). As a surface plant it becomes tougher and reaches 20 to 40 cm (8 to 16 in) in length. It is wide at the base and tapers off towards the top. The species will live in comparatively low light and is often found in our own rivers and streams. The plantlets which grow on the end of the stolons can be taken from their natural habitat and placed in the aquarium.

TRAPA

This genus is better known as the Water Chestnut. The plants it comprises have floating leaves arranged in a rosette, while the underwater leaves are linear. In its natural habitat the plant multiplies very quickly and can present a hazard to navigation.

■ *T.natans*

pH: 6–7.2	Temp.: 20–22°C (68–72°F)
°dH: 4–8	Surface plant

Family: *Trapaceae.*
Scientific name: *Trapa natans* Linnaeus.
Synonyms: more than a hundred.
Common name: Water Chestnut.
Geographical area: Worldwide.

The leaves grow on reddish petioles and form a rosette on the surface of the water on either side of a central axis which may reach between 60 and 300 cm (24 and 120 in) depending on the depth of the water. The floating leaves are diamond-shaped with serrated edges. The upper surface of the leaf is pale-green and shiny with conspicuous veins. The petiole is between 4 and 20 cm (1½ and 8 in) long and dilated at the middle. The plant should be grown in strong light in the form of a fluorescent tube for fourteen hours a day and the temperature of the water should never exceed 22°C (72°F). The plant makes a

T.natans

very good decoration for an outdoor pond, where it should flower and produce its fruit, which looks like a chestnut. The *bispinosa* variety from Senegal seems better suited to a tropical aquarium.

UTRICULARIA

A very large number of species go to make up this genus: most of them are found in tropical and subtropical areas, where they live in almost any environment including out of the water: some species are epiphytes, i.e. they live on other plants without being parasitic. The

Utricularia are very specialized plants: they have thread-like leaves with capillary segments and a bladder with a valve which traps minute animals. They can therefore be regarded as carnivorous plants.

■ *U.vulgaris*

pH: 6.5–7.5	Temp.: 15–22°C (59–72°F)
°dH: 3–8	Surface plant

Family: *Utriculariaceae.*
Scientific name: *Utricularia vulgaris* Linnaeus.
Synonyms: many.

Utricularia sp.

Common name: Common Bladderwort.
Geographical area: Europe and North Africa.
This is not an easy species to maintain, partly because it requires so much light and partly because it grows slowly and is very prone to invasion by algae. The Common Bladderwort has a horizontal central axis bearing finely-divided, alternate leaves. The bladders measure up to 4 mm (¼ in) in diameter, spread across the leaf and serve both to feed the plant and maintain buoyancy. The plant will form a carpet of vegetation on the surface of the water. The yellow flowers are borne on an aerial shoot. The plant is not suitable as a surface plant for breeding tanks, as it

will trap smaller fry. The plant requires strong light and soft water. It will not reproduce sexually in an aquarium, but like other species of the genus it reproduces by division of the stem and the production of turions, or 'winter buds', at the end of the stem.

VALLISNERIA

There are seven or eight different forms of this genus which are found in aquariums, and they are particularly popular plants. Unfortunately they cannot be told apart except by their flowers, which rarely appear in an aquarium. Vallisneria are very useful aquarium plants; depending on which species they are, they can form a curtain of vegetation along the middle or back of the tank or along the sides.

■ V.asiatica

pH: 6.4–7	Temp.: 20–26°C (68–79°F)
°dH: 3–8	Water depth: 30 cm (12 in)

Family: Hydrocharitaceae.
Scientific name: Vallisneria asiatica Miki.
Synonyms: V.spiralis var.tortifolia, var.torta, var.tortuosa, var.torsada.
Common name: Asiatic Vallisneria.
Geographical area: Asia.
This plant should be planted in groups in an aquarium which is more than 40 cm (16 in) deep. The leaves are ribbon-like and grow up to 40 or 60 cm (16 to 24 in) in length by 1 cm (½ in) wide. In the wild, the leaves are slightly smaller. The species will cover a large area of the background of a tank but requires bright light falling on the whole plant. It is

therefore important not to plant the stems too close together and to ensure that each one gets plenty of light. Like all Vallisneria, the plant will live in most types of environment. It reproduces by growing plantlets from the stolon.

■ V.gigantea

pH: 6.5–7.2	Temp.: 22–28°C (72–82°F)
°dH: 3–10	Water depth: 50 cm (20 in)

Family: Hydrocharitaceae.
Scientific name: Vallisneria gigantea Graebner.
Synonyms: none.
Common name: Giant Vallisneria.
Geographical area: New Guinea, Philippines.

V.gigantea

This is a very tall plant when grown in an aquarium, sometimes reaching more than 2 m (6 ft 6 in) in length, with ribbon-shaped leaves 3 cm (1½ in) wide. When the plant starts taking up too much room, one or two stems should be selected and the rest removed. The plant should not be trimmed by cutting off leaves whole or in part, as this will endanger the whole plant. A sudden change in the amount of light or the composition of the aquarium will often kill the plant. The best place for it is at the back or sides of the aquarium.

■ V.spiralis

pH: 6.5–7.5	Temp.: 22–28°C (72–82°F)
°dH: 3–15	Water depth: 50 cm (20 in)

Family: Hydrocharitaceae.
Scientific name: Vallisneria spiralis Linnaeus.
Synonyms: many.
Common name: Straight Vallisneria or Tape Grass.
Geographical area: Native to southern Europe and North Africa: now widespread in tropical and sub-tropical areas.
This is a very popular aquarium plant which makes an excellent decoration for the background of a tank. It grows to more than 50 cm (20 in). The ribbon-shaped leaves are not twisted and there is often confusion on the part of aquarium owners because of the name of the species, which in fact refers to the floral peduncle rather than the leaves. The plant grows to a maximum of 60 cm (24 in) and the leaves are between 4 and 12 mm (1½ and 5 in) wide with three veins. The end of the leaf is straight with fine teeth, and it is this feature which distinguishes the species from the Sagittaria. The species can be kept in a tropical or cold-water tank and grows very easily and rapidly. When it stops growing, the whole group should be removed. The plant reproduces frequently and easily using runners.

VESICULARIA

There are more than 130 species in this genus. They are

V.dubyana

found only in tropical and sub-tropical areas, but only a few rare species are purely aquatic. The Java Moss has many uses in the aquarium and is an amphibious species which will quite happily live underwater for long periods.

■ *V.dubyana*

pH: 6.5–7.0	Temp.: 22–25°C (72–77°F)
°dH: 3–10	Water depth: 10 cm (4 in)

Family: *Hypnaceae.*
Scientific name: *Vesicularis dubyana* (C. Müller) Brotherus.
Synonym: *Hypnum dubyanum.*
Common name: Java Moss.
Geographical area: South-East Asia, Malaysia, Java, India.
This is a very adaptable species of moss which has many uses both in the aquarium and the humid paludarium. It is a very undemanding plant but grows rather slowly. The stems are thin and flexible with two sets of small, bright-green, lanceolate leaves. In a decorative aquarium it makes a good cover for a rock or root. It simply needs to be fixed to the part of the substratum to be covered, using an elastic band; the plant is held in place by hapterons, or root-like organs and it starts to grow more rapidly. It makes a good support for egg-laying in a breeding tank as well as providing protection for the eggs against hungry parents. Unfortunately, it is liable to become covered by algae in an aquarium and by fungi in a paludarium. The plant can also be left to float near the surface of an aquarium if it is fixed to a number of floating objects such as a cork cut into slices. The plant prefers soft water and low light and reproduces by division.

WOLLFIA

These plants are morphologically similar to the Duckweeds, but much smaller. They are found both in temperate and tropical regions and are the smallest flowering plants in the world.

■ *W.arrhiza*

pH: 6.5–7.5	Temp.: 15–28°C (59–82°F)
°dH: 3–20	Water depth: 5 cm (2 in)

Family: *Lemnaceae.*
Scientific name: *Wolffia arrhiza* (Linnaeus) Horlel ex Wimmer.
Synonyms: *Lemna arrhiza, Lemna globosa, Grantia globosa, Bruniera vivipara, Wolffia michelii, W.delilii, W.arrhizia.*
Common name: Dwarf Duckweed.
Geographical area: Widespread throughout the world.
This is the smallest known species of flowering plant, with a body of only 1 mm ($\frac{1}{20}$ in) in diameter. It is round to ovoid, bright-green and has no roots. If grown under strong light it becomes slightly reddish in colour. The species is difficult to distinguish from the seven others making up the genus. In the wild, the plant spreads extremely fast and in South-East Asia it is harvested and eaten. Plant-eating fish are very fond of it. It is best kept in strong light and water with plenty of trace elements. It reproduces by growing plantlets.

Non-aquatic plants, such as the genera Aglaonema, Didiplis, Dracaenia *and* Cordylina, *which are sometimes sold as aquatic plants, have been deliberately left out of this chapter. They cannot be grown properly in an aquarium; and even if they are, they have a very short lifespan.*

GLOSSARY

A

Acuminate : denotes tapering leaf.

Adventive : applies to root growing directly from stalk.

Alternate : describes leaves arranged in two (but not opposite) rows. It can also be used to describe leaves in a spiral arrangement.

Amphibious : denotes plant having parts both above and under water, or being able to grow above and below water.

Anaerobiosis : existence in the absence of free (useable) oxygen. Anaerobic fermentation refers to a chain of respiratory reactions which certain bacteria and other micro-organisms can perform in an oxygen-free environment.

Apex : top of plant.

Aquaterrarium : two-section tank displaying aquatic and terrestrial environments.

Aquatic : under-water plant producing flowers at water level.

Argillo-humic compounds : argillaceous compounds all have a high proportion of clay in their make-up—humic ones have a high organic content. Argillo-humic compounds are therefore fine-grained substrates which have an organic component.

Atrophy of the air bladder : reduction in the size of the air (swim) bladder. This results in the loss of buoyancy and is typical of many species which live on the substratum and/or in fast-flowing water.

Autofertile : self-fertilizing. An autofertile flower is fertilized by its own pollen or by that of a flower from the same plant.

Axil : angle formed by leaf and stalk.

Axillary : located on axil.

B

Bell jar : a piece of laboratory equipment (usually bell-shaped and made of glass), used for collecting gases and/or (as in this book) for bringing them into contact with a liquid surface across which diffusion can take place.

Bivalent iron : iron atoms having two free electrons available for combination with other chemicals. Bivalent Iron is usually referred to as Ferrous Iron and is represented chemically as Fe^{++}. Trivalent, or Ferric Iron is written as Fe^{+++} in chemical shorthand.

Bract : organ resembling small leaf, often at base of peduncle or flower.

Brackish : fresh water mixed with sea water.

Bulb : collection of tightly-packed, stored fleshy leaves. The onion is a bulb.

C

Candle (Candela) : a unit of luminous intensity.

Candle Test : a test used to detect the presence of a leak of carbon dioxide (the gas, if present, will extinguish a lighted candle).

Cephalic Glands : temporary structures found in some types of newly-hatched egglayer fry (larvae) which allow them to attach themselves to plants, the substratum or other objects.

Chlorophyll : the pigment which gives green plants their characteristic colour. Chlorophyll is essential for photosynthesis.

Cordate : heart-shaped.

Cosmopolitan : plant species found throughout the world.

Cutting : fragment of stalk, root or rhizome which when planted produces another individual.

D

Decantation Tank : a small 'tank' or compartment within an aquarium, usually used as a first chamber (in a series of chambers) which goes to form an integrated filtration system. The 'decantation tank' receives detritus-laden water from the main aquarium and acts as a sedimentation site for the largest particles of debris.

Decussate : pairs of opposite shoots each at right angles to the pair below.

Denticulate : edged with small serrations.

Disbudding : propagation by cuttings.

Discoidal : disc-shaped.

Distichous : leaves arranged in two vertical lines on opposite sides of the stem.

Dutch Tank : an aquarium in which the emphasis is on a carefully chosen and abundant selection of plants. Although Dutch tanks can (and often do) also contain fish, these are generally few in number compared to other types of aquarium and usually consist of non-polluting, non-herbivorous species.

E

Elliptiform : ellipse-shaped.

Endemic : denotes species found in one specific area only. A plant can be said to be endemic to Central America.

Epiphyte : plant which grows on another.

Eutrophic : said of environment rich in nutritional elements, often due to man's presence. One speaks of eutrophication of a lake.

F

Family : systematic unit in which genera are grouped.
Filiform : threadlike.
Foliar : of leaf.
Frond : name given to 'leaves' of fern. Fronds carry fruit-bearing part of fern: sporangium.
Fructification : the formation of fruits.

G

Genus : systematic unit of species.

H

Heliophile : applies to plants living in full sunlight.

I

Inflorescence : arrangement of flowers of plant.
Infusoria : single-cell organisms which develop in water and provide food for fry in the first days of their life.
Internode : space between two nodes.

L

Laciniate : irregularly divided into narrow segments.
Lamina : wide part of leaf, usually connected to stalk by petiole.
Lanceolate : spear-shaped.
Linear : Long, narrow leaf with parallel edges.

M

Microphthalmia : the possession of very small eyes, often typical of species that live in turbid or dark environments.
Monotypic : group of plants or animals comprising one species.

N

Neotropical : denotes plants originating in tropical zones of the New World (North America, Central America and South America).
Nervures : leaf veins.
Neuration : distribution of nervures of leaf.
Node : point of plant at which leaves spring.

O

Ovoviviparous : fish producing young by eggs hatched within body of female.

P

Paludal : plant living in marshy environment.
Paludarium : tank creating marshy environment for amphibious plants and fish.
Palustral : marshy.
Pantropical : species found in all tropical zones of world.
Perennial : plant living more than two years.
Petiole : plant organ connecting leaf to stalk.
pH : This is an indication of the acidity/alkalinity of a medium. The scale is logarithmic and runs from 1 to 14. Neutral conditions are indicated by a pH value of 7. Anything below this is acidic, while anything above is alkaline. Because of the logarithmic nature of the scale, the size of the units differs. For instance, pH 6 indicates a level of acidity 10 times higher than that represented by pH 7. A water sample having a pH value of 5 would therefore be 10 times more acidic than one having a pH of 6 and 100 times more acidic than one having a value of pH 7. The same, of course, also applies on the alkaline side of the scale.
Photosynthesis : the process by which green plants manufacture food (carbohydrate) from carbon dioxide and water. Light and chlorophyll are essential for this process which generates oxygen as a by-product.
Summary Equation :

$$6CO_2 + 6H_2O \xrightarrow[\text{Chlorophyll}]{\text{Light}} C_6H_{12}O_6 + 6O_2$$

(carbon dioxide
– six molecules

(water – six
molecules)

(carbohydrate
one molecule)

(Oxygen –
six molecules)

Plumiform : feather or plume-shaped.
Polychrome : displaying several colours.
Polymerization : the process by which molecules having similar chemical composition join up to form larger, heavier molecules.
Polymorphous : having several shapes. One speaks of foliar polymorphy with regard to amphibious plants, because under-water leaves are often shaped differently from floating leaves.

R

Radicle : small secondary root appearing on major root. Also used to describe the primary root of a seedling.
Reniform : kidney-shaped.
Reproduction : way in which living beings produce others like themselves. For plants this can be:
● plant multiplication, where a new individual arises from fragment of mother plant (sucker, stolon);
● sexual reproduction, where sexual organs, gametes of plant are involved.
Rheophiles : plants and animals living in currents.
Rhizome : subterranean or creeping stalk emitting aerial roots and stalks.

Ribboned : leaf whose laminae is ribbon-shaped.
Rosette : circlet of leaves around root neck.

S

Sessile : leaf attached directly to stalk without petiole.
Asexual : reproduction without sexual organs or gametes. Also known in plant kingdom as multiplication.
Shaft : flower-bearing stalk off root-neck. Does not bear leaves.
Spathe : modified leaf surrounding inflorescence.
Spatuliform : enlarged leaf spatula-shaped at end.
Spike : closely-arranged flower cluster at stalk end.
Sporangium : typical reproductive organ of lower plants containing spores.
Spore : reproductive organ of plants. In lower plants (moss, fern) a spore gives birth to a new seedling bearing reproductive organs. In higher, flowering plants, male and female spores unite to give birth to a new individual.
Spring Tides : tides which occur when the sun, moon and earth are in a straight line (or nearly so). As a result, high tides are higher (and low tides, lower) than at other times.
Station : habitat of plant.
Stolon : creeping offshoot on which roots appear. One speaks of stolons of strawberry plants.
Sublacustrine : almost lake-like.
Submerged : under-water leaf.
Sucker : shoot which appears on root.

T

Terrarium : tank where an environment is maintained to suit terrestrial plants and animals.
Thallus : lower plant organ not differentiated into root, stem and leaves.
Topping : removal of top of plant.
Tuber : swelling of root or underground stalk; a tuber is filled with nutrients.

V

Verticil : circle of organs around the same point on the axis. One refers to a verticil of leaves.
Villi : small threadlike projections producing a rough surface.

X

Xanthoic : a yellow–pigmented form of a particular species.

Z

Zeolites : a general term used to refer to compounds (usually fine-grained) which are characterized by their ability to exchange certain ions for others. For instance, zeolites are very good at absorbing ammonia from fresh water. They can also be 'recharged' in saline solution, whereupon they release their ammonia in exchange for sodium.

UNITS

Lumen : a unit of illumination variously described as a 'unit of luminous flux' (the total visible energy emitted by a source of light), or 'the light emitted by a source of one international candle (candela) intensity per unit space angle in a second'.

Lux : a unit of illumination expressed as the number of lumens received per square metre of surface. Units which appear in the text:

lm/dm^2 = no. of lumens per square decimetre (10 decimetres = 1 metre)

lm/l = no. of lumens per litre (c. 4.5 litres = 1 gallon)

Å (Ångström) : a very small unit of measurement usually employed in stating light wavelength.

10.000,000 (10 million) Å = 1 metre

°K (Degrees Kelvin) : refers to absolute temperature whose zero point is 459° below zero on the Farenheit scale and 273° below zero on the Centigrade scale.
Therefore, to convert °F to °K, add 459; to convert °C to °K, add 273.

CRI (Colour Rendering Index) : this is a measure of how close, or otherwise, a source of light is to sunlight (the solar spectrum). Sunlight is considered to have a CRI of 100.

$\mu S/cm^2$ (Micro-siemens per Square Centimetre) : a siemens is a unit of conductivity related to the amount of dissolved chemicals in the water. As a result, hard water samples have higher conductivity figures than soft water ones. For example, some of the soft slightly acid waters of Peruvian rivers have a conductivity value as low as 17 $\mu S/cm^2$ compared to 600 $\mu S/cm^2$ for Lake Tanganyika.

TFf° : Total Hardness of a water sample in French degrees. For comparison, 1° of French Hardness = 1.8° German Hardness = 1.4° English Hardness.

ppm (Parts per Million) : the amount of a certain substance (measured in parts) which occurs in a solution containing one million parts of water.

TH (Total Hardness) : made up of general or permanent hardness (GH) and Carbonate, Bicarbonate or Temporary Hardness (KH).

GH : General or Permanent Hardness of water caused by the sulphates, nitrates and chlorides of calcium and magnesium.

KH : Carbonate, Bicarbonate or Temporary Hardness of water caused by the bicarbonates of calcium and magnesium. Temporary hardness can be reduced by boiling while general hardness cannot.

°d : German degree.

°a : English (Clark) degree.

Temperature

C = 5(F–32)/9 or C + 40 = 5 (F + 40) 9

°f : French degree.

AFC : (Acid Fixation Capacity or Acid Binding Capacity) : this factor is used to determine the alkalinity of a water sample and is recorded as the number of cubic centimetres (cm^3) or millilitres (ml) of 10HCl (Ten–molar Hydrochloric Acid – see entry mmol/l) required to neutralize the alkaline materials present in 100 cm^3 of a water sample. Consequently, the more alkaline the water, the higher its AFC.

mEq/l (Milli-Equivalents per Litre) : the equivalent of a compound is the number of parts by weight of that compound which will react with (or yield) one part weight of hydrogen. One milli-Equivalent = 1/1000 of one Equivalent.

mmol/l (Milli-Moles per Litre) : a mole is defined as one gram-molecular weight of a substance. The Gram-molecular weight of a substance is its molecular weight expressed in grams. For example, Oxygen has an atomic weight of 16. Each molecule of oxygen consists of two atoms. Therefore, the molecular weight of oxygen is 32 and its gram-molecular weight is 32g.

One Milli-Mole = 1/1000 of one Mole.

Metric, with British Equivalents

1 millimetre	=	0.039 inch
1 litre	=	1.76 pints
1 milligram	=	0.015 grain

INDEX OF SPECIES

INDEX OF GENERA

BIBLIOGRAPHY

Benl, G., *A Key to the Genera of Aquarium Plants Based on Vegetative Characters* (Bayleya, Ithaca N.Y., 1971)

Cook, C.D.K., *Water Plants of the World. A manual for the identification of the genera of freshwater macrophytes* (The Hague, 1974)

De Witt, H.C.D., *Aquarienpflanzen,* (Verlag Eugen Ulmer, Stuttgart, 1971)

Haslam, S., Sinker, C., Wolseley, P., *British Water Plants* (Field Studies Council, 1982)

James, B., *A Fishkeeper's Guide to Aquarium Plants* (Salamander, 1986)

Mühlberg, H., *The Complete Guide to Water Plants,* (E. P. Publishing Ltd., 1980)

Rataj, K., and Horeman, T., *Aquarium Plants,* (T.F.H. Publications, Inc. 1977)

Swindells, P., *Waterlilies* (Croom Helm, 1983)

Terver, D., *Les Plantes: Généralités, Manuel d' Aquariologie* (Réalisations Editoriales Pédagogiques, 1983)

Wendt, A., *Die Aquarienpflanze in Wort und Bild* (Stuttgart und Essen, 1952)

PICTURE ACKNOWLEDGEMENTS

ALLGAYER : 10, 12 ; **BLANC :** 23, 116 top ; **CHAUMETON/
NATURE :** 49, 57, 76, 80, 83, 97, 99, 100, 101, 102, 103, 106, 108, 110,
111, 113, 115 top, 116, 117 bottom, 121, 122, 123, 124 bottom left, 125,
126, 127, 128 top, 129 bottom, 131, 132, 134 bottom, 137, 138 middle,
139, 140 middle, 142, 143 right, 144 middle ; **CHAUMETON-KIEFFER/
NATURE :** 47 ; **FERRERO/NATURE :** 63 bottom ; **GROPAS/
NATURE :** 124 bottom right; **ISSEMAN :** 14 ; **KLAUS PAYSAN :** 26, 27,
75 ; **LAMAISON/NATURE :** 130 ; **TETON :** 2, 6, 7, 11, 15, 17, 20, 22,
25, 40, 41, 42, 48, 50, 51, 53, 54, 55, 56, 58, 60, 62, 63 top, 66, 67, 70, 74,
78, 79, 82, 89 top, 92, 93, 94, 95, 98, 102 bottom left, 102 middle right,
104, 105, 107, 108 middle left, 109, 112, 114, 115 bottom, 117 top, 119,
120, 128 middle left, 129 top, 135, 138 right, 140 right, 141, 142 bottom
right, 143 middle, 144 bottom right ; **TOMEY :** 87, 88, 89 bottom, 90.

We are grateful to the Société Eden Aquatique, 1, rue Charretière, 6300 Clermont-Fd, for
trusting us with plants illustrated in this book.